THE STORY OF EDGEWATER HOUSE

1910 — 2016

Nancy Glidden Coffey

ISBN: 978-1-891906-13-8

Cover images: Front: *American Country Houses of Today*, 1913, p. 150. Courtesy Boston Public Library. Back: Courtesy Jeffrey and Carol Horvitz.

To Jeffrey and Carol Horvitz, who conceived the idea of the book,

and to all those who made it possible by sharing their stories

Contents

Prologue   Setting the Scene 1

Chapter 1   The Rise of Mary Carver Leiter...4

Chapter 2   The Building of Edgewater House and Mary Leiter's Years There: 1910-1912 11

Chapter 3   The Joseph and Juliette Leiter Years: 1913-1932 20

Chapter 4   The Widow Juliette Leiter and Her Children: 1932-1942 49

Chapter 5   Tommy and Oatsie Leiter: 1942-1950..63

Chapter 6   The Kaisers: June 1950-April 1951 69

Chapter 7   Oliver and Ellen Ames, Year-Round Resident Owners: 1950-1980 86

Chapter 8   Dennis and Susan Fabry: 1980-1991...98

Chapter 9   Jeffrey and Carol Horvitz: The Rebirth of Edgewater, 1991-Present 104

Epilogue   The Leiters After Edgewater House 128

Acknowledgements...135

About the Author 137

Bibliography 138

Notes..139

Prologue
Setting the Scene

The widow Mary Leiter was a woman in a hurry. When she put the contract for her Beverly Farms estate out to bid in March of 1910, she stipulated that it was to be completed by September 20. Lateness would result in a penalty. L. D. Willcutt and Sons Company of Boston was awarded the bid in March and completed house and carriage house on schedule. Edgewater House had arrived.

Now, over a hundred years later, Edgewater House still stands. The story of the house and its inhabitants reflects the story of the North Shore's Gold Coast, and of the nation.

For 40 years Edgewater House remained in the Leiter family. Sold to Herbert Kaiser in June 1950, it faced partial demolition. Ellen and Oliver Ames rescued the house in November of that year and made it a year-round home for their growing family. Speculators Dennis and Susan Fabry of California and Nevada bought the house from Ellen Ames in 1980; personal financial crises led to foreclosure.

Present owners Jeffrey and Carol Horvitz purchased the house in 1991. Under their stewardship, Edgewater House has regained its original grandeur.

This is the Edgewater story.

* * *

The summer community in Beverly Farms was just over 50 years old when Mary Leiter purchased three acres of shorefront property in 1909.

The coming of the railroad in 1847 had quickly transformed a sleepy and neglected rural section of Beverly into desirable real estate. The land grab preceded the laying of the track. Once the board of directors of the Eastern Railroad had made its decision to run a line from Beverly to Gloucester, board members and their friends started buying up land. By the time the train passed through the Prides Crossing and Beverly Farms sections of the city of Beverly in 1847, all of the property along the shore, with the exception of a small strip owned by the heirs of Thomas West, had been purchased by merchants and bankers from Boston and Salem. Charles Paine had purchased a large tract at the Allen's Head end of the beach with the intention of subdividing it. In April of 1846, Franklin Haven purchased 20 acres from farmer Josiah Obear for $500. By the end of the century he and his son Franklin Jr. owned a total of 80 acres from the ocean to the railroad line.[1]

As the nineteenth century progressed, Paine's land was subdivided. As available oceanfront land diminished, the ledges and swamps of the town's old common land were bought up and turned into magnificent woodland or ocean-view estates. For the next 50 years Beverly Farms developed a thriving business district that was increasingly focused on serving the needs of its growing summer community.

1

Although attempts to secede from Beverly in the 1880s were unsuccessful, Beverly Farms had become a separate community in all but governance.

Throughout the second half of the nineteenth century, the North Shore, running from Nahant to Gloucester, was an enclave of Boston society. Back Bay and Beacon Hill neighbors were North Shore neighbors as well. Those who mingled at the Myopia Hunt Club, the Essex County Club, and the Eastern Yacht Club in the summer were the same men and women who frequented the Somerset Club and the Chilton Club in the winter. They had gone to school together. Their children married each other.

For the most part, the summer residents represented old money. The Brahmins traced their inheritance back to the China trade. Although the census listed at least one "gentleman of leisure",[*] most of them continued to work and add to their family fortunes. The estate owners were bankers, businessmen, mill and factory owners, lawyers, and doctors. There was also a respectable group of intellectuals and academics.

The growing class of wealthy millionaires and the access created by railroads had led to the growth of similar summer communities throughout the country. On the northeast coast, Bar Harbor in Maine, Oyster Bay on Long Island, and Newport in Rhode Island became summer playgrounds for the wealthy of New York and Washington. Each community had its own appeal. Bar Harbor was perhaps the most rugged, with its amusements focused on sailing and hiking. Newport was the grandest of all, with a dizzying season of balls and social events. By most standards, the North Shore summer community of the 1880s and 1890s was rather staid and maybe even a little stodgy.

Nonetheless, by the end of the nineteenth century, when outsiders began to acquire property, fissures began to develop in this closed and somewhat parochial community. Perhaps new millionaires spawned by the post-Civil War industrial boom craved the kind of old-money respectability that North Shore society offered.

In the first five years of the twentieth century, three Midwestern millionaires arrived and startled their neighbors with their huge summer houses in Prides Crossing. All three houses were designed by the architectural firm Little and Browne of Boston. The first was built for Edwin Swift of Chicago. Swift and his older brother Gustave were Cape Cod butchers who prospered, moved to Chicago, and founded Swift and Company in 1873. Edwin's beachfront estate, Swiftmore, was built between 1900 and 1902. Over 1901-1902, William Henry Moore, a New York lawyer and investor with roots in Chicago, built his Rockmarge estate next door. The two families shared a pier and built side-by-side bathhouses. Between 1901 and 1906, Henry Clay Frick, the self-made man and steel magnate from Pittsburgh, built his fabulous Eagle Rock high on a hill above the water. These families offended many of their more conservative neighbors with their ostentation, but eventually they would find their place in North Shore society.

---

[*] Eleonora Sears' father, Frederick Sears, Jr. listed his occupation as a "gentleman of leisure" in the 1880 census. His father had listed his as "gentleman".

The beginning of the twentieth century was bringing a transformation to the Beverly Farms waterfront. In 1907, Neal Rantoul, grandson of original summer resident David Neal, tore down the old Neal house and built the beautiful brick house designed by his architect brother William Rantoul. A local architectural review dubbed it the loveliest mansion on the beach — perhaps a subtle criticism of the newly built behemoths at the far end.

Three years later, in 1910, three more estates were built on the beach: Philadelphia investor Sydney Hutchinson's Sydith next to the West Beach Corporation, Marion Sargent's Rockedge at the far end of the beach on Allan's Head, and Mary Leiter's Edgewater House in the middle.

Unlike the houses built by Swift, Moore, and Frick, Sydith, Rockedge and Edgewater still stand today.

Chapter 1
The Rise of Mary Carver Leiter

Mary Teresa Carver was born near Utica, New York, in 1845. Her parents, Benjamin and Nancy Carver, later moved to Chicago, where Benjamin became a moderately successful banker. Their daughter Mary was a young schoolteacher when she met Levi Zeigler Leiter. When Levi and Mary married in 1866, he was 32 and she was 21. The marriage set Mary Carver Leiter on a trajectory that would propel her into a world far beyond anything she could have imagined. Her husband, Levi Leiter, was to become one of the most important men in Chicago.

No one could have predicted that Mary Carver would one day be an internationally known figure. From modest origins, Mary would rise to become a leader in Chicago and later Washington society. Everyone who was anyone would come to the lavish parties at her Washington mansion, reputed to be the finest private home in the District of Columbia. Unlike most, perhaps all, socially ambitious mothers of America's Gilded Age, she would manage twice to achieve the ultimate prize: two of her daughters would marry British nobility. The eldest, Mary Victoria, would become Lady Curzon, Vicereine of India, and the youngest, Margaret, would marry Henry Molyneux Paget Howard, 19th Earl of Suffolk and 12th Earl of Buckingham.

A brief sketch of Levi Leiter's early life from the Leiter family papers summarizes his rise to prominence.

Levi Leiter, one of Chicago's leading nineteenth-century businessmen, was an early partner of Marshall Field and Potter Palmer in dry-goods merchandising, and later a major investor in real estate, stocks, and securities. He was born November 2, 1834, in Leitersburg, Maryland, the son of Joseph Leiter and Ann Zeigler.[*] After moving to Chicago in 1855, Levi Leiter met Marshall Field while both were employed as clerks for Cooley, Wadsworth and Company, a wholesale drapery house in which they soon became partners. In 1865 they sold their interest to John V. Farwell and purchased controlling interest in a dry-goods firm founded by Potter Palmer, which became the department store known as Field, Palmer and Leiter. Palmer retired in 1867, and the name was changed to Field, Leiter and Company. Field was the merchandiser; Leiter specialized in credit and finance.

Levi Leiter also began investing in land and buildings, and in 1881 sold his share of the dry-goods business to Marshall Field. Over the years Leiter invested heavily in downtown Chicago real estate, including an eight-story building on State Street known as the Leiter Building, which was completed in 1893 and leased to the department store Siegel, Cooper & Company. In addition, he owned 7500 acres of coal lands in Franklin and Williamson counties in southern Illinois, half

---

[*] Leitersburg was named for Levi's ancestor Andrew Leiter, who purchased land there in 1811.

interest in 13,000 acres of ranch lands in Wyoming, mine claims in several Western states, as well as a number of other properties. His diverse investments in stocks and securities included major holdings in the Chicago City Railroad, Illinois Trust and Savings Bank, the Grand Pacific Hotel, and Pullman Palace Car Company.

An active promoter of Chicago business and philanthropic interests, Leiter served as director of the Chicago [Fire] Relief and Aid Society from 1874 to 1880, helped fund the erection of a new Chicago Historical Society building in 1874, helped to organize the Commercial Club in 1881, and became the second president of the Art Institute of Chicago in 1881.[2]

The family's official version of the Field-Leiter split suggests that Levi Leiter sold out to Field in order to pursue other interests. In fact, Field forced him out. Marshall Field was a visionary, Levi Leiter, a cautious business man. When Leiter refused to support Field's plan to create an entirely new kind of department store, asserting that it was too risky, Field and the upper level managers of the business gave Leiter no choice. In selling out to Field, Levi Leiter loosened the ties that bound him to Chicago.[3]

Levi and Mary Leiter had four children: a son, Joseph, in 1868, and three daughters, Mary Victoria in 1870, Nancy in 1872, and Margaret (Daisy) in 1879. Joseph was sent to St. Paul's School and Harvard. The girls attended a private academy that educated the daughters of Chicago's elite families. The family lived on the then fashionable Calumet Street and summered at Linden Lodge, their elegant estate on Lake Geneva in Wisconsin.[4]

Unlike her husband, Mary Leiter does not appear to have had much interest in the arts or in any intellectual pursuits. Her chief concern was establishing her place in society. While she certainly wanted this for herself, as the mother of three girls she was primarily focused on ensuring that her daughters would be well placed to make advantageous marriages. To that end Mary Leiter eventually persuaded her husband to move the family from Chicago to Washington, D.C., which he did in 1881. For many years the family lived in a rented house on fashionable Dupont Circle. A newspaper article from 1909 suggested that the move had been a wise one.

Levi Leiter was among the earliest of the Western merchant princes who deliberately and advisedly came East to establish himself and his family in Washington society. Mr. and Mrs. Leiter succeeded in ten years in becoming the leading resident hosts of the Capital and moved the social center to Dupont circle.[5]

Soon after her arrival in Washington, Mary Leiter had joined the Ladies of Mount Vernon, where she became well enough acquainted with the wives of prominent Washingtonians to invite them to dinner. The Leiters gave lavish parties, and the people who counted came — Cabinet members, Supreme Court justices, and members of Congress. By time Mary Victoria made her debut in 1888, the family was established. Mary Victoria's intelligence, charm, and good looks made her the belle of Washington society. Much to her mother's delight, she also became a close friend of President Cleveland's young wife, Frances.

In addition to Mary Leiter's efforts in Washington society, during the 1880s and '90' she and her husband saw to it that their older daughters received the appropriate moral upbringing and education to make them suitable candidates for good marriages. Like other wealthy families, the Leiters made several trips to Europe where they and their daughters went on the Grand Tour, had their portraits painted, were fitted for dresses by Worth, and managed introductions to the local nobility. Both at home and abroad Mary Leiter kept a fairly tight rein on her daughters.

In 1895 two of Mary Leiter's fondest dreams came to fruition. After years of renting, the Leiters finally built their own home in Washington. Following his graduation from Harvard in 1891, son Joseph had become his father's business agent in Chicago. By 1895 Joe Leiter was firmly enough established for Levi Leiter to finally sell the Chicago house and leave his son to oversee the family business. The 52-room mansion that the Leiters built at 1500 New Hampshire Avenue on the corner of Dupont Circle was considered to be the finest private dwelling in Washington at the time. In spite of the move, for business reasons the Leiters retained Chicago as their legal residence.

But the real highlight of 1895 was the marriage of daughter Mary Victoria to British nobleman George Curzon, son and heir of Lord Scarsdale, Marquess of Kedleston. Levi Leiter provided 140,000 pounds outright and an annual income of 6000. Curzon had hoped for 9000 a year, but since his annual income at the time was only 1000 pounds, he settled. While the financial arrangements were of utmost importance to Curzon, he and Mary did indeed love each other. The wedding took place at St. John's Church followed by a reception at the Leiters' new home. Although protocol prohibited the President from attending, his wife Frances and much of the rest of official Washington were there. A week later the newly married Curzons sailed for England. Mary Curzon never returned to the United States. Mary Leiter traveled to England to be present at the birth of her first grandchild in January of 1896 and visited her daughter there three times over the next two years. [*]

Mary Curzon's biographer, Nigel Nicolson, painted a rather unflattering picture of Mary Teresa Leiter.

> She was a firm believer in Christian Science, convinced that physical well-being depends entirely upon an effort of will, and her manner was correspondingly extrovert, even jovial at times, demanding constant entertainment, in search of which she would flit from Chicago to New York, from London to Paris. But she could turn unexpectedly severe, when her high moral tone caught up with ebullience, and her victims were usually children, servants, or women of inferior means. She had no natural wit, but was considered eccentric in a rather engaging way, due chiefly to her lapses into malapropisms, as when she exclaimed, "At last I am back on terra cotta" on landing from a stormy Atlantic crossing, or when she announced that her husband would be attending a fancy dress ball "in the garbage of a monk."[6] [†]

_____

[*]Was Mary Victoria Leiter the model for Cora, the American heiress who married Lord Grantham in the BBC series *Downton Abbey*? In her book *The World of Downton Abbey*, Jessica Fellowes entitles one entry "The Real Life Cora: Lady Curzon." Author Julian Fellowes says Cora is a composite of many, including Mary Victoria Leiter, inspired by his reading of *To Marry an English Lord* by Gail McCall and Carol Wallace. Cora and Mary Victoria do have a lot in common: both were the daughters of very wealthy self-made men and social-climbing women, both bore their heir-seeking husbands three daughters and no sons. When the Honorable George Curzon became engaged to the daughter of Levi Leiter, English aristocracy speculated that the Leiters were Jewish. Fellowes gave Cora the maiden name Levinson.

[†] Nicolson also writes: The best joke of her life was probably inadvertent, when she protested that a public urinal that was to be erected outside her Washington house would be better sited on P Street

Her daughter Mary Victoria Curzon wrote of her a little more charitably.

> There is a high moral tone to all of her infantile stories, which I remember well as a child. I am afraid I am not made of such strong fibre as she is. She would show absolute composure in an earthquake, and always accept the inevitable without a shadow of discomfiture. She is self-centered, which I suppose is natural to anyone with such absolute self-confidence, and all our talk seems to revolve about small episodes in her existence.... She is peculiar but magnificent. [7]

According to Nicolson, George Curzon was not so kind. "He imagined Mrs. Leiter as a frequent self-invited guest at Kedleston Hall, perhaps sleeping in his dead mother's bed and patronizing his father's servants, and he did not look forward to the prospect at all."[8] After the birth of the Curzons' first child, both Mary and her husband came to appreciate Mary Leiter's finer qualities. She was an attentive and affectionate mother and grandmother.

A *Vanity Fair* article from 1897 gives some insight into Mary Leiter's social pretensions and successes at the time of her daughter Nancy's debut.

> Washington is coming to be a very sanguinary social battle-field. As the seat of government, and consequently the residence of foreign diplomats, it is a very desirable point of vantage from which to assail the citadels of New York society. If a socially ambitious woman can take the diplomats into camp — and this is not a difficult matter, for they are cosmopolites who are prone to take the gifts the gods provide and are particularly susceptible to the fascinations of a good cook — she acquires a standing that soon opens the charmed portals of New York and Newport to her.

> Mrs. L. Z. Leiter has done this and is emphasizing the fact in a way that has convulsed the feminine East. She came out of Chicago some ten years ago, backed by her husband's millions and the unquestionable charms of a very beautiful daughter, and the latter's marriage, year before last, to the Hon. George Curzon has made her position almost impregnable. This winter she has had a second daughter to bring out, and she has disrupted social Washington in doing so. The present Miss Leiter was brought out at a reception and cotillion which were given on the same evening that the Small and Early Dancing Class — patronized by Mrs. Henry Cabot Lodge, Mrs. Archibald Hopkins, the wife of Admiral John G. Walker, and Mrs. Ward, the grandmother of Mrs. William C. Endicott Jr. — had selected for their dance. As Mrs. Leiter had expressed her disapproval of young women dancing in public halls, the patronesses of the Small and Earlies felt that the gage of battle had been thrown down, and the people who were invited to both affairs were in a quandary as to which they would attend. Many of them were in doubt as to the reception they would receive at Mrs. Leiter's hands, for it is on record that at a cotillion which she gave during the Brice regime, there was actually a silken ribbon hung through the ball-room to separate the socially elect among her guests from the hoi polloi. However, at this present dance, Mrs. Leiter secured the cream of the diplomatic corps, and her position is now more assured than ever.[9]

In 1898 George Curzon was appointed Viceroy of India. A few months later he was created Baron Curzon of Kedleston, and thereafter referred to as Lord Curzon. As Vicereine, Mary Curzon became the second-highest-ranking woman in the British empire. Mary Leiter visited India once, in 1903, for the great coronation Durbar honoring King Edward VII's becoming emperor of India. The *New York Times* reported on her arrival in New York.

> Mrs. Levi Z. Leiter, in company with Miss Leiter, arrived last evening from Liverpool on the White Star liner *Oceanic*.... It was learned that Mrs. Leiter had a narrow escape from falling into the sea on Tuesday. She was sitting in a steamer chair on deck, as were scores of others. The sea was exceedingly rough at the time and most of the chairs were lashed, but Mrs. Leiter's was not. The ship was plowing through heavy seas and a huge wave caused it to lurch more than ever. Mrs. Leiter was pitched out of her chair and sent, with the chair, toward the rail. Several men leaped after her. Mrs. Leiter was dazed, and had she been alone she would almost certainly have been pitched under the rail and into the sea. As it was, she was severely shaken up. Neither Mrs. Leiter nor her daughter would say anything about the occurrence.

> Mrs. Leiter said her arrival in New York was the end of an almost continuous journey from Asiatic shores. She no more than touched England than she left for America. When asked as to her feelings of beholding her daughter the most important woman in all India, she threw up her hands in partial deprecation and walked away.[10]

Mary Leiter's daughters Daisy and Nancy visited their sister in India several times. It was there that Daisy met Lord Curzon's equerry Henry Molyneux Paget Howard, 19th Earl of Suffolk and 12th Earl of Buckingham, and her older sister Nancy met a second equerry, Major Colin Campbell — the two men whom the sisters would later marry.

The year 1904 was a momentous and difficult year for Mary Leiter. As had become their custom, the Levi Leiters went to Bar Harbor in May to spend the summer at the cottage they rented from the Vanderbilts. On June 6, Levi Leiter had a heart attack and died. He was 70 years old. His estate was valued at $30,000,000.

In the early fall Mary Leiter received word that her beloved daughter Mary was very, very ill. Lady Curzon was in England, having gone there earlier in the spring to give birth to her third child. Alexandra Naldera Curzon had been born on March 20. Lord Curzon had come to spend time with his wife and daughters. In midsummer Mary developed an illness that grew increasingly worse. By mid-September she was close to death. Mary Leiter rushed to her daughter's side. As soon as Mary Curzon recovered, Mary Leiter returned to Washington to oversee the weddings of her two younger daughters. On November 29, Nancy Leiter married Major Colin Campbell. On Boxing Day, December 26, Daisy married Henry Molyneux. These quiet family weddings were held at the Dupont Circle house. Both couples soon left to live in England.

Two years later, in 1906, Mary Curzon died at age 36, leaving three young daughters and a grieving husband. Mary Leiter spent much of the next two years in England in order to be close to her motherless granddaughters as well as to her daughters Nancy and Daisy. Among Mary Leiter's four children, only her son Joseph was still unmarried and living in the United States. As the head of the Leiter business enterprises and chief trustee of his father's estate, Joe Leiter spent much of his time in Chicago.

Perhaps it was during this period after the marriages of Daisy and Nancy and the death of Mary Curzon that Mary Leiter found the time to devote herself to what on the surface appears to have been an unlikely avocation. The sometimes bumptious and pretentious social climber became a skilled horticulturalist and plant breeder. Writing of a party at the Leiter house in the spring of 1908, Evalyn Walsh McLean and Boyden Sparkes wrote:

> By the time of our party, Mrs. Leiter had become a horticulturalist. She mixed some pollen and named the resulting blue verbena after Alice Roosevelt. Later on she brought about a yellow verbena she called "Ethel Roosevelt." Still later, she produced a pink one that she named for Helen Taft.[11]

Mary Teresa Leiter made her first appearance on Boston's North Shore in 1908. The front cover of the May 2, 1908, issue of *North Shore Breeze* magazine features a photograph of Undercliff, a Manchester estate built in 1900. The caption reads:

> *"Undercliff," the Charles Head Residence in Manchester,*
> *to Be Occupied This Season by Mrs. L. Z. Leiter of Chicago*

Why Mary Leiter chose to come to Manchester is unclear. Several Washington families summered on the North Shore, so it is likely that she came because she had friends in the area.

In June Mary Leiter returned to Washington briefly to attend the wedding of her son Joseph to Juliette Williams. The newlyweds joined her in Manchester later in the summer and then accompanied her to Europe. Upon their return, the three took up residence together at the Dupont Circle house. For the next few years, the young Leiters would go on to spend most of their time in Chicago with extended visits to Washington.

The summer of 1909 brought Mary Leiter to Beverly. In November of 1908, her Dupont Circle neighbor William Howard Taft had been elected president. Apparently Mary Leiter was friendly with Taft family and felt particular affection for Taft's wife, Nellie. When the Tafts announced that they would spend the summer at Stetson Cottage on the Evans estate in Beverly Cove, Mary Leiter rented the nearby Dudley Pickman house on Brackenbury Beach. Nellie Taft had suffered a stroke in May of 1909, and Mary Leiter may have come to give her support. A *New York Times* story from July 5, 1909, stated that Mary Leiter would be a leader in the Taft circle in Beverly, and that "the Taft cottage will see more of Mrs. Leiter than her own house." The article also noted that Mrs. Levi Leiter was not spending the summer in England, "the cause being that a rift had occurred between Lord Curzon and his mother-in-law."[12]

With the Tafts in residence, members of Washington society, as well as many foreign ambassadors and their staffs, scrambled to find accommodations on the North Shore. It was expected that Beverly would be the location of the summer White House for at least three and possibly seven more years. At some time during that summer at the Pickman house, Mary Leiter decided to build her own summer residence in Beverly.

Mary Leiter's decision to build a summer house on the North Shore may also have been rooted in her desire for a kind of respectability that is not easily bought. With the marriage of two daughters to English nobility and a third to a member of the English gentry, the Leiter money had done its work. By this time in Mary Leiter's life, Newport, a place where the newly rich could flaunt their wealth, held little appeal. On the North Shore, where proper Bostonians dominated the social scene, she had found the rough equivalent of the English aristocracy.

On October 7, 1909, a member of that Yankee aristocracy, the widow Mrs. Lucius Sargent (nee Marion Coolidge) purchased a little over three acres of Beverly Farms ocean front property at Allen's Head from Henry Lee Higgenson, her son-in-law's father. Three days later ground was broken for a Georgian brick mansion designed by Manchester architects Roberts and Hoar. A month later, Mary Leiter took the first step toward building her own Georgian mansion half a mile down the beach.

On November 6, Mary T. Leiter purchased three acres of oceanfront property in the Beverly Farms section of the city of Beverly from Mary Haven of Beverly and Charles Thornton Davis of Marblehead, trustees to the Franklin Haven Estate. The land was at the northeast corner of the Haven property, abutting the land of Robert S. Rantoul.

Mary Leiter's three-acre parcel was the first piece of the Haven estate to be sold off. The price that Mary Leiter paid is not recorded. The deed, typical of the time, reads "the sum of one dollar and other valuable considerations to be paid by Mary Leiter." Since there are no tax stamps on deeds, there is no way of knowing the true price. That the Havens were willing to sell it at all implies that Mary Leiter paid a substantial sum.

The deed contained restrictions forbidding the cutting of trees near the Haven property line without permission and forbidding the construction of new out buildings near the property lines. The restrictions were to be in effect for twenty years.[13]

Chapter 2
The Building of Edgewater House and
Mary Leiter's Years There: 1910-1912

Mary Leiter chose the Boston architect J. Harleston Parker to design her summer home by the sea. Parker had impeccable social as well as professional credentials. After graduating from Harvard in 1893 he had gone on to study architecture at MIT, in Italy, and at the École de Beaux Artes in Paris. He and his wife, the former Edith Stackpole, owned a summer home in Manchester and were members of the Myopia Hunt and Essex County Clubs. In 1904 Parker had designed Avalon, the handsome Frederick Ayer estate in Prides Crossing. Later he would design the Harvard Club and in 1914 the new buildings for the Essex County Club.

By February of 1910 the architectural plans were complete, and the project was about to go out to bid. A *New York Times* article of February 26 reported that Mrs. Levi Leiter had paid $50,000 an acre and went on to say:

> Mrs. Leiter has plans made for a mansion in the Old English style, which it is said will eclipse even Eagle Rock, the mansion of Henry Clay Frick in Prides Crossing.... Estimates of the cost of the Leiter mansion have varied from $500,000 to $1,000,000, and to build and furnish such a palace in 6 months' time is a task. It will mean the employment of hundreds of men, perhaps a thousand, from excavators to high-priced decorators.[14]

The March 4 edition of the *North Shore Breeze* reported that estimates were being made to be submitted the next week for Mrs. Leiter's house in Beverly Farms and that local contractors were not participating because of a contract requirement that the builder must finish the project by September of 1910 or be penalized. Mary Leiter was perhaps engaging in a personal race with Marion Sargent whose house was already under construction. The *Breeze* of March 18 published two stories about the Leiter house. The first reported Mary Leiter's reaction to the February 26th *New York Times* article.

> Mrs. Leiter has been rather troubled by reports that have been current regarding the new summer house she is having built in Beverly Farms. She says that she is not putting up a palace as has been suggested, nor has she ever paid $50,000 an acre for land anywhere as reported, and that it will be about 1/5 of the $500,000 which it is credited to cost when finished.

The second reported that L.D. Willcutt and Sons Company of Boston had won the contract for building the house, which was to be built of tapestry brick and would be when completed one of the handsomest houses on the North Shore.

> Work has already been started with a large force of men. The contract calls for the house to be completed by September 20th, and it is understood that the contractor will work most of the time with 2 or 3 shifts. Work on the stable and garage was started some weeks ago.

A third article reported that as a result of two weeks of splendid weather "work is going apace for building estates." Mrs. Lucius Sargent's estate was among those listed.

The laborers who constructed the Edgewater buildings most likely commuted to Beverly Farms from Boston by train. It is possible that construction may have slowed down in May, when carpenters in Beverly Farms went on a three-day strike to prevent contractors from enforcing a new rule to set uniform work hours that were inconvenient to the train schedule. The workers won. Independent carpenters were unionized, and by May of 1910 North Shore carpenters were getting $21 a week for 44 hours. Before the 1910 agreement, they were getting $19.68 for a 48-hour work week. Day laborers working in construction were earning about $9 for a 60-hour week.[15]

Three weeks later the *Breeze* reported: "Mrs. Leiter will sail for Europe in June to remain until September. Upon her return she will go to Beverly Farms when it is expected her new villa will be ready for occupancy." During her absence, work moved along quickly. The cover of the July 29 *Breeze* featured the newly completed Leiter stables.

In August Mary Leiter returned from Europe and again settled into the Dudley Pickman house in Beverly Cove. She quickly reestablished her place in society by holding a dinner party at her home to introduce a group of her friends to President Taft and his wife. Her son, Joseph, and his wife, Juliette, joined her at the end of the month, bringing with them their newborn son, John. The younger Leiters left in mid-September. The September 23 *Breeze* reported:

> Mrs. Levi Leiter is to remain in the North Shore until well along in October attending to the furnishing of her new home in Beverly Farms. She will not live in it in the autumn, but plans to leave it in such a way that it will be ready for occupancy next spring when she comes from Washington for the summer.

L. D. Willcutt and Sons had met the challenge and completed the building of stable and the estate house by the September 20 deadline, a phenomenal accomplishment. The September 30 issue of *North Shore Breeze* reported:

> Mrs. Lucius M. Sargent concluded her summer stay at Manchester with her father. Her new summer mansion at Prides is making rapid progress although March is the time designated for its completion. Work on grading the grounds was started this week by Connolly Bros. of Beverly Farms.

If Mary Leiter had been in an unacknowledged race with Marion Sargent, she had won, but it had been close. Both women would open their new summer homes for the 1911 season.

Edgewater House was an immediate success. Contrary to *New York Times* predictions, it was not another huge mansion on the order of Eagle Rock, Swiftmore, or Rockmarge. In keeping with the image she wished to establish on the North Shore, the house Mary Leiter built was spacious but restrained. The October 7 issue of *North Shore Breeze* carried the following article:

Description of Mrs. Levi Leiter's New Summer Mansion

By Mary Taylor Falt

The imposing new tapestry brick and marble mansion of Mrs. Levi Z. Leiter at West Beach, Beverly Farms, is a notable addition to the array of costly estates being located on the North Shore.

The mansion, which contains over 60 rooms, sets a little back from the beachfront at West Beach, with an enclosed marble terrace, and with balustrades in the foreground. In the rear of the house, the grounds of which sweep out toward the ocean on one side and to the Haven estate field on the railroad line, is the gardener's lodge, stable, and garage with belfry and clock tower. These buildings have been built also of tapestry brick and marble.

The mansion will be approached by long, tree-bordered concrete avenues. Preliminary work for Italian gardens, 120x46 feet, has been started. The mansion itself is a fine example of a most complete and ornate home, with lofty halls and living rooms, family suites and guest rooms, billiard hall, library, and servants apartments, while the culinary, laundry and other practical apartments of such a mansion are most up-to-date and equipped to every detail. The front, side, and back entrances are supported by stately white marble columns, and marbled-tiled, roomy balconies open from the upstairs suites of Mrs. Leiter, Sr., and Mrs. Joseph Leiter. The waterfront terrace of the mansion opens into a loggia of green latticework and ornately carved papier mache inserts, the medallions depicting classical and mythological subjects.

Much mahogany is used for the heavy doors of the mansion, while the library, finished in gumwood, has very beautiful hand-carved decorations.

The reception room is in white wood with a hand-carved mantle. The dining hall, 22x28, is carried out in mahogany and papier mache carvings* with a statuary marble mantle. The dainty breakfast room opens on the terrace and is finished in white and green latticework. The finish of the billiard hall is black cypress and grey stone. The guest rooms number eight. The long, sweeping staircase on the first floor has black ornate balustrades topped with mahogany, and on the second floor it is carried out in colonial style in white enameled wood.

The contractors for the mansion were L. D. Willcut and Sons Co. of Boston, and the architects were Thomas, Parker, and Rice of Boston, whose landscape gardener is laying out the Italian gardens. Linehan of Beverly Farms has the grading contract.[16]

Fisk & Company, Inc., with offices in New York and Boston, were "the proprietors and manufacturers of Tapestry Brick," which they advertised as "the most artistic and permanent building material in the world." Their ad also claimed that "a house built of Tapestry will usually be less expensive than one built of concrete."

The company used a photograph and description of the "House of Mrs. Levi Z. Leiter in Beverly Farms, Mass." in an advertisement in *The Brickbuilder*:[17]

---

* It is odd that Falt refers to "papier mache carvings." Perhaps the long-gone insert medallions in the lattice of the loggia were paper mache but the dining room carvings are plaster.

Prominent in the "North Shore Colony" is a beautiful "Tapestry Brick" house, the front view of which is shown in the above picture.

The brick in this house is our standard, full-range "Red Tapestry Group" laid with a one-half-inch gray mortar joint, rough cut flush with the face of the brick. The brick is laid in Flemish Bond, with headers of random color. Viewed from a distance, the color scheme is soft and dignified and in keeping with the character of the house, yet there is a beautiful play of color upon closer examination. Two interesting panels appear in the picture.

It is such use of "Tapestry Brick" that has made it *The Aristocrat of Building Materials.*[18]

The window frames were painted white. The shutters as well as the exterior of the breakfast room doors were painted a soft green, most probably the same color as the interior latticework. An early postcard of the exterior shows the library and reception room shutters closed. The front terrace off the loggia was fitted with an awning, as was a section of the upstairs porch adjoining Mary Leiter's bedroom.

First floor   The furnishings of the downstairs rooms were chosen for both style and comfort. A photograph from the time records a grouping of a sofa and two floral-printed upholstered chairs in the front hall. The reception room (parlor) was furnished with French provincial sofas and chairs, Feraghan rugs in senna leaf and allover floral design, assorted card tables including a "rare old George I walnut card table with top fitted with tills, cabriole legs carved on the knees, lion claw feet," and a Louis XVI ormolu mounted commode.[19]

A photograph of the dining room shows a simple Sheraton table and chairs. The inventory from the 1948 auction, in which all the furnishings were sold, described them "a very unusual Sheraton mahogany dining table consisting of five pedestal tables and two extra leaves" coupled with matching Hepplewhite mahogany shield-back chairs covered in golden cut velvet," a total of 22 side chairs and two armchairs.

The green lattice in the loggia suggests that it would have been furnished in the style of the day with wicker furniture and potted plants.

Mary Leiter may have at least partially furnished the library shelves with sets of books considered suitable for an educated person's home at the time: novels, histories, essays, biography, and travel — among them 15 volumes of de Maupassant, 17 of Bacon, 13 of Oliver Wendell Holmes, 20 of Eliot, 18 of Twain, 15 of Oscar Wilde, 20 of Carlyle, and 32 of the Irish author Charles Lever.

Second and third floors   The second-floor layout demonstrates how clearly the house was designed to serve the needs of Mary Leiter. The entire southwest end of the floor was devoted to her needs. The large (29'x 27') corner bedroom opened onto her balcony and connected to her bathroom and boudoir. Her bedroom was decorated with delicately painted, enameled cream furniture in the style of Louis XVI. Mary Leiter's personal maid had the corner room across the main hall. In the original plans, the elevator was located in the main hall next to her bedroom, but it was relocated to the main hall.

The ocean-view bedroom in the east corner (29'x 23') was designed for Juliette Leiter and included an adjoining dressing room for her husband. The bath for this room was equipped with both fresh and saltwater taps. Apparently the younger Leiters were taken with this recent fad. Bathrooms at The Breakers in Newport are similarly equipped.

The second floor had four additional guest bedrooms: one bedroom and bath on the main hall overlooking the driveway; two bedrooms with a connecting bath on the corridor of the wing[*]; and a bedroom, dressing room and bath suite at the end of the corridor. Beyond that suite and inaccessible from the main hall were rooms for male servants.

Four additional guest bedrooms were located on the third floor. The bedroom in the east corner included a dressing room. The bedroom in southwest corner connected through a shared bath to a small bedroom beyond. A large linen room was also located on the main corridor of the floor.

Service area   The great summer estates required well-designed service areas in order to operate efficiently. Edgewater House was designed for a staff of 20 or more. During Mary Leiter's time, these included a butler, a valet, footmen, two lady's maids, downstairs and upstairs maids, a head cook and her assistants, one or more chauffeurs, a groom, a caretaker/head gardener, several under-gardeners, and perhaps a houseman.

The service area was located in a wing perpendicular to the main house. Opposite the dining room, on the first floor, the butler's pantry served as the portal from the house to the service wing. The current owners have retained it much as it was. It is a room of richly polished wood and gleaming glass with wooden storage cabinets beneath work counters, and glass-enclosed cupboards for glassware and dishes above. A polished-wood serving table dominates the room. At the east of end of the room are the plate-warming shelves, a safe for the silver, and three dumbwaiters from the kitchen below. High on the south wall is the annunciator, the electric call system with connection to the public rooms, Mary Leiter's bedroom, Juliette Leiter's bedroom, and the eight guest rooms.

Beyond the butler's pantry was an airy servants' hall with a small exterior porch. The hall served as both dining room and gathering place for the staff. The servants' staircase, near the butler's pantry, led to the second and third floors. At the far end of the wing was the male servants' area: the valet's workroom, the butler's office, a full bath, three bedrooms for the butler and two male servants, and a stairway to the second floor.

The primary work area was in the basement. A stairway from the service hall led down to a large kitchen dominated by a big coal-burning cast iron stove. Two welled windows on the courtyard side provided light, as did two smaller windows in the open pantry. Closed utility cupboards were built in beneath the windows. Just to the left of the stairway was the scullery, with two soapstone sinks and built-in cupboards. To the right were the three dumbwaiters and a door into the laundry area. At the opposite end of the kitchen, a hallway behind the stove led to the utility boxes, a cold room with large refrigerators, a wine room, and the cook's storeroom. A staff toilet was located at the end of that hallway.

The laundry area, which was located behind the servants' stairs and the scullery, included two rooms: the laundry room with large soapstone sinks, a stove, and a supply closet, and a heated drying room.

---

[*] Oliver Ames Jr. remembers that although they no longer carried seawater, this bath also included the saltwater taps.

Since line drying in sunlight and fresh air was preferred, there was an outdoor drying area as well. Stairs from the laundry led directly out to a sunken gravel surfaced clothes yard.

The basement area under the main part of the house was devoted to utilities and storage. Two large coal bins were designated for furnace coal and kitchen coal. Next to them was a pump room. The engineering plans labeled two large round vats in the main basement as "filters." These were needed for filtering the seawater that would be pumped to two of the bathrooms in the east corner of the house. The eastern corner of the main basement is devoted to the furnace room, which was, and still is, fitted out with a metal door.[20]

Staff Housing   Most of the Edgewater staff was housed on the estate. The main house included ten rooms for female servants and seven rooms for the men. On the second floor, above the butler and male servants' suite, were additional male servants' quarters of four bedrooms and a full bath. With the exception of Mary Leiter's personal maid, who had a room near her lady's bedroom, all female servants had rooms on the third floor of the service wing. There was only one bath serving nine rooms of varying size, some of which probably housed two servants.

Garage, Stable and Gardener's cottage   The gardener and his family, as well as additional male staff, lived in the building that housed the garage, the stable, and gardener's cottage. A bell in the clock tower of that building was used to call the servants to meals. *American Country House of Today* ran a photograph and short review of the exterior that building:

Garage and Gardeners Cottage
Upon the Estate of Mrs. L. Z. Leiter, Beverly Farms

The octagonal clock tower is a very serviceable and decorative accent, adding greatly to the individuality and distinction of the group. Here is a lookout as well as a bell-cot, permitting an excellent view of the distance. It is interesting to see the way in which the rich tone of the bricks brings out the white of the stone and painted woodwork. The bricks are so laid in the tower and the bay of the cottage as to count at the angles as a decorative note. A landscape effort has also been made in the roof whereby the breadth is preserved to a measure and the dormers are kept as small as possible. In many ways the group recalls the material and serious spirit of the house. Attention has been vouchsafed the two gables, one belonging to the cottage and the other to the stable. The flat arches which span the entrance of the garage recall the proportions of a cloister. The approach is on the main axial line and is well planted on each side with maple trees so that shortly it will add still further to the attraction of the place, harmonizing with the splendid oaks and chestnuts, the tall elms and round-topped maples so prominent in the picturesque setting.[21]

Inside, the building was divided into three distinct areas. The stable/carriage house, which occupied the short wing, included stabling for three horses, a carriage room, and a carriage wash area. Over the stable section and accessed by a circular stairway in the tower were bedrooms and a bath for four male servants. The chauffeur(s) and perhaps under-gardeners lived here. The next section, on the other side of the bell tower, was a garage with three bays and a car wash area. Above it was a hayloft. The final section was a comfortable gardener's cottage. The downstairs included a kitchen and pantry, a dining room, parlor, and loggia opening to the back. Three bedrooms and a bath occupied the second floor.

A *North Shore Breeze* article about the building written after Mary Leiter's death commented on the utility of the bell tower. "The big bell in the tower on the barn is an unusual feature on a sea-shore home. It is said that during the time when Mr. Leiter's mother occupied the place several years ago, a great number of men were employed upon the premises and the bell tolled out the working hours, seven, twelve, one, and five."[22]

Grounds   The drive into Edgewater House split just as it came around the stable: the service branch curved behind the building and ended behind the service wing. The main drive swept around a large lawn curving into a circle in the entrance courtyard. According to the landscape plan, a large vegetable garden was to cover much of the ground between the gardener's cottage and the service wing. The plans also called for the loggia to open out onto lawns terraced to two levels down to the embankment to the beach. An Italian garden was to be laid out in the area beyond the south porch.

***

Once the main buildings were completed, Mary Leiter turned her attention to the creation of greenhouses. On September 16, 1910, she purchased an additional 72,942 square feet of land from the Haven heirs; this was located across the drive and bordering on West Street.

The October 21 issue of *North Shore Breeze* reported:

> Mrs. Levi Leiter closed her Beverly Cove cottage last Sunday and has returned to her winter residence, Dupont Circle, Washington. Mrs. Leiter is an early comer and late stayer on the North Shore. She intends to open her new estate at Beverly Farms next May to reside until November 1st. During the autumn the large fruit and vegetable houses of glass will be erected.[23]

A task Mary Leiter had completed before leaving for Washington was the hiring of a gardener/caretaker. She followed the example of many of her neighbors in choosing a Scotsman. Lechlan Cameron was 33 when he emigrated from Scotland in 1906 with his wife, Jessie, and two-year-old son Duncan. Cameron had trained in Scotland and had been working as an under-gardener on the Henry Frick estate when Mary Leiter hired him. The Camerons probably moved into the gardener's cottage in the fall of 1910 so that Cameron could begin work on the gardens as well as serve as onsite caretaker for the newly completed and furnished estate.[24]

***

The Leiters arrived at Edgewater in mid-May of 1911 with plans to stay a month before sailing to Europe for an early summer visit. *North Shore Breeze* reported on the projects that had been completed since Mary Leiter had left in October.

> Since then improvement of the grounds has gone on with excellent results, and a series of greenhouses has been constructed by the Lord and Burnham Company of Boston. Another new feature on the Leiter estate is the revolving sun house. It is a small round building so planned that shelter from too glaring sun or from the wind is afforded. E.A. Abbott and Sons are the builders[25]

17

The only image of the impressive Leiter greenhouses is in an aerial photograph of the property taken in the early twenties. The greenhouse complex consisted of two greenhouses 31' 4" wide and 106' 6" long, four hot frames 53' 3'' long, a brick potting shed, and a large underground cistern. One greenhouse was divided into two heating zones, for early and intermediate potted fruit. The second was designated intermediate and late potted fruit.[26]

The sun house was a phenomenon. The *New Orleans Picayune* of May 29, 1911, gave a more detailed description:

> It stands at the end of some small gardens on a terrace overlooking the beach and sea. Its roof is constructed of small poles and is supported by rustic posts covered with rough bark. Around three sides of the structure heavy plates of glass are set. Curtains within are so arranged that the occupants can protect themselves from the hottest glare of the sun's rays. The structure is balanced upon ball bearings as nicely as the carriage of an expensive telescope.[27]

Following Mary Leiter's return from Europe, she, Joe, and Juliette settled into a routine of entertaining. Mrs. Leiter loved to entertain out of doors. A photo of the period shows the front lawn set up for tea. In August, *North Shore Breeze* reported:

> Mrs. Buckner M. Randolph of Washington has been spending the week with Mrs. Levi Z. Leiter at Edgewater House....Miss Helen Taft is a very frequent caller at the Leiter cottage with its broad verandas opening onto West Beach and with a cool breeze always blowing in from the ocean. Mr. and Mrs. Joseph Leiter have given several informal luncheons in Miss Taft's honor, including one on Monday this week....Luncheons are a popular medium for social intercourse. Mrs. L. Z. Leiter gave one on Wednesday to some forty guests.[28]

In late August, Joe and Juliette spent time in Newport, taking in tennis week and visiting with friends. Mary Leiter stayed home.

> Mrs. Levi Z. Leiter...has, it seems, been spending much of her time in a labor of love and memory, the completion of her late husband's collection of Southern books and manuscripts of the Civil War, after many years of wearisome labor. The collection is said to be the largest in existence of letters, papers, books, and records, etc., of the war between the North and South. There has been an enormous task of indexing and cross-indexing the contents. An expert from the Congressional Library did this work. It is a matter of speculation whether the valuable collection will remain at the Beverly Farms mansion or will be sent to Mrs. Leiter's Washington residence.[29]

In September Mary Leiter held a large dinner party that included Mrs. Jack Gardner (Isabella Stewart), who stayed on for a few days as Mary's guest.[30] Over the years Mrs. Gardner often stayed at Alhambra, the Prides Crossing cottage on the estate of her husband's nephew William Amory Gardner. At the time of her stay at Edgewater, she was devoting most of her fortune and attention to her art collection and the development of Fenway Court. She spent as little money as possible on other things and was well known for cadging invitations to stay with friends and acquaintances on the North Shore.[31]

In October Mary Leiter engaged Connolly Brothers to build "an attractive stone entrance wall and pillars at the first entrance of the estate."[32] The new structure caused immediate controversy with her neighbors the Rantouls, whose land abutted the driveway. In 1848, David Neal had sold Franklin Haven a 50 x 212 feet strip of land to provide Haven with access to his estate from Hale Street. A few years later

Neal gave a portion of land between his house and the Haven estate to his daughter, Harriet Neal Rantoul. In building her grand entrance, Mary Leiter had encroached on Rantoul land. The problem was solved by a memorandum signed by Robert S. Rantoul and Mary Leiter and filed with the registry of deeds. Mary Leiter did not have to remove her gate, but she acknowledged that she did not have right of passage over the portion of land on which she had encroached.[33]

It is not surprising that the Rantouls felt under threat. The clapboard Rantoul cottage was one of the oldest and most modest residences on the waterfront and had been built quite close to the Haven boundary line. The view from the Rantouls' western windows had always been of spacious fields with the rambling old Haven cottage in the distance. All of that had changed dramatically with the building of Edgewater House. The Rantouls' immediate view was now of the sunken clothes yard and the looming three-story service wing.

***

In early June of 1912 Mary Leiter returned to Edgewater House and, in the words of the *North Shore Breeze,* "is giving personal supervision to her gardens which are very fine."[34] Apparently Lechlan Cameron did not appreciate Mary Leiter's personal supervision. She had a reputation for being condescending and a bit imperious to her social inferiors including servants. A gardener's cottage in close proximity to the main house was not always an advantage. The cause is not documented, but in early August Cameron tendered his resignation, effective in September.[35] He worked for a year as a mechanic and then returned to work as a gardener at the Frick estate, where he eventually became superintendent. He continued to be employed with Frick until his death in 1934.[36]

During that summer Mary Leiter entertained Joe and Juliette Leiter as well as many out-of-town guests. Locally, Edgewater House became well known as the site of many social events, including well-attended luncheon parties. Although no mention is made of it in the *North Shore Breeze*, the Tafts may well have been among those entertained there during the summers of 1911 and 1912. Over the five summers Mary Leiter had spent on the North Shore, she had become a part of the social community. In August of 1912 she was among the patronesses at a fete given by Mrs. John Hayes Hammond to raise funds for a memorial arch to honor women who died on the *Titanic*.[37]

The death of Mary Leiter's sister in August of 1912 caused her to leave Edgewater before the season ended. The August 30 issue of the *Breeze* reported.

> Mrs. Levi Leiter will be one of the first of Beverly Farms residents to desert the charms of the North Shore. Mrs. Leiter leaves Tuesday for New York, from which she will sail for Europe to be abroad for the winter. Mrs. Leiter has been one of the foremost entertainers of Beverly Farms, and her departure will be regretted by many who know her.[38]

Mary Teresa Leiter was never to return to Edgewater House. On March 7, 1913, she died of a cerebral hemorrhage at her home in Washington. She was 68. Her will, written in Beverly Farms on June 3, 1912, gave her son Joseph life tenancy of Edgewater House on condition that he never rent it out or use it for anything other than a private dwelling.[39]

Chapter 3
The Joseph and Juliette Leiter Years:
1913-1932

Joseph Leiter was in most ways the polar opposite of his father. Levi Leiter was a self-made man who had risen from store clerk to financier. He was a cautious businessman, the epitome of prudence; a serious man who led the relief effort after the Chicago fire; a cultured man who collected Civil War manuscripts and rebuilt both Chicago's Historical Society and its art museum. Joe Leiter was a romantic, flamboyant adventurer with big ideas. He could be wildly impetuous, leaping into new ventures with great optimism. Some knew him as a totally charming man, a gourmet cook, and genial host. Others experienced his mercurial temper and saw him as a bully. In every way he was a larger-than-life character who ignored convention and did as he pleased. The one characteristic father and son shared was a fierce determination to let nothing stand in the way of getting what they wanted.

Joseph Leiter was born in Chicago in 1868, the eldest child and only son among Levi and Mary Leiter's four children. He attended school at St. Paul's in Concord, New Hampshire, and Harvard University, where he became a member of Spee, one of college's exclusive final clubs.[*] Shortly after his graduation in 1891, Joe Leiter went to work at his father's Chicago office, and proved so capable that Levi Leiter gave him $1,000,000 to engage in speculation on his own account. He soon made a fortune, principally in mining and railway stocks. During this time he became director of the City Railway Company, the South Side Rapid Transit, and the Chicago Edison Company as well as the First National Bank of Topeka, Kansas.[40]

In an 1893 letter, Joe's sister Mary Victoria wrote her fiancé, George Curzon, "You will like Joe — he is the jewel of the family. He calls forth an affection from every sort of living thing."[41] Curzon would later have reason to lose any affection he may have felt.

Joseph Leiter is best known for his cornering the wheat market in 1897. For a short time he looked like a 29-year-old boy wonder. The scheme began to unravel when Philip D. Armour used icebreakers to bring in Canadian wheat and flood the market. This, in addition to predictions of a bumper United States wheat crop the following year, led to Leiter's losing close to $10,000,000 and being suspended from the Chicago Board of Trade. The loss couldn't have come at a more inopportune time for his brother-in-law. Just then Curzon was negotiating to be appointed Viceroy of India, a position that depended upon his wife's income.

---

[*] Not quite as prestigious as Porcellian, Spee was in the upper echelon of clubs. Both Jack and Ted Kennedy were among its 20th century members.

"Through an arrangement between Levi Leiter and the banks, the unsold wheat was gradually marketed without disturbing its value, and by September 1898 every creditor had been paid in full and all bank obligations wiped out."[42] Although Curzon did become Viceroy of India in 1898, he never again trusted his brother-in-law's financial management ability. Undaunted, Joe Leiter dusted himself off and continued to speculate — with apparent success. He soon became involved in a combine of Chicago street railways, a milk trust, and a Canadian meat trust.[43] Joe Leiter's wheat-cornering fiasco lived on as the seed for muckraking novelist Frank Norris's Chicago novel *The Pit*.[44]

In the early 1900s, Levi Leiter gave his son specific control of the nearly 8000 acres of family-owned coal fields in southern Illinois. In 1903 Joe Leiter established the mining town of Zeigler, named for his father's mother's family. Following in the footsteps of George Pullman, Joe Leiter attempted to create a model company town complete with paved streets, electricity, schools, a model farm, and a hospital. Zeigler was laid out in a wagon wheel pattern like Washington, D. C. Company headquarters and Leiter's house were built on the central ring, facing a park. The mine itself was electrified and fitted out with state-of-the-art equipment designed to improve efficiency and safety in the mine. In 1904, citing the use of labor-saving devices, Leiter lowered the tonnage pay rate for miners. The United Mine Workers ordered a strike. When violence broke out, Leiter called in the militia to restore order and hired unsuspecting immigrants to run the mines. All hope for a utopia was destroyed when Zeigler became an armed camp surrounded by stockade walls.

A terrible explosion in 1905 led to the deaths of over 50 miners, many of them Greek and Lithuanian immigrants. A fire followed by another fatal explosion in 1909 led to a temporary closing of the mine. The following year Leiter leased the Zeigler mine for royalties. In spite of the early problems, the Zeigler Coal Company went on to become one of the largest coal producers in the country.[45]

After his father's death in 1904, Joseph Leiter and non-family trustee Seymour Morris assumed complete management of the vast holdings of the family estate. Although his mother and sisters were co-trustees, Joe had a free hand in managing the affairs: his mother had no interest in business, Mary Leiter Curzon was in India, and his sisters Daisy and Nancy were in England.

In 1908 Joe Leiter married Juliette Williams, considered one of the most beautiful young women in Washington society. Joe was 40, his bride 21. Juliette was the daughter of Colonel John and Maie Hewitt Williams. The Leiters were Episcopalians; the Williamses Catholics. A quiet family wedding in the Williams's apartments was followed by a reception at a Washington hotel. The bride and groom sat at a heart-shaped table with 18 close friends — Representative Nick Longworth and his wife, Alice Roosevelt Longworth, were among them.*

Events that occurred outside got as much press as the wedding itself. As one of Washington's most eligible bachelors, Joe Leiter had become a favorite of local gossip columnists. He had anticipated that photographers might be lying in wait for him when he arrived at the Williams' apartments for the

---

* Nick and Alice Longworth often vacationed at the senior Longworths' estate in Prides Crossing.

ceremony. Since he knew that they would expect him to drive from his mother's house in his "silver-gray racing auto," he outwitted them by taking a taxi and going in the back door.

So that, with the earlier victory of the day a pleasant memory, he was made very angry when his auto containing himself, his bride, and her mother Mrs. Williams drew up at Rauscher's, where the reception was to be held, and discovered a camera man named Pridgeon ready to make a plate of the party as they alighted.

Pridgeon's head was under the cloth and he failed to see the spring with which Mr. Leiter landed on the sidewalk. Before the operator even had a chance to squeeze the bulb and snap the shutter, Mr. Leiter was upon him. Mr. Leiter weighs about 200 pounds.

He forcibly pushed down on the mound of the cloth which represented Pridgeon's head, and the photographer was borne to the sidewalk wildly waving his arms and legs, trying to disentangle himself from the cloth and asking in a muffled voice what might be the trouble.

But he did not try to rise. Mr. Leiter then quite adequately smashed the camera, breaking the tripod legs to bits and shattering the glass of the lens and the two plates in the holder.[46]

Following a honeymoon that included a visit with Mary Leiter in Manchester, Joe and Juliette set up residence in Chicago. For the next few years they divided their time between their home in Chicago and Mary Leiter's house in Washington. Their first child, John, was born in 1909 and died the same year. A second son, Joseph Jr., was born in 1910.

In 1911, the year his mother moved into Edgewater, Joe Leiter bought land and made plans to build a new house of his own. The October issue of *North Shore Breeze* reported:

Joseph Leiter, who is abroad with his mother, is building a mansion in Virginia, which is on the site of the Potomac River. The estate will be laid out like an English park, and one of its principal features will be a game preserve. The estate is said to have nearly 2 miles of river frontage.[47]

Joe, with the help of his mother, had purchased 520 acres of waterfront farmland in Fairfax County. The estate was called The Palisades, named for the natural formation along the riverfront. The rambling shingle and stone house that Leiter built there came to be known as the Glass Palace. With 72 rooms and 17 baths, it dwarfed Edgewater House. State-of-the-art technology provided water and electric power. The estate included a greenhouse, a barn, and a caretaker's house. Although it was operated as a working farm, The Palisades served primarily as "a spot for entertaining Washington socialites and for conducting business."

In order to ensure easy access to Washington, Leiter paved the Georgetown Turnpike, making it the first macadamized road in Fairfax County. He managed to persuade the county to both reimburse him for the costs and exempt him from paying the toll on the completed highway.[48]

Upon his mother's death in 1913, Leiter acquired the family mansion on Dupont Circle. Although he and Juliette left Chicago and made the Dupont Circle house their winter residence, they kept Chicago as their legal residence. Since the Leiter estate was administered from Chicago, Joe Leiter maintained an apartment there for the rest of his life. The *Social Register* always included the Leiters in its Chicago section. By 1913 Joe and Juliette had two sons: in addition to Joseph Jr., born in 1910, Thomas had been born in February of 1912. The *Summer Social Register* for 1913 listed the summer residence of Mr. and Mrs. Joseph Leiter of Chicago as "The Palisades, Langley, Virginia."[49] Mary Leiter had left Edgewater House to all of her children in equal, undivided shares. Joseph, the only heir then living in the United States, was given life tenancy on condition that Edgewater never be rented out.[50]

The 1913 spring and early summer issues of *North Shore Breeze* made no mention of Mary Leiter's death or of Joseph Leiter. It appears that the only inhabitants of the estate were the new gardener/caretaker and his family. At some time in August of 1912, Mary Leiter had hired William Swan to replace Lechlan Cameron. Swan had emigrated from England sometime between 1890 and 1898. Before coming to Edgewater, Swan had worked in Manchester for Mrs. Lathrop Brown and before that for her father, R. C. Hooper. In the fall of 1912 Swan, his wife, Katherine, and their young sons, William and Frederick, moved into the gardener's cottage. Edgewater was a summer residence, but it required year-round maintenance. In addition to providing security for the house, Swan kept the large greenhouses working throughout the winter and spring.

The sole mention of the Leiters in the *North Shore Breeze* of 1913 was in the August 15 issue.

> Mr. and Mrs. Joseph Leiter of Washington and Beverly Farms are planning to start on a trip around the world in September and have chartered the *Niagara IV* of Howard Gould for the cruise. They will sail from New York and be absent for a year. Accompanying them on their trip will be their children, a physician, and several friends. It is understood that Mrs. Leiter's parents, Col. and Mrs. John Williams, will join them in Europe and travel with them. The *Niagara* has 12 staterooms and 9 baths, a music room, a library, a dining room, a breakfast room, extra rooms for the physician, secretary, valet, and maids, a steam laundry, and other equipment equal to that of the average fashionable house. The cruise will start from New York and then to British waters. They will go to the Mediterranean Sea, where they will remain until the first of the year, and then go to the East through the Suez Canal, visiting India, Ceylon, China, Japan, the Philippines, and Honolulu, returning by way of San Francisco and the Panama Canal. They plan to be back in time for the America's Cup races during September, 1914.

The *New York Times* issue for August 12 headlined its column:

LEITER PLANS WORLD CRUISE
Charters Howard Gould's Yacht to Take Forty Around the Globe

According to the *Times* article, the *Niagara IV* required a crew of 65. The *Times* and the *Breeze* may both have exaggerated the numbers, but Howard Gould's yacht, completed in 1911 for an estimated $500,000 (over $1,000,000 in 2015 dollars), was indeed a floating palace.[51]

Joseph and Juliette Leiter were not to take possession of Edgewater until the summer of 1915. The story of the estate during 1913 and 1914 is primarily the story of its gardeners.

***

Once news of the Leiters' plan for a year-long cruise became public knowledge, gardener William Swan may have considered his position uncertain. In any case, at the end of the summer he accepted the position as head gardener on Louis Frothingham's summer estate in North Easton.[52] The *Gardener's Chronicle of America* wrote:

> William Swan, for many years head gardener of the R. C. Hooper estate in West Manchester and more recently with Mrs. Levi Z. Leiter of Beverly Farms, succeeds W. M. Craig at Longwater, North Easton. Mr. Swan worked at North Easton for several years before going to West Manchester, and is noted as a first class gardener.[53]

Before leaving on his cruise, Joseph Leiter hired a new gardener, Joseph Tillson, who had been working on the Spaulding Farm off Greenwood Avenue in Beverly Farms. Tillson had been born in Wales in 1886 and probably trained in England as a gardener. In 1910, he immigrated to Massachusetts and must have come to Beverly Farms right away. It is possible that the Spaulding brothers had recruited him to oversee their fruit greenhouses. In 1911 he joined the North Shore Horticultural Society and in 1913 was a featured speaker at one of the Society's meetings. According to the minutes:

> The president then introduced Mr. Joseph Tillson of Beverly Farms, who presented a very able paper on fruit growing. Questions were freely asked and replied to, after which it was voted to close the discussion. A vote of thanks was extended to Mr. Tillson for his able talk.[54]

At the Spaulding Farm, Tillson was one of many gardeners under the supervision of Superintendent Frank Cole. At Edgewater he would be the head gardener/caretaker of an estate with two superb greenhouses and a fine house for his family. When Swan left in September of 1913, Tillson and his wife, Jane, moved into the gardener's cottage, and Tillson became gardener and caretaker for an empty estate.

During the year when the Leiters were traveling around the world, Joseph Tillson was busy improving the gardens and further developing the complex system of horticulture in the greenhouses. By mid-June of 1915, Tillson was preparing the house for the Leiters' arrival. *North Shore Breeze* reported:

> Edgewater, the home of Joseph Leiter of Chicago and Washington, is one of the attractive places at Beverly Farms. Just now the approach to the house leads through fine rows of rhododendrons. The house is being made ready for Mr. Leiter, who will spend the last week of June here. During July and August, Col. and Mrs. Williams, parents of Mrs. Leiter (Juliette Williams), will occupy the place.

During the last week of July, 1915, more than two years after Mary Teresa Leiter's death, Joseph Leiter and his family finally came to take possession of Edgewater. *North Shore Breeze* combined the announcement of their arrival with a vivid description of the gardens and greenhouses:

> Mr. and Mrs. Joseph Leiter (Juliette Williams) and two children of Washington arrived this Wednesday at Edgewater House, their beautiful home in Beverly Farms. They have been spending several weeks at their country home near Washington. Mrs. Leiter's mother, Mrs. John R. Williams of Washington, will be with them this summer.
>
> Edgewater House is one of the many attractive estates at Beverly Farms. The large brick house has a very old and distinguished air about it and can be seen plainly from the water. A revolving sun-parlor is a unique feature of the garden. A sunken garden and a rose-garden are things of beauty now. The rose garden is very striking in its simplicity, being simply a square filled with various roses

and surrounded by a fence completely covered with pink ramblers. The square has an arched entrance on the four sides, over which the rambles hang in great profusion.

The estate has immense hothouses in which an English plan is in operation for raising fruits and vegetables. The Leiter family has been supplied all spring by the products of their greenhouse in Beverly Farms. The English gardener, Joseph Tillson, has been experimenting in many unique ways. Luscious figs, nectarines, peaches, tree tomatoes, and melons are some of the special novelties seen now in the hotbeds. The melons are especially attractive growing on small vines running up the side walls, and each melon so heavy (2 to 4 pounds) that it is encased in a little nest tied to the ceiling. The peach and nectarine trees are trained fan-shaped on netting and make a very ornamental sight. The visitor would think it was all arranged for an artistic fruit show, but the gardener assures one that it is all for a very utilitarian purpose. He has rooms of various temperatures, some extremely hot in which fruit is forced and others cooler in which the fruit will mature later. In this way he hopes to extend the crop as long as the family remains at Beverly Farms. Various small garden supplies [sic] were raised in the hothouses and sent to the Leiters in Washington all winter.[55]

***

The Beverly Farms that the Leiters came to in the summer of 1915 was representative of the North Shore Gold Coast at the height of its development. The 1913 *Who's Who on the North Shore* listed 123 summer homes in the broader Beverly Farms area; the vast majority of them were owned by wealthy and socially prominent residents of Massachusetts.[*]

Beverly Farms and Prides Crossing, although part of the city of Beverly, each had its own post office, railway station, and express company. A fire station in Beverly Farms served both communities. By 1915 AT&T had a telephone exchange on Vine Street.

The commercial center of Beverly Farms during this period catered to year-round residents and to the practical needs of the summer residents. There were contractors, carpenters, painters, plumbers, a tree transplanter, a florist, wood-and-coal and hay-and-grain dealers, blacksmiths and farriers, two harness shops, livery stables and an automobile service station and garage, a doctor, a dentist, and a veterinarian specializing in the care of horses. The commercial establishments on West, Hale, and Vine Streets also included grocery and provision stores, a fish market, a Chinese laundry, an apothecary, shoe and dry-goods stores, cobblers, barbers, a seamstress, three tailors, a small restaurant, and a summer photographic studio.

Beverly Farms had three churches: the old Baptist Church on Hart Street, St. Margaret's Roman Catholic Church, built in 1887, and St. John's Episcopal Church, completed in 1902. The town also had two function halls that primarily served the year-round residents: Marshall's Hall above the apothecary on

_____

[*]Atlases of the period sometimes designate the sections of Beverly between Boyle's corner (where Hale and Boyle streets meet) to the Manchester border as West Farms, Prides Crossing, and Beverly Farms. In this book they are generally referred to as Beverly Farms unless there is a specific Prides Crossing location.

the corner of Hale and West streets, and Neighbor's Hall above the shopping arcade on West Street.[56] The elegant brick library would be completed in 1916.

The Farms' only hotel reopened as the Tunapoo Inn in 1915. *North Shore Breeze* described it as "one of the quiet, homelike places on the North Shore where one can be in touch with all the activity of the shore and yet enjoy the quiet and homelike atmosphere of a modern inn. The inn is proving very popular as a tearoom. Afternoon tea is served in a pretty, screened part of the big veranda, which is one of the attractive features of the place." Its first overnight guests were a group of young women from Wellesley College.[57]

The broader North Shore community provided social clubs, exclusive shops, restaurants, and public entertainments. The yacht clubs of choice for most Farms-Prides residents were the Eastern Yacht club in Marblehead and the nearby Manchester Yacht Club. Horsemen and golfers belonged to the exclusive Myopia Hunt Club in Hamilton. The Essex County Club in Manchester was a more general club, to which most summer residents belonged. The facilities included a fine golf course and tennis courts. The club's elegant new clubhouse, designed by Edgewater architect J. Harleston Parker, opened in 1915 and became a popular venue for luncheons and dinner dances.

Magnolia, with its grand Oceanside Hotel, was the shopping and entertainment mecca for the northern section of the Shore. The hotel and its cottages could accommodate 750 people. The hotel's large ballroom hosted regular dances and elaborate musical entertainments, with nationally famous artists. The new North Shore Grill on Magnolia Avenue became "the place de resistance for the smart set who arrived in their automobiles." In 1914 the grill had set up an outdoor dance floor and engaged the Imperial Hungarian Orchestra. The shopping arcades on Lexington Avenue catered to the summer residents and included branches of many exclusive New York and Boston shops.

Social life on the North Shore during the early part of the twentieth century, in spite of the influx of millionaires from beyond Massachusetts, remained relatively sedate. Proper Boston society continued to set the tone. The outsiders were eventually woven into the social fabric, but seldom dominated it. It would be several years before the Leiters became fully connected to the summer community.

From the very beginning, Boston Brahmins' sense of *noblesse oblige* manifested itself in the summer community by the intertwining of social activities with good causes. The Boston ladies brought their favorite charities with them and planned fairs, musicales, and luncheons for their benefit.

By the summer of 1915, the war in Europe had cast a shadow over the summer idyll. Many of the summer residents as well as their servants had family or social connections in Europe. A few sons of North Shore residents volunteered in the Lafayette Escadrille. The community spread their charitable work to include those in Europe. The Leiters' neighbors Harriet Rantoul, Mrs. Fred Bemis, and Elizabeth Perkins were leading members of the North Shore Fund for the French Wounded. Down the road in Prides Crossing, Mrs. Robert Bradley hosted a musicale in support of the fund in early July. Mr. and Mrs. Francis L. Higginson of Paine Avenue held a concert in support of Polish sufferers. Although the United States. was not yet involved in the war, mobilization was beginning. The largest Beverly Farms fundraiser of the summer was a mid-July fair held at Sydney Hutchinson's beachfront house in support of the Navy YMCA.

Although the Leiters did not host any events that summer, they would certainly have attended them. Edgewater may have been among the summer estates affected by one war related event. By June, Italy's entry into the war led to an exodus of young Italian men from the North Shore. Many of them had worked as under-gardeners.

Except for an extended motor trip to Washington in early August, the Leiters spent the rest of the summer and early fall in Beverly Farms.

***

Sometime in the spring of 1916, Joe Leiter wrote a short biographical piece for the Harvard class of 1891's twenty-fifth anniversary yearbook. His summary gives some insight into the nature of the man at this point in his life.

> On leaving College I went to work in my father's office in Chicago, July 1, 1891. On January 1, 1892, I was given charge of the office. On July 1, 1892, I was given charge of all affairs coming into the office. During 1892 and 1893 I was made director in many corporations representing our interests. In 1896, 1897, and 1898, in addition to my other work, I ran a speculation in wheat and corn which caused some comment but was not profitable.

> From 1898 to 1902 I was engaged in manufacturing and in putting together consolidations with success. I went into coal mining about this time and, objecting to the unions running my business, had a strike on my hands for three years, during which time the properties ran with non-union men in spite of a good deal of killing and destruction of property. This sort of existence proving a little too exciting for my wife, [so] I rented the property out to another concern.

> Since then I have reorganized a gas company and several other concerns, but am not now actively engaged in the conduct of any business in a managerial way, but in many as director.

> From September 1913, to September 1914, I took the family and a number of friends around the world in a yacht.[58]

***

In the summer of 1916, Juliette Leiter and her children arrived at Edgewater in late July to be joined later by Joe Leiter. Juliette's parents, Colonel John and Maie Williams, and Juliette's elder sister, Mrs. W. F. McCombs, had rented houses in Beverly Farms. As a young mother with two small boys, and pregnant with a third child, Juliette must have been delighted to have her family nearby.[*]

---

[*] Some written sources state that this third child, Nancy Leiter, was adopted. Nancy's daughter and other family members are certain that this is not true, that Nancy was indeed Joe and Juliette's natural child.

Less than two weeks after she arrived, Juliette faced a domestic crisis when the estate superintendent abruptly resigned. The Beverly Farms column in the local news section of the August 4 edition of *North Shore Breeze* reported:

> Mr. Joseph Tillson, who has been superintendent of Edgewater, the Leiter estate, has resigned his position and for the present will be employed by John L. Chapman, who recently went into a commercial nursery and gardening business. Mr. Tillson and family have moved into the "Endicott" cottage owned by Patrick Barry on High Street.[59]

Edgewater House had lost its third superintendent in six years. There is no record of what caused Tillson to resign, but the decision appears to have been a sudden. It was unusual for a caretaker to quit in mid-season. For Tillson to have given up a prestigious position, state-of-the-art greenhouses, and an especially fine gardener's cottage suggests that he found something about his situation untenable.

Joe Leiter arrived the following week and hired a replacement, an English-trained gardener named Percy Huxley. Huxley and his pregnant wife, Jessie, moved to Edgewater immediately. Percy Huxley had been born in Wales in 1891 and immigrated to the United States in 1911. Huxley stayed on as superintendent for ten years.

Once the caretaker issue was resolved, the Leiters settled in for a quiet summer. Both of them were pleased to have the Williams family nearby. Juliette's younger sister, Francise Williams, was a beautiful and lively young woman who quickly became involved in local social and charitable activities. Like the rest of the nation, the North Shore community, year-round and summer residents alike, continued their aid to Europeans and also began to prepare for the expected United States entry into the war.

Even at home, Juliette and her family would have been exposed to military preparations. The revolving sun house at Edgewater was an ideal spot for viewing activities taking place on the water. The September 13 *North Shore Breeze* reported:

> West Beach frequenters...have an opportunity to see an aeroplane in action nearly every day. Godfrey Cabot of the Beverly Farms summer colony, who is much interested in aviation, has his seaplane out every fair day. Last Saturday and Sunday he made more than thirty flights along the Shore. Mr. Cabot is building a hangar on Mystery Island * and many of the summer colonists are interested in a plan for the organization of an aviation corps as an auxiliary to the government service.[60]

The Leiters did host one major social event in September of 1916, the wedding of Juliette's sister Francise and John Ballantyne Pitney. Pitney was a Princeton graduate from a prominent New Jersey family. He had a strong interest in the military and was about to take an examination for a lieutenancy in the Army. Colonel and Mrs. Williams held a prenuptial dinner at Myopia Hunt Club. The wedding was held at Edgewater House at noon on September 22. Father Walsh from St. Margaret's Roman Catholic Church officiated. *North Shore Breeze* described the setting.

---

* Promoters had recently so renamed Misery Island in hopes of making it more inviting.

Edgewater House was decorated for the event with quantities of blue hydrangeas, effectively massed and also with many pink gladioli....The bride wore a bridal gown of white tulle over white satin and the full train was also of tulle. The gown was trimmed with rich lace and with it a bridal veil of tulle was worn, held in place with orange blossoms. The bride carried a bouquet of white orchids.

At the reception which followed, the host and hostess, Mr. and Mrs. Joseph Leiter, and the bridal couple welcomed 150 to 200 guests. It was in part al fresco in character, as the guests wandered out of doors where the lawns and flower beds make the estate most attractive. The tables from which the wedding breakfast was served were set out on the lawn and the members of the bridal party were seated as they were served. Boernstein's orchestra from Washington came from there to furnish the music, playing first indoors for the wedding, and out on the lawn for the reception.[61]

By mid-October the Leiters had left Edgewater. Juliette and the children may have taken the special train that carried summer residents from Beverly Farms to their home cities of Philadelphia, Baltimore, and Washington. Since a train that would carry passengers south, skirting Boston by way of the Grand Junction[*] was unusual, it was the object of considerable interest, and a large number of local residents witnessed the departure.[62]

Joe Leiter had left earlier to oversee the building of yet another Leiter vacation house.

Mr. Joseph Leiter of Beverly Farms is spending much time at Marsh Island near the mouth of the river at New Orleans, where he is overseeing work on his new hunting lodge. It will be a rustic building plainly finished externally, but luxuriously furnished for a hunting home. The work is being rushed in order to have it ready for November 1, when the hunting season opens. Mr. Leiter is preparing to spend the winter between Marsh Island and New Orleans, where he will take part in social activities. The total property includes 8711 acres, or 12 square miles.[63]

Leiter wasn't the only summer resident to own a huge hunting preserve in the South. A few years earlier his West Beach neighbor Sydney Hutchinson had purchased the Foshalee quail-hunting plantation in Leon County, Florida. By 1914 he had expanded it to 14,000 acres, or 22 square miles.[64]

Over the next three years the Joe and Juliette Leiter spent very little time at Edgewater. The entry of the United States into the war on April 6, 1917, led to fears that the Atlantic coastline might not be safe. Later in the spring there were rumors of submarine sightings off the North Shore. A local insurance agent advertised "war insurance" for seaside residents. The ever-optimistic *North Shore Breeze* reported that in spite of these scares, the North Shore was more popular than ever, that every possible rental property was engaged, and that potential renters were being turned away.

Joe and Juliette Leiter were among those who chose to stay away during the war years. Perhaps they felt safer spending the summer at their country house in Virginia. Juliette had given birth to a daughter, Nancy, in November of 1916. It is also possible that the Leiter family enterprises kept Joe Leiter in Washington and Chicago. During 1918 he was working to increase the profitability of the Leiter estate's vast Wyoming land holdings.

---

[*] The Grand Junction runs on freight tracks from Chelsea, through Somerville and on to South Station. It is used today to move rolling stock between North and South Stations.

Although Mary Teresa Leiter's will prohibited Joe Leiter from renting Edgewater House out, the estate did not stay empty in his absence. The July 20 *North Shore Breeze* reported that Juliette Leiter's older sister, Mrs. W. F. McCombs, spent the summer of 1917 at Edgewater. Juliette Leiter made a brief visit in August. *North Shore Breeze* wrote:

> Edgewater was the scene of a family gathering last week. Mrs. W. M. McCombs was joined by her parents, Col. and Mrs. John R. Williams of Washington, who will spend the summer. Mrs. Williams' mother, Mrs. Hewitt of St. Louis, joined the party. Mrs. Leiter came for a brief visit only, as did also her sister, Mrs. John Ballantyne Pitney (Francise Williams), whose wedding took place at Edgewater last September.[65]

During the summer of 1918, Juliette's mother, Maie Williams, her sister Francise (Mrs. John. B. Pitney), and Francise's infant son spent time at Edgewater.

Edgewater itself seems to have been untouched by the war, but there were changes in its immediate surroundings. Neighbor Mary Haven donated a portion of her land for a public garden where fifteen local men, some of them gardeners from other estates, were given substantial plots for raising vegetables. Farther down the beach, the Dexters turned their side lawn into a potato patch.

The view from the Leiters' revolving sun house to Misery Island changed dramatically. Summer resident and aviator Godfrey Cabot set up a training school for a naval aviation squad on the island, where they experimented with seaplanes. An odd-looking raft, invented by Cabot, was anchored off shore. Gasoline was stored on its top. Aeroplanes successfully flew over it and proved that the gasoline could be grabbed without necessitating a halt in the flight. Volunteer submarine spotters patrolled the beach. The U.S. Navy, through Godfrey Cabot, obtained permission from the West Beach Corporation to use the bathhouse for a lookout on the rooftop veranda, and naval dormitories in the men's dressing rooms. The lawn to the west of the bathhouse was to be used as a hangar. In the end none of these uses materialized, and the beach remained open for bathers throughout the war.[66]

During the summers of 1917 and 1918, the North Shore summer community threw itself into support for the war. Musicales, fairs, Judge Moore's horse shows, an Essex County Club's golf tournament — every possible social event became a fundraiser for one of the many war-related causes. Mrs. Curtis held an apron sale to raise funds for the Lafayette Fund, which supplied kits to French soldiers in the trenches: a rubber coat, a full set of underclothing, socks, and a wool muffler. Summer residents and locals worked side by side at bandage rolling in the Beverly Farms Library basement, canning home-grown produce in a summer resident's garage, collecting scrap metal, and trading tips for meatless and wheatless meals. Mrs. Robert Bradley, a stalwart supporter of frugal use of resources, went so far as to instruct her cook to can the leftovers from dinner![67]

Juliette Leiter's mother, Maie Williams, was a gregarious woman, active in local charities in Washington. Although there is no record of any war-related activities or fundraisers at Edgewater, Mrs. Williams would certainly have participated in the war effort in Beverly Farms. Not to do so would have reflected badly on the family.

In August of 1918, *North Shore Breeze* made a point of reporting on the Leiters' contribution to the war effort:

> Mr. and Mrs. Joseph Leiter of Beverly Farms are both active in Red Cross work in Washington. Mrs. Leiter is the head of the information bureau, a position which she fills with much aptitude. Mr. Leiter has had to leave his work in Washington to make a short visit to their ranch in Wyoming. Mrs. Leiter has accompanied him, leaving the children in the charge of her mother, Mrs. John Williams, who is staying at Edgewater. Another daughter of Mrs. Williams, Mrs. John B Pitney, and baby are also at the Leiters'.[68]

The visit to the Wyoming ranch was for business, not pleasure. The 13,000 acre ranch in the high plains was a Leiter Trust property that Joe Leiter was trying to make profitable. A sheep-raising venture initiated by the Trustees had been curtailed in 1911, and the land was being leased to ranchers. In 1916 the trustees decided that the only practical use for the land was to divide it up into small farms which would be leased or sold. The Trustees authorized the building of housing for tenant farmers. The one great barrier to this plan was a reliable water supply; a local river usually dried up in mid-July. Engineers concluded that a large scale irrigation project would be necessary. In July of 1918 Leiter went to Wyoming to investigate possibilities for purchasing Lake DeSmet as a reservoir. He was able to purchase it the following year and the irrigation project went forward.

Edgewater appears to have remained empty during the following summer. A 1919 *North Shore Breeze* reported:

> Edgewater House is looking lonely, and the beautiful roses in the garden are blooming unseen by the sea at Beverly Farms. Mr. and Mrs. Joseph Leiter have remained in Washington late, but it is understood that South Hampton, L.I., has been chosen for their summer vacation this year, and the Beverly Farms home will not be opened.[69]

During the seven years since Mary Leiter's death, Joseph Leiter and his family had spent only two summers at Edgewater. This was not entirely uncommon among summer residents.[70] Many owned more than one summer home, sometimes including more rustic men's hunting camps in New Hampshire and Maine. Each year some went to Europe for all or part of the summer. *North Shore Breeze* had a regular column devoted to the travels of summer residents. It was also common practice for a family to rent out its North Shore house and rent another one elsewhere. Maybelle Swift Wichfield and her husband spent eight summers in Europe, sometimes renting out Swiftmore, sometimes closing the house entirely.*

The year 1920 marked the beginning of Edgewater's glory days. During the next ten years the Leiters settled into Edgewater House as their primary summer home and became an integral part of the summer community. Joe Leiter was 52 and Juliette 33. They had three children: Joseph Jr., age 10, Tommy, 9, and Nancy, 4.

The family spent only about a month at Edgewater that year, but it was a start. Joe Jr. and Tommy became involved in the activities organized by Bunny Woods for children of summer residents, which

---

* After her divorce, Maybelle left Beverly Farms for good and allowed Swiftmore to be foreclosed. Ada Small Moore purchased it in 1933, demolished the buildings and extended her gardens. Only the bathhouse remains.

included swimming lessons at West Beach taught by Harvard-connected swim coach Joseph Fowler. Then, in early August, the family was off to Montreal to spend several weeks with Joe Leiter's sister and brother-in-law, Nancy and Colonel Colin Campbell and their children.

As had become their custom, shortly after Christmas that year, the Leiter family and a group of friends went to Marsh Island, Louisiana, where they vacationed at Chateau Canard, the hunting lodge Joe Leiter had built five years before. On January 10, the *New York Times* reported a tragic accident:

Joseph Leiter Jr.
Ten-Year-Old Son of Millionaire
Dies in Father's Duck Blind

The *Times* quoted from a telephone conversation with Joe Leiter:

"Joseph," said Mr. Leiter, "went to one of the duck blinds this morning with a party of hunters. I was not with him. According to those in the blind with him, Joseph fired at a duck, and reloaded the gun without anyone seeing him do it. He laid the gun down on the floor of the blind. Nobody knew it was loaded and therefore I suppose no particular attention was paid to it. When Joseph again picked up the gun, it exploded. Just what caused it to explode I do not know."

It was with a choking voice that Mr. Leiter told of his son's death, and he could scarcely be understood over the long-distance telephone. It was with an effort that Mr. Leiter held himself together when he was asked his son's age. He said, "Only ten years old last July." Then he broke down. He could be heard sobbing over the telephone.[71]

The *Times* article reported the official version. The family story is even more tragic. Young Joseph's nine-year-old brother Tommy was also in the duck blind. It was Tommy who caused the accident that killed his brother. The family never discussed the circumstances of Joseph's death.[72] A commemorative diptych painted shortly after the accident depicts the two brothers on one panel and a single portrait of Joseph on the other.[*] The accident and his role in it haunted Tommy Leiter for the rest of his life.

During the summer of 1921 Edgewater became a refuge for the Leiters. They came in early July and remained until late September. Juliette's sister Francise and her children were there for part of the time. *North Shore Breeze* reported on the Leiters' arrival and noted: "The Leiter family are all in deep mourning this year owing to the sad death by accident of their older son last winter." Joe Leiter and son Tommy participated in activities at the Manchester yacht club, but the family was absent from accounts of other summer social activities. The only Edgewater event reported by *North Shore Breeze* was in September, when it announced an early birthday party for Nancy, who would turn five in November.

Little Nancy Leiter, daughter of Mr. and Mrs. Joseph Leiter, of Edgewater House, celebrated her fifth birthday Thursday, by having a party for her small friends.[73]

---

[*] The painting now hangs in the home of Tommy Leiter's daughter, Victoria Leiter Mele.

***

Juliette Leiter took a serious interest in the Edgewater rose garden and joined the North Shore Horticultural Society in 1922. Estate owners and their gardeners had established the Society in 1888 as a serious professional organization with monthly meetings on horticulture. In 1917 the Society had erected a beautiful meeting hall in Manchester, where they held two yearly competitive shows: a rose show in July and a general flower and vegetable show in late August. West Beach neighbor Ada Small Moore and Manchester resident Mrs. Lester Leland were consistent winners in these competitions for many years. In 1925 Juliette Leiter and her gardener Percy Huxley won two prizes in the rose show, one for hybrid perennials, the other for tea roses. Juliette herself won a second prize for "a basket of roses, arranged for effect."[74]

Juliette's interests ran to more than gardening. Like her Beverly Farms friend Eleonora Sears, Juliette Leiter liked to drive. Although there is no record of Juliette's driving in Beverly Farms, it is very likely that she did so. There is a photograph of a roadster parked in front of Edgewater. An article about the Leiters in their Virginia house includes the following:

> The story has been told of Mrs. Leiter and her driving habits. Juliette enjoyed very much taking rides in the family's Stevens-Durant roadster. Often she would operate the vehicle herself with the chauffeur close behind in case of an emergency. It seems that Juliette drove excessively fast — because she soon attained the reputation as some kind of crazy driver.[75]

Over the next few years, the Leiters established themselves as prominent members of the Beverly Farms summer community. They loved to entertain, and Edgewater House became well known for its weekend house parties with guests from Chicago and Washington. Local people considered seaside luncheons and dinner dances at Edgewater among the gayest events on the Shore.

On August 29, 1924, the Leiters hosted a dance that was one of the largest and most anticipated social events of the season. Invitations went out to 200. The local invitation list included the cream of North Shore society as well as British attaché Sir Esme Howard, his wife Lady Isabella, and various members of Howard's staff. Guests from Washington were H. B. Spencer, Undersecretary of the Treasury, and Mrs. Spencer; Leland Harrison of the State Department; Garrett Winston; Juliette's parents, Colonel and Mrs. Williams, and her sister Francise and her husband John Pitney. Throughout the North Shore, prominent summer residents planned dinner parties to precede the dance. Mr. and Mrs. Rodolphe L. Agassiz of Hamilton would hold a dinner for fifty. *North Shore Breeze* bubbled with delighted anticipation.

> A guest that all would welcome most cordially at the dance would be the Prince of Wales, coming in on the *Berengaria*.

The Prince of Wales did not attend. On August 29 the *Berengaria* was on its way to Washington, where the Prince dined with the President on August 31. When Prince Edward actually came to the North Shore in October, the Leiters had returned to Washington.

By the beginning of November, the last of the summer residents who had remained on for the royal visit had returned to their winter homes. The estates were closed for the season, and Beverly Farms

33

anticipated a quiet fall and winter, quieter perhaps, but not as quiet as in earlier years. Since the onset of Prohibition in January of 1920, the off season saw the ever-increasing activities of rum runners off the coast. At the end of 1924, rum running made Edgewater and Joe Leiter front-page news throughout the country.

Joe Leiter had long been known as a bon vivant who took particular pride in his extensive wine cellar and stock of fine liquor. He, like many other men of wealth, had worked out a way to get around the law.

In the fall of 1919, after the Eighteenth Amendment had passed but before the law went into effect in January of 1920, Joe Leiter had spent $300,000 ($3,985,558 in 2015 dollars)[*] on what he expected to be a lifetime supply of wine and liquor. He stashed it in a newly fortified, burglar-proof cellar on his country estate in Virginia. On October 2, 1921, while caretaker Robert Thornton was in Washington, "automobile bandits" used oxy-acetylene torches to cut through the three-inch-thick steel door and emptied the place. The press loved it. Papers as far away as Singapore carried the story.[76] *Life* magazine editor John Ames Mitchell used Leiter's plight to poke fun at the absurdity of Prohibition.

That three hundred thousand dollars' worth of alcoholic stimulants has been abstracted from the cellar of Joseph Leiter's house in Washington [actually Virginia][77] was an extraordinary story that stirred such emotions of the American public as were not already taut about something else. Not anywhere has so great a confidence in the stability of prohibition been shown as by Mr. Leiter in making so large a provision against it. Here is one man at least that has faith in prohibition. The papers say that the officers of the law are on the trail of his lost liquids and hope to recover them. Let us hope they may. Confidence like his in prohibition and its enforcement deserves all the support and all the vindication that the utmost powers of the Drys can muster. Any law-abiding citizen who has his lawful rum stolen from him ought to have his loss made up by the government, and the Drys should see that it is done.[78]

Joe Leiter's cache was indeed "lawful rum," since it had been purchased before Prohibition went into effect and had the customs stamps to prove it. The burglars were apprehended in November. "They were said by the police to be bootleggers who had, over a period of months, gained the confidence of the caretakers of the estate in preparation for the robbery. Several cases of rare Champagne and several thousand dollars were recovered."[79]

In spite of the theft, Leiter entertainments throughout the twenties were never dry. Joe Leiter had no intention of obeying the Volstead Act and liked nothing better than outwitting the government. He had lost his legal cache, but there were other supply lines. Rum running off the coast of Massachusetts had become big business very quickly; "Rum Runner's Row" was 12 miles out to sea. Everyone with a fishing boat, schooner, or pleasure boat could do well ferrying liquid cargo to shore. The *Boston Globe* for the period carried innumerable stories of rum-running gangs, chartered schooners, arrested fishermen, high-level police collusion, and corruption in the Coast Guard. The beach at Edgewater was an ideal landing spot, and

---

[*]2015 dollar equivalents throughout the book are based on the Bureau of Labor Statistics CPI Inflation Calculator, which uses the average Consumer Price Index for a given calendar year. This data represents changes in prices of all goods and services purchased for consumption by urban households. This index value has been calculated every year since 1913. For the current year the latest monthly index value is used.

Joe Leiter had the money to insure that nothing would go wrong. He equipped his wine cellar at Edgewater House with an alarm system that alerted the Beverly Police Department. As an added precaution, he employed Allen J. Harris, a night watchman supplied through the alarm company. But as he might have known from the 1921 theft, even fool-proof schemes could be compromised.

On November 22, 1924, the *Beverly Times* reported the theft of more than $50,000 worth of liquor from the Leiter cellar:

> ...the watchman on duty is reported missing and the telephone and burglar alarm system wires were cut....Hijackers raided the mansion — making a break over the front door, working through the house into the cellar, and evidently overpowering the watchman — helped themselves to the liquor, opened a rear door, bundled the liquor on a truck, and went off.

> The break was discovered by Percy Huxley, caretaker on the estate. He had noticed a truck leaving the estate a few minutes before and became suspicious after stories of hijackers raiding wine cellars. Entering the house he found things topsy-turvy. In the basement near the wine cellar, which had been jimmied open, he found the watchman's gun, flashlight, cap, and vest on the floor.

> The raid was the largest one ever made on the Shore. The Leiters had closed their mansion house and had gone to Washington earlier in the month. The wine cellar, a massive one, was under the protection of the Holmes burglar alarm system of Boston.[80]

Two nights later, thieves struck again. This time, Percy Huxley was able to telephone the police when he saw a large truck with eight men and more of Leiter's liquor leaving the estate. The report of subsequent events reads like a script for the Keystone Kops:

> Officers Edwin Egan and James Dolliver started out in the police automobile, held up the truck, arrested the eight men, and placed them in the police machine. Officer Egan drove the truck to Beverly police headquarters. Missing Dolliver, he returned to the scene, found his brother officer lying badly beaten on the road and the police car and eight prisoners gone.

> Patrolman Dolliver. who is at the Beverly Hospital, says that he got on the running board of the car after he had ordered the rum runners inside and had detailed one of them to operate the machine. As they approached the Prides Crossing railroad station, the gates were down and one of the men said, "Step on it." Another demurred saying that the train was too near, and received the reply, "What of it, we might as well be killed as not." Just then Dolliver reached for the emergency brake, and as he bent over, one of the men struck him in the jaw and took his pistol, with which he had them covered, away from him, pushing him into the road and leaving him in a dazed condition. He soon came to and started for the men again, but they beat him off and got away, the train having passed Prides Crossing.

> Savoya Colantonio, 20, of 20 Sheafe Street, Boston, who was found asleep by the side of the road near the Manchester line yesterday, is well known in that city's North End as "Ben Turpin."

> Questioned during the day, after he had been discovered fast asleep in the driver's seat of an automobile parked near the Leiter estate, Colantonio gave a fairly plausible account of himself.

> But last night, on being re-examined, he admitted that he had driven two North End men from Boston to the Leiter residence early yesterday morning, and that he was waiting for them to return to the car when found by authorities. ....Following an hour's grilling....Colantonio gave the police the names of six residents of Boston's North End.

At the District Court in Salem this morning, Colantonio of Boston was charged with breaking and entering and larceny of liquors valued at $10,000 ($139,067 in 2015 dollars) from the estate of Joseph Leiter on November 24 and was held on $20,000 until December 2.[81]

A Beverly police report revealed something the newspaper did not. The thieves probably wouldn't have made it to Boston in any case, as their truck had broken down on route to the police station. The report also listed the liquors found on the truck:

CHAMPAGNE 1 bottle	Generale, 119 bottles	Cordon Rouge, 15 bottles
Burgundy Dijon, 16 bottles	Piper Heidsick, 8 bottles	Old Bourbon; RUM, 4 bottles
Bourgogne Mouseaux VERMOUTH, 24 bottles	Martini, 1 bottle	Rhum Charleston, 1 bottle
Grenadine syrup	and 2 barrels, 52 gallons each, of some kind of liquor[82]	

Several days later the story got even more interesting. The December 3 *Beverly Evening Times* headline read:

FEDERAL OFFICERS RAID LEITER WINE CELLAR
WATCHMAN ARRESTED
Sensational Turn in the Now Famous Raid on the Joseph Leiter Wine Cellar

A sensational turn in the now famous raid on the wine cellar of Joseph Leiter in his Edgewater estate at Beverly Farms came yesterday when federal officers visited the cellar and took more than six hundred bottles of high class wines and liquors ... which they declare was not of the pre-prohibition stock, apparently only recently smuggled into the country... Later in the evening police arrested Allen J. Harris of Maplewood Avenue, Malden, a watchman at the estate, on the technical charge of larceny from a building. There was a hint today that the federal authorities are investigating reports that the Leiter estate, unbeknown to the owner, was being used as a base for rum-running and that two previous robberies by the hijackers were faked.[83]

The arrested watchman, Allen J. Harris, claimed that he had had nothing to do with the thefts, that he had been away celebrating his 45th birthday on the night of the first theft and asleep the night of the second.

Somehow local authorities were prepared to believe that the liquor in Joe Leiter's basement was not his.[*] Three days later, agents went to Gloucester and arrested George L. Green, reportedly a "keystone man" in the rum-running ring operating off the North Shore, on the allegation that he was the owner of the liquor stored at Edgewater and mastermind of the thefts. Green's chartered Canadian schooner, the *Marjorie E. Bachman,* had been seized offshore near "rum row" and taken to Boston after its captain sold 25 cases of liquor to Coast Guard agents in October.[84]

Four months later, the March 13, 1925, *Boston Daily Globe* carried another sensational headline:

---

[*] There was some justification for this assumption. In November of 1923, police had charged William J. Sullivan of Salem after they arrested him and ten employees unloading 154 cans containing 500 gallons of alcohol from a boat onto Sydney Hutchinson's pier. (Beverly Police report, November 23, 1923)

In an effort to clear himself, former watchman Allen J. Harris swore that during the time he worked as a watchman at the Edgewater, he had seen Leiter's caretaker Percy Huxley, chauffeur William F. Collins, and personal secretary Eugene O'Neill haul liquor from the beach to the wine cellar.

On March 24, Percy Huxley and William F. Collins pleaded not guilty when arraigned in Federal Court in Boston on charges that they "did smuggle and clandestinely introduce into the United States …and fraudulently and knowingly facilitate in the transportation and concealment of a certain large quantity of intoxicating liquor" at the Leiter estate in Beverly Farms. They were held on bail of $500 each, awaiting trial. Joseph Leiter and Eugene O'Neill, charged with the same offense, were out of state. According to news reports they were to be arraigned later.[85]

The indictments included an inventory of the liquor remaining in and confiscated from the Leiter cellar and garage during the federal raid. The list did not include the truckload of liquor the police had rescued from the thieves after the second break-in. The inventory described "a large quantity of intoxicating liquor as defined in the Act of Congress of October 28, 1919, and commonly known as the National Prohibition act, to wit, 585 bottles of intoxicating liquors consisting of:

Apricot Brandy	13 bottles	Cacao Chouva	19 bottles
Cherry Brandy	11 bottles	Alayla & Co. Champagne	22 bottles
Crème de Menthe	45 bottles	Dawson Scotch Whiskey	5 bottles
M. Misa Port	30 bottles	Burke Old Irish Whiskey	2 bottles
Cinzano Tonic	19 bottles	Lawson Scottish Whiskey	2 bottles
Gordon Rouge	51 bottles	Porto D'Origine	2 bottles
Chastenet Port	16 bottles	Cherry Brandy	1 bottle
Vine Mousseux	24 bottles	Benedictine	30 bottles
Oude Pollen Gin	4 stone jugs	Sauternes	20 bottles
Haut Sauternes	46 bottles	Oude Schiedam Gin	7 stone jugs
Spark. Brachette	77 bottles	Pilsner Beer	26 bottles
Ayale Champagne	22 bottles	Spark. Burgundy	14 bottles
Carte D'Or Champagne	12 bottles	Gordon Rouge	53 bottles
Crème de Menthe, etc.	3 bottles		

Court records include Capias orders issued on April 24 for both Leiter and O'Neill. The colorful language of the Court reads:

To the Marshal of our District of Massachusetts or to either of his deputies,
Greetings:

We command you that you take the body of Joseph Leiter of Chicago in the State of Illinois (if he be found in your precinct) and have him before the District Court of the United States, now holden at Boston, within and for the Massachusetts District, forthwith, then and there to answer to an Indictment pending against him in Court.[86]

Neither Leiter nor O'Neill was found in Massachusetts.

As one might have expected, Joseph Leiter chose to fight the charges. On May 12, 1925, his lawyer, John P. Feeney of Boston, filed a motion to quash the indictment on the grounds that the evidence presented to the grand jury had been obtained by federal officer Andrew B. Stroup in trespassing upon the premises of the defendant and without a license, leave, or authority of law. The May 14 *Boston Globe* carried a surprise headline:

LEITER GUILTY OF POSSESSING
Fined $500 After Plea in Federal Court
Motion filed previous to Quash Federal Indictment
Action of Chicago-Beverly Man a Surprise

After the motion was filed yesterday, persons at the Federal Building expected a legal combat. It was expected that the motion would be heard on Friday. Leiter came in at 2:30 when things were rather quiet. He had pleaded guilty and left the building before most people were aware that he was even in Boston.[87]

Apparently John P. Feeney had arranged a plea bargain. Joe Leiter pleaded guilty to the lesser charge of possession and was slapped on the wrist with a $500 fine. He pleaded *nolo proli* to the greater charges of smuggling and transportation. The next day, Eugene O'Neill pleaded guilty to the same charge with the same result.[88]

The cases of Percy Huxley and William F. Collins were left pending. A letter in the case record dated April 5, 1926, states that Collins did plead guilty to possession of illegal liquor and *nolo proli* to the other charges. Huxley presumably did the same. There is no record of the disposition of their cases.[89] Percy Huxley stayed on as gardener/caretaker through the summer of 1925. In 1926 he and his family moved to North Carolina.

North Shore Breeze, which printed only flattering stories about summer residents, published nothing about any of these events. Evading the Volstead Act was so commonplace along the North Shore it was hardly news in any case. Leiter's indictment cast nary a shadow. The emptied wine cellar was refilled by summer, and entertaining on the grand scale continued. If anything, Edgewater House and the Leiters reached the height of their popularity during the summer of 1925.

In the spring of 1924 Joseph Leiter had made the first of three changes that transformed Edgewater from a staid estate designed for an aging widow to a more suitable playground for a man of the twenties. The first change was the elimination of the formal garden at the west end of the house to make room for a swimming pool.

By the 1920s swimming pools were all the rage. The Magnolia Swimming Club pool, built in 1913, had quickly become one of the most popular destinations on the North Shore. At least one summer home in Gloucester had a pool as early as 1917. Connolly Brothers of Beverly Farms became the premier builders of pools and tennis courts. In April of 1924 Joe Leiter hired them to build a tennis court as well as a swimming pool that he and Juliette personally designed. In late August *North Shore Breeze* carried a vivid description of the pool.

Swimming pools of various kinds dot the Shore, all carrying some idea of the owner in their construction. The one completed this summer at the Joseph Leiter place at Beverly ranks with any in the county for beauty and originality, and practical purposes.

A saltwater basin, 30x60 ft., was constructed at one side of the house in an open, sunny lawn just above the sea and by the revolving summer house, long a feature here. The deep and large open pool has an adjoining addition not seen in any other similar construction on the Shore — a plot of sand, a space about half as large as the pool and enclosed by the same low masonry as the pool. On this sandy "beach" at one end (looking across it and seaward) have been placed beach chairs and gay umbrellas — a regular Palm Beach in miniature — and enjoyed merely by stepping out of the house. Here all the comforts of private pool and beach combined are, with the ozone from the sea below enveloping one as if down by its own rocky shore.

In the center of this sandy spot has been placed a sundial made by Philip S. Sears, sculptor, of Prides Crossing. Connolly Bros. of Beverly Farms constructed the pool.[90]

The swimming pool became the focal point of outdoor entertaining for as long as Leiters lived there. In 1925 and for the next couple of years Tommy and Nancy's friends came to the pool for swimming lessons.

Edgewater house, the Joseph Leiter place in Beverly Farms, is another place where swimming classes meet, Mrs. Leiter giving the use of the great, new pool made last year close to the house and having unusual features for a swimming pool. Pupils who enjoy their dip here come from all around, and among them may be mentioned Wingate Graham Charlton just over from England; also Anne Chilton, daughter of Counsel of the British Embassy Henry G. Chilton, Audrey and Gweneth Butler, Olivia Ames, Conway Felton, Francis Sears Jr., Francis Wendell, Francis and Betty Chalifoux, Russell Burrage Jr., Frederick and Mary Lippit, Marjorie Motley, and Duncan Williams.[91]

As the new pool took center stage, the patio and lawn in front of the loggia became less important for casual entertaining. Throughout the twenties, the Leiters regularly entertained their local friends at poolside luncheons and dinner parties. Among their immediate social circle were Bryce and Anna Allen and Mr. and Mrs. Preble Motley of Prides Crossing; Representative Nick Longworth and his wife, Alice Roosevelt Longworth, when they were visiting Nick's parents; and Judge Moore's sons Paul and Edwin. British attachés who summered in Beverly Farms were included in the group.

Photographs from 1928 document a house party of Chicago and Washington friends relaxing at poolside. The west porch served as the bar. Every afternoon was mint julep time.

The Leiters were members of the Essex County Club, where one of the major events of the season was the Women's Invitational Tennis Tournament held in July. In 1925 Juliette Leiter hosted a poolside luncheon for the players and other guests that would become an annual event:

Edgewater House, Beverly Farms home of Mr. and Mrs. Joseph Leiter of Washington was a very gay place on Monday when visiting tennis players, their friends, and all friends of tennis were invited to an informal luncheon served outdoors at tables placed near the beautiful new swimming pool. About 50 guests were present.[92]

That same year the ever-savvy ladies who planned the annual fair in support of Boston Children's Hospital recognized that the Leiters' new pool would be a great draw for the event.

The annual garden party for the benefit of the Children's Hospital in Boston is an affair of importance on the later August program. The date having been set by Mrs. William Gordon Means of

Prides Crossing, who has charge of the affair, for Saturday afternoon, Aug. 29. Mr. and Mrs. Joseph Leiter will open their Beverly Farms estate Edgewater for the garden party, and the magnificent grounds, the lovely gardens, and the attractive swimming pool will make a charming setting.[93]

North Shore Breeze described the estate as it stood ready for the Leiters' arrival in

June of 1927. George Ferrier, the Scottish gardener who had replaced Percy Huxley, proved to be very good at his work.

> Edgewater House, the Beverly Farms summer home of the Joseph Leiters of Washington, is being made ready for their coming about the middle of the month. They were in Europe part of the winter, but returned to Washington in March. Fifteen-year-old Thomas will join his parents and younger sister, Nancy, as soon as the school which he is attending, St Paul's in Concord NH, is closed. The Leiter estate has its own vegetable garden and greenhouses. There are long rows of lettuce growing in huge heads like cabbages, and the peas are three feet high. Prize peaches and other fruits are also grown on the estate. The large tennis court on one side of the house is being resurfaced, and hedges and lawns are being trimmed meticulously. This place is one of the most completely equipped on the North Shore for all the outdoor pleasures. There is an outdoor swimming pool, so that it is not necessary to wait for high tide before taking a swim. Iron settees are placed invitingly under the shade trees. A rustic arbor is on the edge of the sea wall, glassed in on the water side. The wide, grassy terrace is an ideal place for teas under colorful table umbrellas.

George Ferrier was born in Broughty Ferry, a town near Dundee, Scotland, on April 8, 1886. He arrived in the United States aboard the *Caledonia* out of Glasgow in 1911 at age 25. The ship's passenger register listed him as a laborer. In 1920 Ferrier, with his wife Catherine and their year old daughter Jean, was living in Manhattan where he was working as a laborer in a garden. It is possible that George Ferrier learned of the Edgewater position from a relative then living in Beverly. A Charles Ferrier from Dundee, who was operating a grocery store in the Ryal Side neighborhood, may have seen Leiter's advertisement for a gardener and informed George Ferrier of the opening.[94]

Sometime in the mid-twenties the Leiters made at least one major interior change to Edgewater — the addition of a fireplace to the loggia. The loggia and its outdoor terrace and lawn had been designed as a fluid space for day and evening entertaining. Three large French doors opened the room to the ocean. An early photo shows Mary Leiter's arrangement of lawn chairs and a large tea urn on the lawn. With the building of the pool, daytime activities had moved to the west-end terrace. Tea on the lawn had been replaced by drinks at poolside. *North Shore Breeze* mentions "teas under the colorful umbrellas," but, Prohibition notwithstanding, tea was not the preferred beverage.

Joe and Juliette Leiter often held large dinner parties as well as weekend house parties. On cool evenings they liked to serve cocktails in front of the fireplace — the library was too small. Given that no one spent much time on the ocean-side lawn during the day, Joe Leiter was quite willing to destroy the south façade of the house in order to build a fireplace in the loggia. A utilitarian but ugly chimney, made of standard rather than tapestry brick, replaced the center French door, slashed through the center of the limestone pediment above it, eliminating half of its central fruit basket, and blocked out windows on the second and third floors. The Art Deco fireplace became the centerpiece of the loggia. The green latticework and classical medallions on the walls were probably also removed at that time.

Joe Leiter was likely responsible for major changes to the service wing. Given his love of cooking, one can assume that it was he who either moved the kitchen from the basement to the first floor or created a new first-floor kitchen for his personal use. At perhaps the same time, the servants' porch was bricked in and became a small room off the kitchen.

Joe Leiter was well known as a man devoted to good food and drink. He was also an accomplished cook, who must have spent time in the kitchen at Edgewater House. During 1926 he spent a good amount of time compiling a cookbook, which he would privately publish the following summer. Joe Leiter may have needed a relaxing diversion that year; he had spent part of the spring in a Chicago courtroom.

Three years earlier, in 1923, his sister Daisy (Lady Margaret Hyde Howard, the widowed Dowager Duchess of Suffolk and Buckingham), sued her brother over his handling of the Leiter estate. His sister Mary's widower, Lord Curzon, ostensibly on behalf of his daughters, joined in the suit. Lord Curzon and Joe Leiter had traded insults ever since the failed wheat deal in 1897. In 1923, Leiter described Curzon as "an imperious and domineering man who thinks himself superior to mere mortals." He also claimed that Curzon was really interested in getting more money for himself and didn't care much about his daughters. There was perhaps some truth to the latter accusation, since Curzon's second wife was proving to be less generous than she had previously been. Joe's newly widowed third sister, Nancy Leiter Campbell, supported her brother.

By the time the case finally came to court in the spring of 1926, Lord Curzon had died, but his daughters continued to support Lady Suffolk. The suit charged that Joe Leiter was an extravagant and reckless adventurer who had jeopardized the family fortune by making unwise investment decisions without the approval of the other trustees. The final blow came when, after the death of the respected non-family trustee, Seymour Morris, Joe Leiter replaced him with his own candidate without consultation with his sisters.

The Chicago press loved it — English nobility and one of Chicago's most flamboyant millionaires were going to fight it out in a city courtroom. What a show that would be! Joe Leiter's excesses filled the papers. Had he really ordered 12 dozen pairs of silk socks at $12 a pair and then not paid up? ($12 times 144 comes to a total of $1728, or about $23,216 in 2015 dollars.) Had he actually tried to buy the Great Wall of China? The Chicago press may have been disappointed that the lovely Lady Cynthia Curzon Mosely did not appear at the trial, but courtroom photos of Lady Suffolk, Nancy Campbell, and Joe and Juliette Leiter sufficed.[95] The public hearing ended before summer. A decision would not be reached until 1931.

***

In the summer of 1927 Joe privately published the cookbook, calling it **Favorite Old Recipes**: *Being a Comprehensive Collection of Favorite Recipes Diligently Gathered from Many Sources.* Like most other Joe Leiter projects, his cookbook was extravagant in its excess. The large-format, 328-page book included so many recipes that the book's recipients, and certainly their cooks, must have been overwhelmed. The

Sauces section alone contained 147 recipes. According to his preface, Joe Leiter wrote the book to please his friends.

> It has originated from the request of some friends for a description of the methods of making salad dressings and certain dishes which on occasion I cooked. Ambition overcame me and I got French, Belgian, Scotch, Yorkshire and Creole cook books to add to the store of recipes I had already collected and to translate them.

> A chapter on menus several friends implored, but it's too large a field. If you have not enough imagination to prepare your own menus, you won't have any use for this book. This is impossible for the book goes only to my friends who are interested enough to have contributed to the conspiracy which led to its hatching or have been interested enough, having heard of it, to ask to be included among those to whom it is sent. This method of distribution was determined upon so that no one could find fault with it, as it is not polite to look into the mouths of gift horses, and, as before explained, as you are my friends you must be polite....[96]

The presentation page of the copy in the Edgewater House library reads:

> *This copy of*
> *"Favorite Old Recipes"*
> *is No. 56*
> *of a limited edition of*
> *one thousand copies*
> *presented to*
> *Ben: P. Moseley*
> *with the compliments of*
> *Joseph Leiter*

Ben: Perley Poore Moseley was a member of the North Shore aristocracy who summered in Ipswich and was a frequent visitor to Edgewater. The copy was a gift to Carol and Jeffrey Horvitz from Jonathan Loring, who had been given it by Mosely's daughter, Ellen Mosely Ames, who with her husband, Oliver, owned Edgewater House from 1950 until 1984.

A Boston newspaper carried the story of the book's publication:

RICH MR. LEITER HAS NOVEL HOBBY
Chicago and Beverly Farms Multimillionaire
Writes a Cook Book and Gives Some Old Recipes

> Joseph Leiter, who in his time has been everything from grain speculator to trustee of one of American's largest fortunes, not to say anything about his being brother-in-law to the former Viceroy of India, appears now in a new, and possibly his favorite role—that of a cook.

> The picturesque multi-millionaire of Chicago, whose proud boast is that his country estate at Beverly Farms dignifies him as a Bostonian, has, through his hobby, cookery, earned a niche in the gastronomic hall of fame. He also stands revealed as an intensely human individual, if love of good things of the table is a human characteristic.

"Joe" Leiter is something more than an ordinary frier and stewer. Indeed, he is the author of a cook book, "Favorite Old Recipes," privately printed and now being circulated in the same fashion among his personal friends. Several leaders of the North Shore smart set are now rejoicing in their possession of the savory volume.

Aside from the 2500 recipes collected from Bombay to New Orleans and covering everything from Irish stew to snails cooked with mushrooms in white wine, this modern Brillat-Savarin has much to say about the selection of meat and fowl. One of the most interesting chapters in the book is that devoted to game and its preparation.

Skimming through the book one sort of becomes conscious of the fact that the author knows very little about the Volstead Act, for in the preparation of many of his famous dishes wines and brandies and other rare liquors are used with liberal abandon. That he has fallen under the gastronomic influence of the Creoles, especially those of New Orleans, is strikingly evident, for many of his recipes have the distinctive flavor of the Rue Bienville and Rue St. Louis and other sections of the Vieux Carre. Of soups and their bouquet, Leiter writes knowingly. He rates the making of a good bouillon as an art in itself.[97]

Contemptuously does Leiter speak of desserts, "These I never eat and know little about."

Late in the book Joe Leiter did make a brief, tongue-in-cheek reference to the Volstead Act in his introduction to the chapter on cooking game.

The description of the following methods of preparation, as I read them over, made my mouth water with the suggestion of addition for so much wine, which in this modern dark age since the Volstead Act, has been taken out of the kitchen supply and carefully locked in the sideboard. Cheer up! That salted, treated and I am sure non-poisonous substitute for the drinking variety which is sold by all first class grocers for cooking will do as well, but remember don't put any salt with it; it has already absorbed as much of it as is possible in order to make it unfit for drinking.

One can be absolutely certain that Joe Leiter never purchased cooking wine in his life. When Leiter cooked with the Burgundy, Sauterne, Chablis, Beaune, Chambertin, Champagne, Sherry, Madeira, Malaga, Marsala, Port, and Cognac called for in his recipes, the wines were the best Europe had to offer. The Edgewater cellar was well stocked with Joe's wines and liquors well into the 1940s.[98]

The legal wranglings that dragged on through the late twenties in Chicago appeared to have had no effect on the Leiters' life at Edgewater. The house parties and dinners continued. Juliette's poolside luncheon for participants in the Women's Tennis Tournament at the Essex County Club was an annual event. The Leiters also entertained the casts of plays and operas held at the new Stillington Theater in Gloucester; in September of 1927 they hosted a dinner in their honor for 100 people. Although no more grand charity fundraisers were held at Edgewater, Juliette attended and supported events such throughout the North Shore.

Like their parents, the Leiter children enjoyed an active social life at Edgewater. In the fall of 1926 Tommy Leiter entered St. Paul's School, his father's alma mater. His West Beach friend and neighbor Ned Hutchinson was in his class. Eleven year old Nancy attended school in Washington. Tommy and Nancy loved the outdoors. In addition to the swimming pool and tennis court, the children had their own horses and a groom transported to Edgewater from the country house in Virginia. Both children participated in horse shows at Myopia. Tommy Leiter was among the young sailors at Manchester Yacht Club. Nancy was among the group of North Shore children who participated in the many charity fairs and events that were held each summer. *North Shore Breeze* regularly reported on their activities.

A pretty sight these nice mornings is too see Miss Nancy Leiter and her groom loping along that sandy stretch of beach near her Beverly Farms home, Edgewater House, with the horses just avoiding the wavelets which seep in, higher and higher. Mrs. Joseph Leiter, her mother, left Monday for a week's trip to Washington. *

The two younger members of the family, Master Tommy Leiter and his sister little Miss Nancy Leiter, have had a delightful time on the Shore this season. Master Tommy is a young sportsman of ability, and all seasons he has been engaged in matches of various kinds. He has ridden in many of the younger set events at the Myopia, and has also been seen on the winning side of the tennis court frequently this summer. Add to this is the fact that Tommy swims "like a fish" and one has an idea of the versatile abilities of this young chap.[99]

On September 16, 1927, 15-year-old Tommy hosted his first dinner dance at Edgewater:

Tonight Thomas Leiter, the 15 year old son of Mr. and Mrs. Joseph Leiter of Edgewater House Beverly Farms, is giving a dance to which about 50 of his young friends along the Shore have been invited. The affair takes the form of a dinner dance with Del Monte's orchestra furnishing the music. It is really a farewell party for Tommy as he leaves September 22 for another term at St Paul's School in Concord, New Hampshire.

Later in life, Tommy would become a celebrated party organizer and host.

In June of 1928 Joe and Juliette celebrated their twentieth wedding anniversary in Washington. Joe was 60, Juliette was 41. They celebrated at Edgewater with a large Fourth of July house party and continued with an active schedule of schedule of luncheons, dinners, and parties throughout July.

Sometime during the twenties Joe Leiter developed a passionate interest in horseracing and began to develop a racing stable, perhaps on his Virginia or Louisiana estate. In 1928, Joe and Juliette Leiter left Edgewater at the end of July to spend the racing season at Saratoga, as did other North Shore residents Arthur Goodwin, Bayard Tuckerman Jr., and Sumner Pingree. These three sent horses from their North Shore estates to be entered in the races.[100] Joe Leiter never kept racehorses in Beverly Farms, but certainly had entries at Saratoga.

The summer of 1929 brought considerable excitement to West Beach. In late July the wedding of Juliette's widowed sister Francise Williams Pitney to Huston Rawls was the occasion for the first bit of excitement. The wedding itself was quiet, but the arrival of wedding guests from New York was a major event. *North Shore Breeze* reported.

The beach folks are still talking about the big plane that flew in from New York with guests for the wedding last Saturday of Mrs. John Pitney and Barbour Huston Rawls. It carried 8 passengers and followed the water route here, making the trip in exactly two hours. The landing was made on the

---

* Sometime during later childhood or early teens Nancy Leiter suffered a back injury that prevented her from ever riding again.

beach directly below Edgewater House, the Joseph Leiter place, where the wedding breakfast and reception were held.[101]

It is not clear whether the plane remained in Beverly to fly the wedding guests back to New York. If so, it could have made the return flight from the new Beverly Airport, which had been established in 1928. Small seaplanes had been a common sight off the beach as far back as World War I, but larger planes were uncommon. Passenger aviation in the United States was still in its infancy; the first airlines and passenger airports made their debut in late twenties.

The second cause for excitement on the beachfront was a cause for fear rather than celebration. A few weeks after the Leiter wedding, Edith Hutchinson awoke at three a.m. to discover a burglar in her room. She screamed, and he fled with her jewelry, including a $100,000 pearl necklace ($1,386,064 in 2015 dollars) as well as diamond rings, more necklaces, and other jewelry. *North Shore Breeze*, the magazine of happy events, printed not a word. The thief was caught, and most of the jewelry was recovered.[102]

***

When Juliette Leiter returned to Washington that fall, she agreed to become one of a group of socialites whose homes were featured in the Simmons mattress company's full-page advertisements for their luxurious new Beautyrest mattresses. The advertisement emphasized the luxury of the Dupont Circle house and highlighted the rare blue Boucher panels in Juliette's salon.[103]

The illustrated magazines and movies of the early twentieth century had created widespread envy and aspirations by giving ordinary women a glimpse into the lives and homes of the very wealthy. In the 1920s American advertising flourished under the leadership of J. Walter Thompson, whose agency played on those aspirations. As early as 1922 employees were advised, "You're not selling the ticket, you're selling the end of the journey." For American women the end of the journey was social acceptance. Over the next couple of decades, society women and celebrities were used to sell everything from soap to home furnishings.[104]

Why would Juliette choose to be included? One reason may well be that to be included was an acknowledgement that she was at the pinnacle of social success. She was certainly in good company. Her North Shore neighbor Mrs. John Hays Hammond, Jr. and her summer home, Hammond Castle, were photographed by Edward Steichen for a similar ad. In 1930 the ads appeared in both the *Ladies' Home Journal* and *Vogue*.[105] Later Simmons ads included Eleanor Roosevelt, Henry Ford, Cole Porter, and the anti-Fascist Italian Duchess of Sermoneta.

Another possible explanation for Juliette's willingness to appear is that, being a businesswoman herself, she may have felt perfectly comfortable in the commercial world. A 1921 photograph is titled *Mrs.*

Joseph Leiter in Her Modest Dress Shop. The shop, called *Francise*, was located in Washington at 191 Q Street NW until at least 1933. Juliette is listed as president of the company.[*]

The summer of 1930 was a difficult one for the Leiters. On June 22, Joe Leiter's widowed sister Nancy Campbell died while on a trip to England with her children, 21-year-old Colin and 16-year-old Audry. Nancy Leiter Campbell had been Joe's ally in the yet unsettled Leiter trust suit brought by his sister Margaret Hyde (Lady Suffolk) and the Curzons. Joe, Juliette, and Nancy Leiter were in Europe at the same time. Colin and Audry Campbell joined the Leiters aboard the S.S. *Empress* on July 5 for their return to the United States by way of Quebec.[106] Colin Campbell went on to California with his mother's ashes. The Leiters and Audrey Campbell went directly to Edgewater. Audrey Campbell spent a few weeks with the Leiters before returning to California. At the end of July, Joe and Juliette left for Saratoga.[107]

Tommy Leiter had not accompanied his parents to Europe. He had just completed his junior year at St. Paul's and may have been attending some kind of summer school. During one or more summers both Tommy Leiter and Ned Hutchinson had been tutored in algebra by Beverly Farms postmaster Fred Wangler. In September of 1930 Ned withdrew from St. Paul's. Tommy withdrew in December.

According to the St. Paul's records, Tommy chose to withdraw so that he could attend Northwestern School of Commerce in Chicago. He was 18, and he (or his father) felt that he was too old to stay in secondary school. Northwestern required a letter verifying that Thomas Leiter was leaving St. Paul's as a student in good standing. The letter was provided, and Tommy presumably entered Northwestern in January of 1931.[108]

It is not surprising that Joe Leiter chose to send his son to a business school rather than to a liberal arts college. A letter he wrote from Edgewater in 1922 in response to an appeal[109] from Harvard classmate and Fogg Museum director, Edward W. Forbes, illustrates his deep contempt for a liberal arts education.

> Mr. Edward W. Forbes,
> Cambridge, Mass.
>
> My dear Sir:
>
> I cannot for the life of me understand why Professor Norton should have his portrait painted or the many wasted hours of young men's time in his classes commemorated.[†]
>
> I look upon him and his courses as the epitome of the expression of educational piffle at Harvard which has gone so far as to make the graduates, when they have gotten a realization of how little they are fitted educationally for the struggle of life, to realize that in spite of the fact that they were objects

---

[*] Juliette's mother, Maie Williams, was also an entrepreneur in Washington. During the mid-twenties she built two luxury apartment buildings on opposite corners of R and 19th streets.
[†] Charles Eliot Norton was Professor of Art and European Culture at Harvard and one the university's most beloved teachers. The Charles Eliot Norton lecture series honors him to this day.

of charity for one-half of the cost of the education which they had received, the other half of the cost had been spent for green goods. [period slang for something counterfeit or useless]

Yours very truly,

Joseph Leiter

***

In March of 1931 the Levi Leiter Trust case was finally settled. An article from the *Scranton Daily Times* reported:

Control of Leiter Millions to Remain in United States

Control of the late Levi Leiter's millions remains in the United States. The appellate court today upheld Joseph Leiter's right to serve as trustee of the $30,000,000 estate of his merchant-prince father, turning back the demand of British nobility heirs that he be ousted for his management. Representing many pages of Burke's peerage, the appellants to receive Judge Sullivan's superior court approval of Leiter's trusteeship were his sister, Lady Margaret Hyde, Countess of Suffolk and Berkshire, and Lady Cynthia Mosley, Irene Curzon, Baroness of Ravensdale, and Lady Alexandra Metcalfe, the daughters of the late Mary Curzon, another sister and the wife of the former Viceroy of India.

Throughout the eight years of litigation over control of the millions amassed in Chicago merchandising and finance, the third daughter of Levi, Mrs. Nancy Leiter Campbell, supported her brother until her death six months ago. As the appellants' counsel indicated there would be no further appeal of today's decision.[110]

Following settlement of the suit in 1931, both Leiter and Lady Suffolk resigned as trustees, leaving the management of the estate to non-family-members.[111]

Joe Leiter was probably happy to resign. By this time he much preferred managing his racing stable to managing the Leiter trust. By 1930 his 24-horse racing stable was among the finest in the country and included his two stake winners, Prince Hotspur and Princess Camilla.[112] By 1931 he was spending more of the winter in New Orleans than in Washington. The New Orleans *Times-Picayune* described him:

On the streets of New Orleans most any day in winter may be seen a massive man, standing well above six feet with powerful jaw, fierce mien topped by a huge Pilgrim hat and wrapped in a flowing, old fashioned operatic cloak. To a stranger he would appear as an ex-prizefighter with a bent for the stage ... But in fact he would be Joseph Leiter, 63, one of America's most colorful financiers and sportsmen. For thirty-four years he has taken the front pages, first in '97 when as a 29-year-old buck he sought to out-trade the greybeards of the Chicago grain pit and corner the wheat market, then as an operator of railroads, mines and public utilities, and later as a big game hunter[*], fisherman and racehorse man.

Born to millions, Joseph Leiter has lived his life on the grand scale. Moderation is a strange word to him. He is a big game hunter with flash and dash in all his operations. He has taken wallops to the chin only to present a stronger chin for the next one.

Leiter has ridden at a gallop with a free rein. He has lost fortunes and made fortunes, and today his income is estimated as well above a million a year. In recent years, his racing stables appeared to be one of his major interests, and that accounted for the transfer of his winter base to New Orleans.[113]

The Leiters do not appear to have opened Edgewater during the summer of 1931. The only mention of the family in *North Shore Breeze* that summer appeared in September and concerned Tommy.

Among those who were very much missed at Beverly Farms this summer was the young man familiarly known to everybody as Tommy Leiter. Not only was he missed by his friends and neighbors but by the tradespeople and all who have seen him summer after summer at the Farms where he always entered so enthusiastically into the sports of the season.[114]

In July, Joe Leiter was in Chicago with his horses where an outburst at the track put him into the news:

Joseph Leiter, custodian of the Levi Leiter fortune, who once almost cornered the wheat market, faced the possibility today of having his large stable of horses ruled off America's finest racetracks. The Board of Stewards of the Arlington Jockey Club fined Leiter $250 yesterday for "intemperate language and conduct" during his protest against the disqualification of his filly Princess Camelia in the third race Tuesday. Turf officials of Kentucky, New York, Maryland, and Canada have had working agreements with Chicago stewards enforcing suspensions on all tracks against jockeys and owners fined for infractions of the rules.

The Arlington stewards said they would accept no more entries from Leiter until he apologized. Leiter left without announcing his plans.[115]

Joe Leiter did finally apologize and continued to race his horses.

***

Joe Leiter died in Chicago on April 11, 1932, of complications resulting from a cold he caught while attending races in New Orleans two weeks earlier. The official cause of death was complications of pneumonia and diabetes. He was 63 years old. His wife, Juliette, 20-year-old Tommy, and 16-year-old Nancy were at his bedside. Nancy, who had been very close to her father, was devastated by his death.[116]

---

[*] Hunting and fishing had been lifelong pastimes. Joseph Leiter's listing in the 1904 *Who's Who* noted under recreation: fishing and hunting birds and big game. The big game may have included buffalo on the Wyoming ranchlands.

Chapter 4
The Widow Juliette Leiter
and Her Children: 1932-1942

At the time of Joe Leiter's death, Juliette Leiter was 45, Tommy 20, and Nancy 16. The tangle of Joe Leiter's affairs left a great deal of uncertainty. Although somewhat overshadowed by her husband during her marriage, Juliette Leiter was a formidable woman in her own right. She would prove herself to be quite capable of sorting out her family's affairs.

Joseph Leiter's estate was valued at about $30,000,000 ($520,740,876 in 2015 dollars). The bulk of it was left to Juliette, who also inherited the house in Langley, Virginia, with the proviso that she in turn leave it to Nancy. Tommy and Nancy each received income from 1/8 of their grandfather Levi Leiter's estate, income from about $2,500,000. Nancy also received the $500,000 that Joe Leiter had been left by his mother, Mary Teresa Leiter. Tommy Leiter, not yet 21, inherited the Washington house, the Louisiana hunting lodge, and a racing stable worth between $3,000,000 and $5,000,000.[117] Juliette was also left with a retrieval suit from the federal government for the recovery of back taxes. Joe Leiter had never believed in the income tax.

After his father's death, if not before, Tommy Leiter had left the Northwestern School of Commerce and returned to Washington. The school had clearly been Joe Leiter's idea. Tommy had neither his father's competitive spirit nor his interest in business. Rather, his passions at the time were playing polo, sailing, planning parties, and making friends. Perhaps equally important, Juliette wanted her son with her in Washington. According to Tommy's widow:

> If Mrs. Leiter hadn't ruined him, he would have been an absolutely marvelous architect or stage designer. He had more taste. If I have any taste today it is because of T. Leiter. Mr. Leiter was dead and T. Leiter was a young man. Mrs. Leiter used to have these huge dinners at Dupont Circle for sixty people at one table, and he would sit next to the wife of the ambassador — oh, the wife of some ambassador every week . He was very young.

> T. Leiter was never educated the way he should have been. He was extremely bright and very well read and knew a lot more than most people but just — he was just Tommy Leiter, Joe Leiter's son. He did as he pleased.[118]

Juliette was able to stay in the Washington and Virginia houses, but her right to inhabit Edgewater House was unclear. According to Mary Teresa Leiter's will, upon Joe's death Edgewater was the property of Joe's siblings or their heirs. As a result, nine people now owned Edgewater in undivided shares: Juliette's sister-in law, Lady Suffolk (Margaret Hyde, Duchess of Suffolk and Berkshire); Mary Leiter Curzon's three daughters, Lady Irena Curzon (the Baroness Ravensdale), Lady Cynthia Curzon Mosley, and Lady Alexandra Curzon Metcalfe; Nancy Leiter Campbell's children, Colin Campbell, Mary Campbell

Clark and Audry Campbell; and finally Juliette and her own children, Thomas and Nancy Leiter. It is not clear whether the recently acrimonious relations between the English and American Leiters had improved by the time of Joe Leiter's death.

Although Juliette did not open Edgewater in the summer of 1932, she did plan to visit her mother, Maie Williams, who had bought a nearby house at 58 West Street in 1929. In late July, *North Shore Breeze* reported:

> Mrs. John R. Williams has come on from Washington to her cottage on West Street, Beverly Farms, near the estate of her daughter, Mrs. Joseph Leiter, although Mrs. Leiter will not occupy her estate this year. With Mrs. Williams is Mrs. Pitney Rawls and her two sons, John and Duncan Pitney. Mrs. Leiter is expected to visit her mother for a short time in September.

> Long a social center for Shore folk in that section, the noted Leiter swimming pool has once more come into use with Mrs. Williams having numerous friends gather for the bathing hour each morning. Gay sun umbrellas dot the gardens and the social groups of other summers find Edgewater House a happy meeting place.[119]

Juliette did come to Beverly Farms for a brief visit with her mother in September. At that time she must also have visited with her friend Eleonora Sears. In 1932 Eleo was still summering in Beverly Farms with her widowed father in the family cottage on Hart Street. Frederick Sears generally closed up the house in late September. Eleo, who was an avid horsewoman, often rented a different house and stayed on for the fall season. Juliette either loaned or rented Edgewater to Eleo for the fall season of 1932. Mary Teresa Leiter's will had explicitly forbidden the rental of the property when Joe was alive, on threat of revoking his life tenancy and giving the house to her residual heirs. Since Joe's death had already given the house to his mother's heirs, Juliette apparently felt no threat.

In September *North Shore Breeze* reported:

> Mrs. Joseph Leiter and her mother, Mrs. John R. Williams, sailed ten days ago for Ireland where they are visiting the latter's daughter and son-in-law, the United States Minister to the Irish Free State, Mr. and Mrs. Frederick Sterling. Mrs. Williams granddaughter [sic], Miss Audry Campbell, has been with Mr. and Mrs. Sterling for some time and will be presented in Ireland at a ball to be given on November 5 at the U.S. legation by Mr. and Mrs. Sterling.[120]*

After Nancy Leiter Campbell's death, Joe and Juliette Leiter had become Audry's unofficial guardians. Audry had been born in Scotland and had relatives on both her father's and mother's sides in the British Isles. Perhaps it was on this trip that Juliette and the English Leiters came to an agreement regarding Edgewater House. In May of 1933 *North Shore Breeze* noted:

---

* Audry Campbell was Mary Teresa Leiter's granddaughter, not Mrs. Williams's.

It is pleasant news that comes to us of the plans of the family of the late Joseph Leiter to make Beverly Farms their permanent summer home. The property belonged to the Leiter estate as it was built originally by the mother of Mr. Leiter. Mrs. Joseph Leiter has now obtained possession in her own name, and she will in future spend as much of the year at Edgewater as weather conditions will permit.

The marble swimming pool at Edgewater is one of the finest in the entire North Shore area and has been the scene of many brilliant parties in the past.

Mrs. Leiter and her daughter, Miss Nancy Leiter, will come on from Chicago about the first of June. Mrs. Leiter's mother, Mrs. J. R. Williams, who owns a small cottage nearby, will spend the summer at Edgewater, and other relatives and friends will be frequent guests throughout the summer.[121]

There is no mention of their actual arrival or of any activity at Edgewater over the summer. The next *North Shore Breeze* reference to Edgewater is a December note referring to Eleonora Sears.

Eleanor Sears has been spending the fall at Edgewater House, the estate of Mrs. Joseph Leiter at West Beach. Her horses are conveniently stabled at the Sears place, Storrow Hill, nearby, which was closed in early fall.[122]

Eleo Sears continued to rent Edgewater every autumn until she acquired Rock Edge in 1940. Juliette Leiter summered at Edgewater until her death.

Juliette Leiter did not obtain full title to Edgewater until 1936. Lady Cynthia Curzon Mosley's death in May of 1933 may have delayed the process until fall. On November 13, 1933, Joe Leiter's sister Daisy, Lady Suffolk, deeded Juliette her undivided ¼ for a little under $6000. Nancy Leiter Campbell's heirs (Colin Leiter Campbell and his wife; Mary Meta Campbell Clark and her husband; and Audry Campbell) and Mary Leiter Curzon's heirs (Lady Alexandra Curzon Metcalfe and her husband and Irene Curzon, Baroness Ravensdale) all deeded Juliette their undivided 1/12 shares for a total of $9500-$10,000. Tommy deeded an undivided 1/8. Since Nancy was a minor, Juliette held her 1/8. Lady Cynthia Curzon Mosley's estate finally deeded her undivided 1/12 to Juliette for $2250 in November of 1936. The assessed valuation of Edgewater house in 1933 is not available; in 1929 it had been assessed at $225,000 ($3,129,013 in 2015 dollars.)[123]

By the time Juliette returned to Edgewater in 1933, the Depression had deepened, affecting the lives of ordinary people of Beverly. An article just under Joe Leiter's 1932 obituary in the *Beverly Times* had announced the city's ongoing efforts to establish a local relief fund for the needy. Unlike the Great War, which had spurred the ladies of the North Shore to great activity in support of European relief activities, the Depression brought few outpourings on behalf of the unemployed. *North Shore Breeze* editors preached the need for hard work and optimism.

A few of the wealthier families had been hurt by the Crash, but the Leiters were among those who came through unscathed. Edgewater in the 1930s continued to be the site of brilliant summer entertainments. If the Leiters experienced any discomfort, it was slight. However, Depression-related desperation may have fueled a minor incident in July of 1934.

> For a dinner party at her Beverly, Mass., summer home, socialite Mrs. Juliette Leiter, widow of Chicago's rich, speculating Joseph Leiter, ran short of silverware, and borrowed what she needed to piece out from her neighbor Mrs. Anna Allan. To return them early next morning, the Leiter chauffeur loaded them carefully into the Leiter Rolls-Royce. Out of the car a few minutes later, as it stood in the Leiter driveway, thieves stole the borrowed silverware: eight salt spoons, two pepper, two salt shakers, two pepper pots.[124]

Juliette and Nancy spent full summers at Edgewater throughout the thirties; Tommy came and went. Social life centered on Nancy, who would make her debut in 1935. Juliette relied on her son to help her plan and host parties. Tommy was handsome, lighthearted, and creative. Everyone loved him for his infectious good humor and energy. Any party he hosted or attended was guaranteed to be a success. Juliette did all she could to keep him nearby. In August of 1935 Juliette and Tommy hosted a party for Nancy. *North Shore Breeze,* which thrived on naming names and describing fashions, reported:

> Mrs. Joseph Leiter gave a dinner dance for her daughter Nancy which was just great, as we prophesied last week. Nancy wore white with a very different-looking trim of a flame color and to add to her costume, she had a beautiful corsage of orchids. Miss Honora Kammerer was Miss Leiter's houseguest from Avon, Connecticut.

> Mr. "Tommy" Leiter had numerous friends present, among who were Miss Serita Bartlett, Miss Audry Campbell, Mr. and Mrs. Sam Batchelder, Mr. Benjamin Beale, Mr. John Hall, Miss Polly Warren, and Alice Burrage. After dinner some of the mothers came to look in on the fair young things having such a wonderful time. Mrs. Dudley Pickman Jr. brought daughter Nancy Cochrane, both in black gowns with pink accessories. The McKean girls, Peggy Parker, Martha Proctor, Marjorie Motley, Anne Cole — usual knockout in a black and orange dress.[125]

Nancy Leiter's debut was to be a dinner dance scheduled for October 1935 at Edgewater House. That summer *North Shore Breeze* duly reported on all of the pre-deb events — who came and what they wore. Nancy Leiter's name was included in those attending dances at the Essex County Club, pre-dance dinners, concerts at the Casino in Magnolia, picnics, and charity fundraisers: "Nancy Leiter in absinthe green," "Nancy Leiter, seen strolling on the terrace in pale blue flecked with silver, her equally smart mother, Mrs. Joseph Leiter, in white."

Nancy loved to dance and enjoyed all the parties, but even in her debutante year, they were not at the center of her life in Beverly Farms. Participating in the social whirl was Juliette Leiter's passion; Nancy Leiter's great passion was sailing. In early August she sailed to the coast of Maine with the Crowninshields aboard *Cleopatra's Barge.*[126]

By the time she was eighteen Nancy was sailing her own Herreshoff-designed yacht *Venture* in S Class races with the Pleon Yacht Club in Marblehead. She was well known as a skilled and tough competitor. Marblehead Race Week in August of 1935 probably meant more to Nancy than her debut. Nancy was the winner of the Corinthian Yacht Club's S Class race. Her brother Tommy watched from the deck of Eleo Sears's yacht.

Tommy went on to spend the remainder of August at Saratoga. He returned to Edgewater to help plan Nancy's debut. The ball, held on October 11, was a great success. It was a beautiful autumn night with the moon shining over the ocean. A Washington paper described the event.

Miss Leiter Makes Her Debut in Beverly

Mrs. Joseph Leiter of Washington and Chicago gave a large ball last evening in her summer home, Edgewater House, at Beverly Farms, Mass., to present her daughter, Miss Nancy Leiter. Many guests from Washington are being entertained by the hostess over Sunday, having gone to attend the party last evening. Mrs. Leiter was assisted by her son, Mr. Thomas Leiter of Chicago, and the dance was preceded by a dinner party for the houseguests. A group of young bachelors acted as ushers and included Mr. George von L. Meyer III and Mr. Charles A. Meyer, grandsons of the late George von L. Meyer, former Secretary of the Navy.

The several hundred guests danced in a tent erected for the occasion close to the house and decorated with quantities of chrysanthemums. A number of dinner parties were given by members of the summer colony who remained to attend Miss Leiter's debut.

Mrs. Leiter's houseguests included her nephews, Mr. Robert H. Pitney and Mr. John W. Pitney of Bernardsville, N.J., sons of Mrs. Huston Rawls of New York, formerly Miss Francise Williams, who with Mr. Rawls is also a member of the house party; Mr. and Mrs. David McKay; Miss Angelica Lloyd, the debutante daughter of Mr. and Mrs. Demarest Lloyd; Mr. Malcolm S. McConihe Jr.; and Mr. Dennis Smith Bingham of Washington.[127]

During the next few years both Tommy and Nancy were prominent members of the North Shore's smart set. *North Shore Breeze* often reported on their activities:

Opening Night of the Casino in Magnolia--Mr. Thomas Leiter arrived "un peu plus tard" with Joseph W. Woods Jr. Three others seen about the Casino were Jack Goodrich, Standish VanVoorhis, and Louis Baer. All which goes to show the Casino is once again launched on another active summer.

At the Casino-- Nancy Leiter was there having a final fling before she goes down to New Bedford for the races (with her S boat) to stay with Angelica Lloyd, daughter of Demarest Lloyd, and a fellow debutante from Washington.

When Nancy returns she will have two houseguests — Charles Gaylord from Buffalo and Joshua Evans III from Washington — to stay with her. They will probably remain over the 25th, when Nancy is giving a dinner before the Essex dance in honor of the return from the West of Miss Marjorie Motley, debutante daughter of the E. Preble Motleys of Hamilton.

Tommy Leiter came in 3rd in the Handsomest Man on the North Shore contest — beaten out by Charles. R. L. Sturgis of Manchester, first, and Randolph Charrington, second.[128]

In addition to her frequent appearances in the Social Notes, Nancy's extraordinary sailing feats were reported in the *Breeze's* yachting section.

Miss Nancy Leiter of Beverly Farms took her Herreshoff S boat *Venture* to New Bedford last week and won the series prize against such talent as Russell Pierre, Demarest Lloyd Jr., Franklin King, and Charles S. Whitman Jr. of Newport.[129]

Miss Nancy Leiter made her debut in the 8-meter class last week when she sailed Charles. P. Curtis's *Ellen* in the Eastern Challenge Cup races, and in the first race defeated William T. Aldrich's *Armida,* Harry E. Noyes's *Gypsy,* and Byrd & Deland's *Egret.* The last-named yacht was sailed by Miss Marion Leeson. Perhaps these two fair skippers may race permanently in the 8s next season.[130]

In August of 1937, Nancy and Juliette hosted a dinner dance at Edgewater for 60 young people who had participated in the Junito races with the Pleon Yacht Club. Ruby Newman's orchestra supplied the music.[131] Nancy had earlier been named the club's fleet captain. In 1938 she donated the Venture Cup for the girls' racing championship to the Pleon Yacht Club.

As *North Shore Breeze* had predicted, Nancy Leiter did continue to race yachts in the 8-Meter Class with great success. With the fortune she had inherited from her father, she was able to commission her own 8-Meter. A Boston paper reported on its April 1938 launching.

The first major class racing boat in this region since 1930 was launched yesterday. The new International Eight-Meter *Venture*, owned by Nancy Leiter of the Eastern Yacht Club, was launched yesterday in the Saugus River from the Britt Brothers Yard to the acclaim of the notables of yachting. It was a colorful launching, both figuratively and practically, as the sleek addition to the coming Eight-Meter campaign at Marblehead was resplendent with her turquoise blue topsides, azure blue decks, white boot top and green bottom....[It was] dressed with a string of code flags from stem to stern and with the owner's private signal, a yellow flag with a green ladder rampant. Miss Leiter kept in the color scheme of her private signal by wearing a smart yellow sweater and green dress. The ladder on the private signal, incidentally, is "Leiter" in German.

Venture was designed by E. Arthur Shuman Jr., C. Padgett Hodson, associate, and built by Britt Brothers to the new international Eight-Meter rule. Mrs. E. Arthur Shuman Jr. of Marblehead broke the traditional be-ribboned bottle on the rounded nose of the new boat, which marked an outstanding occasion since no one has christened an Eight-Meter for eight long years hereabouts. *Venture* will race against a coterie of crack skippers including Charles Francis Adams at the helm of the champion *Thisbe*.

A luncheon for 100 guests followed the launching, and the Britt Brothers shed was changed to resemble something like a big yacht club on regatta day.[132]

On June 4 *Venture* won the Corinthian 8-Meter race, beating out New York Yacht Club president and former Secretary of the Navy Charles Francis Adam's *Thisbe* by 14 minutes, 43 seconds. It was reported that even the usually taciturn Mr. Adams called to Miss Leiter after her craft turned the windward mark, "You've got something there."[133]

Later that summer Nancy Leiter was the first "maiden lady" admitted to the New York Yacht Club. Married women become club members as wives of their member husbands; Nancy was invited to join based her merit as a sailor.[134] In addition, she was slated to be a member of the United States sailing team in the 1940 Summer Olympics in Tokyo. The games were canceled as a result of the war.

Tommy Leiter also loved to sail. He would sometimes race the *Venture,* but preferred coastal sailing. He often chartered yachts through Arthur Shuman and cruised the East Coast. Tommy also loved to ride and play polo, though he never brought his ponies to Beverly Farms. A *Time* magazine article in July of 1937 referred to him as "polo playing Tommy Leiter." Tommy always spent some time during the summer at Edgewater. He was often present in Beverly Farms for Race Week and the Labor Day weekend.

In 1939 the Leiters were given the opportunity to expand the Edgewater property when the adjacent Haven estate came up for sale. On the death of Ellen Haven Ross in 1938 the property had been left to Harvard College. In the summer of 1939 Harvard decided to sell off all 67 acres, which included two large houses and in places extended from the waterfront to the railroad tracks. Beverly Farms businessman Samuel Batchelder immediately purchased the upper house and 17 inland acres for a paltry $7000. A consortium of men on the North Shore purchased the remaining property. According to *North Shore Breeze*:

> The purpose of the group making this purchase is to preserve the natural beauty of the place and to attract to Beverly Farms new homeowners who will continue to preserve its present residential character. To this end a subdivision has been planned, which provides for five residential lots on the beach, each with a frontage of from 230 to 300 feet, and five rear lots varying from three to seventeen acres, each with access to the beach. That the plan has met with approval is indicated by the fact that four lots are already under agreement to separate owners.[135]

On July 7, Tommy Leiter purchased the 3.5-acre beachfront lot immediately adjacent to the Leiter swimming pool for $9000 ($153,974 in 2015 dollars).[136] A year later he purchased lot 2, the adjoining three-acre lot, for $9500 ($161,368 in 2015 dollars).[137] His combined purchases gave the Leiter family a total of about eight acres. It is not clear whether Tommy Leiter bought the lots for privacy or with the intention of building a house of his own.

During the later years of the 1930s and through 1940, the Leiters continued to entertain many out-of-town guests. One of them was Marion Saffold Oates, a young woman whom Nancy had befriended in New York, and who would later marry Tommy Leiter. In a 2013 interview, Marion Oates Leiter Charles recalled her own early experiences as a guest at Edgewater. Although she came from a family with servants, Edgewater was the place she learned to "ring the bell." She also remembered a lunch when Mrs. Leiter offered her a nectarine from the greenhouse. "I had never eaten a nectarine and must have declined. Mrs. Leiter said, 'Just eat it!' I never much liked fruit, but I did as I was told."

Mrs. Charles also provided a first-hand account of summer days at Edgewater in Juliette's time:

> We had the sand pile which was right in the front of the pool. The terrace was here and you would go down two or three steps and there was a cement sort of thing like this, square, and that was filled with sand, so we didn't have to go to the beach. We just sat there and looked at Misery Island.

> The sand pile had a sundial statue in the middle of it which was quite a lovely statue, a young man sitting. It was small and low and was in the middle of the sand. Everybody would spread out towels in the sand pile — it was marvelous, just like going to the beach. I hope it's still there.

> I'm sure Joe Leiter thought of it. It was always there. The sand was raked every morning and was lovely by noontime. Out we would come, and then the bar was between the two doors, one for the library and one for the sitting room. The bar was there, always ready and waiting.

> Mrs. Leiter had a great friend called Tama from Washington. Tama was absolutely — all of these people were characters, they were wonderful people, not just dull, ordinary, go-to-the-market people. And I remember once when Tama came down the steps to the pool she had on a bathing cap and was stark naked and she carried a geranium right here.[138]

Marion Oates Leiter Charles recalled how much fun the weekend parties were and how Juliette thrived on the pleasure her friends experienced at Edgewater. She often read the effusive thank-you notes aloud. Mrs. Charles chuckled at the memory of a note from Chicago friend Eugene Pike that was short and to the point. "Dear Juliette, Thanks for the damn fine time."[139]

During the thirties one of the Leiters' butlers boarded with the Coughlin family on Hale Street and often hired local girls to help out when there were weekend guests. Two Beverly Farms women remembered that as teenagers they worked at Edgewater parties. Alice Malone was hired to help serve Champagne. She recalled that the butler wasn't satisfied with her serving ability and quickly relegated her to washing dishes. Josephine Fiore (later LeBlanc) was brought in to babysit for an out-of-town couple during the afternoon. In the evening she was asked to wash crystal during the cocktail hour. Over 60 years later she still remembered a beautiful blonde woman "like a movie star," who was quite taken with the butler who was serving Champagne. The woman kept pouring her Champagne into the plant pots so that she could sidle up to the butler for another glass.[140]

Local guests at Edgewater were often Nancy's sailing friends. Dinner parties at Edgewater had become a highlight of Marblehead's race week.

> Mrs. Joseph Leiter and Miss Nancy Leiter entertained a number of their friends at dinner last Saturday at the end of race week. One guest was honored with a birthday cake on which Snow White and the Seven Dwarfs bounded merrily. Among the admirers of this chef-d'oeuvre were Mr. and Mrs. Gordon Abbot, Mr. and Mrs. R. Bennett Forbes, Mr. and Mrs. E. D. Wigglesworth Jr., Mr. and Mrs. George Clement, Mr. and Mrs. Arthur Shuman Jr., Mr. and Mrs. Joseph Robbins, and Miss Nancy Nye.[141]

Together Nancy and Juliette Leiter also hosted numerous dinners and informal dance parties for soon-to-be-married and newly married couples. One memorable party was reported in *North Shore Breeze*:

> Friday night Mrs. Leiter gave a wonderful party for Alice Burrage and George Aldrich, who were married the next day. It was the most original party with a "hillbilly" band and wonderful Southern boys and girls who danced for the King and Queen of England on their visit last year.[142]

William Loring Vaughn, son of an old New England family, was among the young men who attended at least one of the parties at Edgewater. Years later he told his daughter Cecily a story about Juliette Leiter that suggests that she had a playful side. According to Vaughn, on the evening he was there, the stately Mrs. Leiter, dressed in a fine gown and wearing a string of pearls, filled a cocktail shaker, slipped out of her shoes, stepped onto a sofa, and jumped up and down to shake the cocktail.[143]

In addition to their purely social activities, both Juliette Leiter and Nancy served as patronesses for various community and charitable events. In 1940 Nancy was named honorary chairman of the Beverly Farms Fourth of July Committee. Her letter in *North Shore Breeze* reflects the increasing solemnity brought by the threat of war:

Fourth of July Festivities

> Come to West Beach the night of July fourth. Celebrate this country's enviable liberty with us in a real American spirit of patriotism! The program is for the enjoyment of all ages. Bring your family to see our movies shown in the open air.

The Fourth of July Committee cordially invites each and every one of you. The movies to be shown are in place of the usual fireworks in view of conditions abroad today. We felt that you would rather see actual pictures of what is happening and what we, as Americans, through the American Red Cross, are doing to help. The movie "Mobilized for Mercy" will illustrate American effort to alleviate the suffering overseas and the newsreels will show clearly the reason this aid is so essential. You will be glad you're an American and can celebrate the Fourth of July, the freedom of our country, our unabridged press, and the privileges enjoyed by us all as free citizens. There will also be comedy shorts, animated cartoons, as well as a band concert to add to the festivity.

The admission is, as always, *free,* through the cooperation of the West Beach Corporation. There will be ample free parking.

If anyone is interested in helping defray the essential expenses of this patriotic celebration either send your donations to the Secretary of the Fourth of July Committee, or to me in Beverly Farms also. Call me for any details; the number is 175 and I will gladly answer your questions.

I am looking forward to seeing you all with us on Thursday night, Fourth of July, about nine o'clock at West Beach.

Nancy Leiter, Honorary Chairman
Frank W. Dix, Chairman of the Committee
Ralph Lawler, Secretary
John Malley, Treasurer[144]

In September of 1940 Juliette Leiter added to her Beverly Farms property by purchasing the 58 West Street cottage, known in the family as Dower House, from her aging mother, Maie Williams.

In spite of the canceled Olympics and fear of American involvement in the war, 1940 was a happy year for Nancy Leiter. In December she became engaged to C. Thomas Clagett Jr. Tom Clagett had graduated from St. John's College in Annapolis in 1939 with a degree in engineering. After graduation he joined the Navy Reserve. At the time of the engagement a Washington paper wrote:

When Nancy Leiter reached her eighteenth birthday a few years ago and received more than a million dollars as an added inheritance, she was a student at the Westover School in Connecticut.

Fortune hunters, no doubt, took heart, but in an interview at the time, Miss Leiter said "He must be six feet tall, have curly black hair, a suspicion of a dimple, and be a good dancer."

Yesterday Mrs. Joseph Leiter announced the engagement of her daughter Nancy to Charles Thomas Clagett, more than six feet tall with curly black hair, an excellent dancer, and perhaps with just the slightest suspicion of dimple in a frank and pleasant face.[145]

Nancy and Tom were married at the Dupont Circle house in February of 1941. Because Tom was an Episcopalian, the bishop would not permit them to marry in a Catholic church. He did, however, agree to officiate at the wedding.* Like many wartime weddings it was a relatively small event. Society columnist

---

* Nancy considered the bishop's position to be hypocritical, left the Catholic Church and became an Episcopalian.

Igor Cassini (who wrote the Cholly Knickerbocker column) was clearly not pleased and took out his venom in print.

> The Leiter-Clagett wedding, by the way, proved to be a complete surprise. The papers played it up none or little, and half of the people who had been scraping at Mrs. Joe Leiter's feet to enter her graces were left out of the invitation list.[146]

Tommy Leiter gave the newlyweds his yacht in Florida for a two-week honeymoon. War was in the air, and the young couple returned to Washington. Soon after the attack on Pearl Harbor, Tom Clagett was deployed and stationed in Stillwater, Oklahoma, before being sent to the Pacific. Sometime before Tom went overseas, he and Nancy purchased a farm in Rockville, Maryland, which they named Duration Farm. Their daughter Judy Clagett McLennan reported: "My father bought a couple of inoperable cars and pieces of machinery and plopped them in various fields around the farm so that Mother could use them to collect gas coupons."

As a lieutenant in the Naval Reserve, Tom was sent to Maui, where he served throughout the war. "He wasn't the top person on the base, but he headed up operations. The base was there to fix airplanes that were damaged in the Pacific theater. If planes could get to Maui from the aircraft carriers, they were repaired there and sent back. That's what Dad was there doing. He loved it."[147]

While Tom was away Nancy threw herself into the war effort. She used the farm gas coupons to get herself into Washington, where she was a tireless Red Cross volunteer. A newspaper article from 1941 shows a photo of Nancy in her uniform. According to the accompanying story, she had begun working for the Red Cross as soon as she returned from her honeymoon. Nancy Clagett continued to volunteer throughout the war and received many awards for her work.[148] In early June *North Shore Breeze* noted that Nancy had accompanied her mother to Beverly Farms, would stay a week, and then return to Washington, with plans to return again for a visit in July. An item in the yachting section of the magazine announced, "It is understood that Mrs. Charles T. Clagett's (Nancy Leiter) famous *Venture* is for sale."[149] Nancy would never again spend carefree summers at Edgewater.

During the summer of 1941, the North Shore threw itself into the war effort. Juliette Leiter was listed among the patronesses for most of the summer benefits. Although *North Shore Breeze* makes no note of it, Tommy probably spent time with her, and most likely Marion Oates would have come to visit.

In 1942 Edgewater opened for the summer a little later than usual. On June 29 Juliette Leiter was in New York for the wedding of her son Tommy to Marion Saffold Oates.

Marion Oates had spent her childhood at Belvoir, her family's home just outside Montgomery, Alabama. She was the only child of lawyer William Calvin Oates Jr. and Georgia Saffold Oates. Both parents were from prominent Alabama families. William Oates's father, Confederate Colonel William Calvin Oates, led the Confederate forces in the Battle of Little Round Top at Gettysburg and later became governor of Alabama. Georgia Saffold was descended from Reuben Saffold, Chief Justice of the Alabama Supreme Court from 1834 to 1836. Georgia Saffold's mother, Mildred Reynolds Saffold, lived with the family.

As a young teenager Marion was sent to an English-speaking girls' school in Belgium, and a few years later was moved to a convent school in Germany. But the war cut short her stay there and she returned to Alabama.

> My grandmother and I got off the train in Montgomery and we were met by Miss Marie Bankhead — Marie Owen she was then. As we stepped off the train, she said — of course she had been brought up in Washington with her brothers — "My, Marion looks just like Mary Victoria Leiter"! That's the first time we had ever heard of the Leiters. So that was quite a compliment, since Mary Leiter was a very beautiful woman. Aunt Marie was Tallulah Bankhead's aunt. Tallulah was always in and out of my life. [*The Bankheads were close family friends. As a child Marion had often visited with "Aunt Marie."*][150]

After her parents' divorce and her mother's remarriage in 1938, Marion Oates moved to Manhattan, where her stepfather, Philip Gossler, had a house at 14 East 56th Street. There Marion renewed her friendship with Brenda Frazier, a friend from her Montgomery days, who gave her the nickname "Oatsie."

> Brenda Frazier was my only friend when I moved to New York. [Her mother] "Big Brenda" had been stationed in Alabama during World I, so she and my mother knew each other. Brenda was known as the glamour girl.* I was known as the representative of the old guard because I was so dignified." Brenda always made me laugh a lot. She is the one who gave me the nickname "Oatsie" We remained friends until she died.[151]

Marion Oates made her debut at a party at the St. Regis Roof. Meyer's Davis's band played. Mrs. Charles recalled:

> It never occurred to me that when you are invited to a party you aren't expected to have a good time. The debutantes used to get absolutely hysterical that nobody would dance with them. This never occurred to me. So when I came out at the St. Regis Roof, I thought I was there to have a good time. So I did.[152]

Oatsie enjoyed the New York social scene and was quite happy to be single. She recalled an interchange with her grandmother at Belvoir:

> I don't know, I don't think I was ever very keen on marriage. My grandmother said to me once, 'Madam, if you don't get married *soon* I'm going to march you down and marry you to the black gardener if I have to.' That was quite a desperate thing to say in those days.[153]

It was during this time, perhaps through the Bankhead connection, that Oatsie became friends with Nancy Leiter. Over the next few years she spent time with the Leiter family at Dupont Circle as well as at Edgewater.

Oatsie had experienced enough of the world not to be overawed by the Leiter wealth. She found the ostentatious Dupont Circle house rather ugly. Moreover, she had been raised to have the confidence and

---

* Brenda Frazier became one of the most famous debutantes of her era. In 1938, her debutante year, she was dubbed America's number one glamour girl. In November her photograph appeared on the cover of *Life* magazine. In 1918 Brenda's father, Frank Frazier, had been sent to Camp Sheridan outside of Montgomery. His wife, "Big Brenda," accompanied him.

social grace to feel at ease in society. As she put it, "I knew how to enter a drawing room." Juliette Leiter, whom many regarded as rather formidable, was immediately charmed by the attractive young Southerner who had been further polished in Europe. Oatsie always felt that it was Juliette who decided that her son Tommy should marry her.[154]

In 1942, Tommy Leiter did indeed propose, and Oatsie accepted. A few days before the wedding, Oatsie's Alabama-born friend, well-known New York designer Wilson Folmer, took her out to dinner.

> After dinner he said, "Let's go see Tallulah. She should be home from the theater by now." So we went up to see Tallulah. And she said, "I *know* Georgia's not going to tell you the facts of life," so she proceeded to tell me. In the meantime, I had [laryngitis and] no voice, so she was giving me bourbon on sugar. She more or less said sex wasn't all it was cut out to be. I woke up the next morning and mother came in with a wedding present and some sort of tissue paper was rustling. "I said "My God, what's that horrible noise?" And I've never remembered what Tallulah told me.[155]

The couple were married in the chapel of St. Thomas's Church on Fifth Avenue. World War II was on, and the wedding was small. Tommy Leiter was 30. Oatsie was 23.

> I think we went straight to Beverly Farms. That's where we spent our honeymoon. I don't know if he was in uniform. I remember we had dinner in the dining room and the servants were all there and everything. And the next day the telephone rang and it was Aggie Church, Mrs. Frederick Church. She said, "Listen, you must be bored to tears, why don't you come and have dinner tonight? So we went on and had dinner with Fred and Aggie that night and then proceeded on our merry way. [*The Churches summered at "The Old Place," three houses down the beach, just beyond the two Rantoul houses.*]

> I don't think Mrs. Leiter was there the night Tommy and I arrived, but she was there shortly afterwards, and she always sat at the head of the table. The first night we came into dinner she said, "Oatsie, dear, you go to the head of the table. You are now the head of the house." And I said, "Not so long as you are alive; you just get right up there where you belong."[156]

A few weeks later, Tommy and Oatsie left Beverly Farms and returned to Washington. On July 25, 1942, Tommy Leiter enlisted in the Army at Fort Myers, Virginia. Unlike most of his friends, who had graduated from college and entered the military as officers, Tommy entered as a private. He spent the summer in basic training at Fort Lee in Richmond, Virginia.

Juliette Leiter spent the rest of the season at Edgewater. Throughout that summer the articles and notices in *North Shore Breeze* not only included all of the usual social events, but also documented the impact of World War II on the summer community. The July 24 issue noted that Mrs. Thomas Clagett was with her mother at Edgewater. The same issue reported that J. Harleston Parker Jr., son of Manchester summer resident and Edgewater's architect, had enlisted in the Naval Reserve. The September 24 issue of the *Breeze* announced, "Mrs. Thomas Leiter is visiting Mrs. Joseph Leiter in Beverly Farms." That issue also included a wartime request.

> Right now I would like to remind everyone again to look through their garages, attics, barns, and kitchens for junk. Mrs. Evans Dick, who has taken over the collecting in Beverly Farms in the absence of her daughter Joan, says the following are useful for salvage purposes — steel, brass, iron, bronze,

aluminum, zinc, paper, cans, lead, rubber, and old keys. Mrs. Joseph Leiter gave her lovely iron gatepost last week.[157]

As part of the salvage drive, Ada Small Moore tore down the old Swift carriage house on her property and donated the iron. Helen Frick gave the massive wrought-iron fence that surrounded her stables. These donations from the very wealthy were good for local morale.

At the end of September, Juliette Leiter left *Edgewater* for the last time and returned to Dupont Circle. Oatsie was living across the street in the house at 3151 New Hampshire Avenue that she and Tommy rented from Juliette's mother, Maie Williams. Nancy was in Stillwater, Oklahoma, with her husband, and Tommy was at Fort Lee.

Shortly after her return to Washington, Juliette Leiter became ill. In late October, Oatsie and Tommy put her on a train to be taken to Johns Hopkins Hospital in Baltimore.

> When she was dying we put her on the train and took her down to Johns Hopkins. I was the only one with her, and I'll never forget it as long as I live. It was like something out of *Zhivago*. There was a light snow falling and there were soldiers and sailors all over the platform. Juliette was lying on a gurney waiting for the ambulance, and she reached up and took my hand and said, "You know you are the only one who has ever shown me any affection." I mean it really makes me cry fifty [sic] years later because I used to sort of ruffle her hair and nobody else ever dared touch her.[158]

Juliette Leiter died at Johns Hopkins Hospital on October 29, 1942. She was 55 years old and died alone.

Juliette had been only 21 when she married 40-year-old Joe Leiter. By all accounts, her husband was a man of monumental ego and changeable moods. Tragedy struck her family twice, with two of her four children dying young; her first-born, John, in infancy and her second son, Joseph Jr., in the Louisiana hunting accident when he was ten.

Throughout her life Juliette was close to her own family. Her mother, Maie "Ma" Williams, lived across the street from her in Washington and spent most of her summers in Beverly Farms, either at Edgewater with Juliette or in her own Dower House across the street. Juliette's sister Francise often visited as well.

Juliette was known in both Washington and Beverly Farms as a premier hostess. Dinner parties and balls at the Dupont Circle house were frequented by Washington dignitaries, foreign ambassadors, and visiting British and European nobility. Juliette hosted similarly elite entertainments at Edgewater House.

Juliette Leiter's relationship with her own children appears to have been attentive but somewhat severe. Interactions between parents and children in her day were often structured and limited. Nancy's daughter, Judy Clagett McLennan, concluded that her mother loved and respected Juliette Leiter but was sometimes at odds with her. Juliette had very definite ideas about how a young lady should spend her time, ideas that didn't always coincide with Nancy's.[159]

Marion Oates Leiter Charles remembered that other people found Juliette rather terrifying.

She was very tall, and blonde, rather distinguished looking. She wasn't a beauty, but very dignified and elegant. She had a very commanding manner and scared the living daylights out of everyone, including her children. They were always very careful around her. I don't know why she didn't scare me, but she didn't. I think she and I just got along from the moment I first saw her. I thought she was a rather lonely woman.[160]

The section of Juliette's will disposing of her Massachusetts properties was filed in the Salem Probate Court. Cecil Whitney of Choate, Hall was appointed executor, as Tommy Leiter declined to serve.

At the time of Juliette's death, the Edgewater property, including the house, garage/stable/gardener's cottage, greenhouses, swimming pool, and five acres (17,242 square feet) of land, was valued at $57,011 ($831,588 in 2015 dollars). Dower House and its 16,325 square feet of land at 58 West Street, which Juliette had purchased in 1940, was valued at $4500 ($65,652 in 2015 dollars).

In her will Juliette left the house at Dupont Circle and Dower House to Tommy. The Edgewater property was left to Tommy and Nancy in undivided equal shares with the provision that if one of the heirs chose to live in the house, the other was to sell his/her share to the other for no more than $20,000.[161]

Chapter 5
Tommy and Oatsie Leiter: 1942-1950

In the late fall of 1942 Tommy Leiter was sent to Cheyenne, Wyoming, for further military training. Following the custom of young women of her class, Oatsie accompanied him and rented an apartment nearby. Although Tommy was only a private, his wealth and social class apparently gave him extraordinary privileges. Mrs. Charles remembers that, despite rules against fraternization, officers flocked to the Leiter apartment every Sunday afternoon. Tommy Leiter had the best liquor supply in Cheyenne. "He was private first class. He always said there were only two things to be in the Army, four-star general or private first class. He stayed a private first class, and all the generals used to come and call."[162]

When Tommy was shipped to Europe, Oatsie returned to their rented house at 3151 New Hampshire Avenue in Washington, formerly owned by Tommy's grandmother Maie Williams. The United States Government had taken over the Dupont Circle house and used it as office space for the duration of the war. A newspaper photo of the time shows the Leiter ballroom lined with the desks of the National Advisory Committee for Aeronautics stenographic pool. During that time the Boucher panels from the salon and possibly other valuable items were removed and eventually sent to Edgewater.

Tommy Leiter was first stationed in France, where he most probably worked as a driver for a behind-the-lines officer.

> He remained a private but seemed to mingle with all the officers, which of course was against the law in those days, because he always had good food and good drink. He was in Paris, I think, but obviously it must have been someplace outside Paris. I remember he was in a jeep with Gertrude Sanford Legendre. She was a correspondent or something, and they got awfully close to the German lines and he was severely disciplined for going so far.[163] [*Unknown to Tommy Leiter and his superiors, Gertrude Legendre was actually a spy working for the OSS. She was later captured and spent six months in a German prison before escaping.*][164]

At some time Tommy Leiter was transferred to London. In *Those Charming People*, a society gossip column in a Washington newspaper, Austine Cassini wrote, "Private Tommy Leiter, previously one of Washington's most meticulous hosts, gets time off occasionally from his duties as an Army cook in London to mingle with the Tatler crowd…"[165] Unlike the wives of most soldiers, Oatsie Leiter apparently did not need to worry about her husband's safety. Throughout his war service, he was never in combat.

Like Juliette before her, Oatsie spent her summers in Beverly Farms. Life at Edgewater during those wartime summers went on much as it always had, if on a smaller scale. The staff was a reduced in size, but still ample. Caretaker and gardener George Ferrier continued to oversee the estate as well as maintain the greenhouses and gardens. Ferrier had been with the Leiters since 1926, when he replaced Percy Huxley. He and his wife, Katherine, had emigrated from Scotland in 1911. In 1926, when they came to Edgewater, their daughter, Jean, was six and son, George Jr., was four. Local people remembered Ferrier as a sober man and strict father. Mrs. Charles remembered him for the gladiolas he raised.

> We had a huge Irish drinking table, which was a big half-moon. You were supposed to sit in front of the fire on one side and warm your feet on the other. You came in the front door and you saw the fireplace; we had sofas around and there was the table. We used to have a huge Steuben bowl, which I still have. There was always an enormous bouquet of gladiolas, which I generally hate but they were beautiful. The gardener, Ferrier, used to arrange the flowers every day; they were huge and simply marvelous.[166]

Two older adults, George Glanville and Gertie Webb, provided the stability to make Edgewater a pleasant refuge for Oatsie.

Glanville, the family butler, who had stayed on after Juliette's death, continued to arrange the moves, supervise the servants, and oversee the general running of the house. Glanville had come to the United States in 1919. Nancy Leiter Clagett's recollection was that he had been valet to either an English nobleman or a prince who had spent some time with the Leiters. Mrs. Charles recalled that Glanville had come with Lord Cook, who was a member of the British delegation in Washington. According to the family story, the young valet had fallen in love with Juliette's French lady's maid, Annette. When the noble or royal visitor was ready to leave, he asked Juliette what he could do to thank her for hospitality. She said he could leave his valet with her. So Glanville stayed on as the butler and married Annette the French maid. Glanville had once been a member of the Brigadier Guards, and Mrs. Charles remembered that sometimes Juliette would persuade him to wear his beaver hat when she had especially fancy parties. The Leiters paid Glanville well: in 1940 he was earning $1800 a year, near the top of the range for butlers at the time.

George Glanville was an extraordinarily capable, trustworthy, and good humored man who was relied on and beloved by the entire Leiter family. He served the Leiters until Tommy Leiter died in 1956. His wife, Annette, stayed on as Oatsie's personal maid. Nancy Leiter Clagett's husband Tom provided for the Glanvilles in their retirement.

The second older adult who spent a good deal of time at Edgewater with Oatsie during the war years was an extraordinary woman named Gertie Webb, companion to Tommy Leiter's cousin Audry Campbell.

Juliette had engaged Gertie Webb as companion to Audry after Nancy Leiter Campbell's death in 1930. Born in Wexford, Ireland, the young Gertie Webb had somehow made her way to Russia, where she served Prince Koudasheff and his family. According to the family story, she helped smuggle the Koudasheff jewels out of Russia during the revolution. Her immigration records indicate that she was trilingual — speaking both French and Russian in addition to English. Sometime after the Koudasheffs came to the United States, Gertie Webb left them and took a position with the wealthy Parker Palmers in Chicago. When Juliette Leiter was seeking companion for Audry, "Mrs. Palmer or someone said, 'There's a wonderful old girl here who would probably love to be Audrey's companion. She's Irish.' And the next thing everybody knew, Gertie arrived in Washington, and she was with Audry for years and years even after Audry was married. She was marvelous, really a remarkable, wonderful character — funny as a crutch, always up to her Irish tricks."[167]

From 1931 on Audry Campbell and Gertie Webb had been regular summer visitors to Edgewater. Tommy Leiter became very close to both of them. Warm, resourceful, and always full of fun, Gertie brought joy and comfort to both cousins through difficult times. Mrs. Charles remembered that it was Gertie Webb who had told her of Tommy's involvement in the hunting accident that had killed his brother, Joe Jr. Shortly after Oatsie and Tommy were married, Audry Campbell and Middleton George Charles Train, son of Admiral Train, married at the Leiters' Washington house. Middleton Train immediately went on active duty in the Navy. Gertie stayed on as Audry's companion.

During the war years, Audry Campbell Train and Gertie were with Oatsie at Edgewater for much of the time. The down-to-earth Gertie could always be relied on to face any situation with good common sense and sometimes antic humor. Like the rest of the Leiters, Oatsie adored her.

Audry and Oatsie were very different but had become great friends. As Oatsie described Audry, "She was 'veddy English' and really didn't know what to make of me when we first met, but we became close friends right away and remained friends until she died." Audry was a rather reserved woman with poor eyesight.

During their summers at Edgewater, Audry and Oatsie apparently found many ways to forget about the war.

> It was just enormously pleasant. Audry and I used to shop like mad. There was a marvelous man, Mr. Rothschild, who had a wonderful shop in Manchester, an antique shop. We used to go all over the place shopping.
>
> I remember Audry and I were driving to Manchester once on a rather foggy, misty day and suddenly we smelled a skunk that had been killed on the road, and Audrey sniffed and said, "Oh, always reminds me mummy. She always had skunk collars and I never smell a skunk that I don't think of mummy."
>
> We played tennis too, Audry and I, but neither of us could ever hit the ball. Somewhere there is a little trophy that says *Edgewater Beach Tennis Championship* that I won. There were only two of us playing. The tennis court was right out in front of the house.
>
> We used to go in to the Ritz quite a lot. We were driven in; Audry had her own chauffeur. I remember once going in and meeting Bill Coolidge for lunch in Boston and he said, "What have you done today?" I never drank a thing in those days — but I had had a sip of some drink and I said, "Why we went to the Goose of the Seven Gobbles in Salem." I've never forgotten it. Life was really quite extraordinary, very comfortable, very easy, and extremely nice.[168]
>
> The war, I hate to tell you, was a terribly pleasant time at Edgewater. The atmosphere in the world was very exciting. You were always waiting for some exciting news. You never knew when the officers were going to be called away. It was just an exciting time.
>
> Although you're not supposed to mingle officers and privates, any friends who were in uniform and showed up in Beverly Farms — there was Harry Brooks and God knows who else —boy, there would be a headlong run to Edgewater House because of the liquor. Old Joe Leiter used to have the bootleggers come up on the shore, so we had all kinds of wonderful stuff that nobody else had. And it was strictly against Army rules, but we didn't care.[169]

Oatsie's maternal grandmother, Mildred Saffold Reynolds, visited as well. Mrs. Reynolds had lived with Oatsie and her family in Alabama and remained at Belvoir even after Oatsie's father died and her mother remarried. "We had an English Triumph that was a two-seater. It was an absolute bliss to drive. When my grandmother would come up to visit we used to get in the car and drive around to look at graveyards, we were Southern crazy about graveyards. She especially liked to drive around in the rain."

In addition to her out-of-town guests, Oatsie also spent time with her many Beverly Farms friends. Aggie Church and Prissy Motely were among her close companions. Despite the difference in ages, Eleo Sears was also a friend, and she and Oatsie often went walking around Beverly Farms and sometimes to Manchester. In 1940 Eleo had acquired Rockedge and was a neighbor on the beach.

> Eleo had a great friend, I don't remember her name, but she was simply charming. She used to come and stay with her in the summer and she collected shells — she had the most beautiful collection of shells I have ever seen. I remember one day being at Eleo's and she said to somebody, Prissy Motely or Aggie Church or somebody, "My dear, are you a concologist?" She was very impressed that I knew what it meant.

With the end of the war, Tom and Nancy Clagett and Tommy and Oatsie Leiter made decisions about Edgewater. Tommy and Oatsie both loved being in Beverly Farms and chose to continue to spend their summers there. Nancy and Tom Clagett chose Newport, where Tom had spent time at the naval base.

In early October of 1945, Thomas Clagett and Nancy Leiter Clagett sold their undivided share of Edgewater House to Thomas Leiter for $44,000, over twice the price Juliette had stipulated in her will. Exactly what share of the property the Clagetts were actually selling was unclear. The final sentence of the deed reads "The undivided interest hereby conveyed is believed to be one undivided eighth part, but all of the interest of the grantor herein is conveyed whether the same be more or less."[170]

During the summer of 1946, for reasons that are not clear, Tommy Leiter didn't open Edgewater House. Instead he and Oatsie stayed at the Dower House, the smaller house at 58 West Street that Juliette Leiter had purchased from her mother in 1940. Mrs. Charles later recalled:

> I can't remember why I was in the Dower House. I believe we didn't open Edgewater one year. I absolutely loved it. We would walk over to the pool and pass the greenhouses on the way. It was absolutely charming. Is it still there? It was a divine house. It was the best small house I've ever lived in.[171]

During that summer at the Dower House and the next, when they were back at Edgewater, Oatsie and Tommy Leiter were full participants in North Shore society. Tommy sailed with his friends and played golf at Myopia. Both played golf and attended events at the Essex County Club. The house was usually full of out-of-town guests and friends from the North Shore community. Tommy Leiter loved to entertain.

> He was a marvelous host and a marvelous party giver and I never had to worry about anything. I just had to come downstairs. He did the inviting; he did everything — dinner parties, balls, picnics. He was wildly imaginative.

During those postwar years Edgewater was still famous for its excellent wine and liquor. This was a time of three-martini lunches and generally heavy drinking at society parties. Mrs. Charles reminisced about a favorite Boston Brahmin couple who were frequent guests.

> The person I remember best was C___. He and his wife M___ were at a party when a friend of mine, who was very elegant, very chic, came down the stairs at Edgewater, and somebody said, "My god, that's a good-looking woman," and M___, who was inclined to drink, looked up and said, "Stand her on her head and what's she got?" Imagine standing Min LeGree on her head! C___ used to have a wonderful trick. He'd take a straight chair, and stand behind it, and jump over it.[172]

Oatsie loved Edgewater House and looked forward to spending many more summers there with Tommy.

> Then one day in 1947 he came to me said, "I'm selling the house." And I said, "Why?" "Because everyone goes Down East in the summer, and none of my friends are here." So off we went. I was so God-damned mad I could hardly speak. It is a lovely house, I think. And I loved everything about the North Shore. I loved all my friends; I loved Boston.[173]

Tommy and Oatsie held one last big house party at Edgewater House, on Labor Day weekend 1947. A professional photographer recorded the Leiters at the pool as well as with their guests at the evening dinner party and dance. Marion Oates Leiter Charles has the photos in a small red leather album with *Edgewater House* embossed in gold on the cover.

On April 9, 1948, Thomas and Nancy Clagett again registered a deed of "all our right, title and interest, believed to be an undivided half interest" in Edgewater House to Thomas Leiter. On April 10 Tommy took out a ten-year, $30,000 mortgage on the combined Edgewater House and Dower House properties from the Suffolk Savings Bank. Bank president and Beverly Farms resident Leward Lister witnessed both documents.

The Beverly City Directory for 1948 recorded that Thomas Leiter had removed to Northeast Harbor, Maine. Edgewater was listed as vacant for the summer, though George Ferrier remained on as gardener/caretaker. Mrs. Charles recalled:

> The next thing I knew we wound up in Northeast Harbor. Well, we went to Northeast Harbor and then we moved to Bar Harbor after the fire and had a house right on the water. I don't remember the name of it; it's now an inn. But I never forgave him for selling Beverly Farms. He sold everything in it, lock, stock, and barrel.[174]

Over July 14 through 17 of 1948, Louis Joseph auctioneers held a four-day auction at Edgewater House and Dower House. Tickets to the auction cost two dollars, with the proceeds from the ticket sales to benefit Beverly Hospital. Everything from the eighteenth-century pastoral room panels attributed to Francois Boucher to mops and brooms were put up for sale. Recent Edgewater neighbor Natalie Glovsky remembered attending the pre-auction showing. Room after room was filled with valuable antique furniture, oriental rugs, draperies, Ming vases, Sung pottery, spinach and mutton fat jade pieces, framed mezzotints, a Japanese netsuke collection, silver and china candlesticks and garnitures — even a 14-foot linen tablecloth reputed to have been presented to Maria Theresa of Austria by Louis XIV. By 1948 the library's collection had grown to 1600 books. It was the sale of the books that especially saddened Oatsie.

The Boucher panels, such a source of pride to both Mary Teresa and Juliette Leiter, did not sell. Current Edgewater owner Jeffrey Horvitz, a collector and expert on Boucher, believes they were in fact from the school of Boucher, not by the master himself.[175]

In the fall of 1948, the young Leiters went to England. It was perhaps on this trip that Oatsie first met the English Leiters; she and they would remain friends throughout their lives. The Leiters spent the summers of 1948 through 1952 in Northeast Harbor and Bar Harbor. Tommy loved being Down East. Oatsie did not:

> I said, "I'm not going to stay in Bar Harbor because you all go off in sailboats and I get terribly seasick." So he said, "All right. You can go anywhere on the East coast that you like." The only other place I knew where I had some friends was Newport, so we rented Land's End (the former Edith Wharton house) from Augustus Paine and in the fall we bought it.[176]

Edgewater House remained empty from 1948 until 1950. Caretaker George Ferrier stayed on until June of 1950, when Thomas and Marion Leiter sold Edgewater House to Herbert Kaiser, a buyer who had a radically different vision for Edgewater's future.

Chapter 6
The Kaisers: June 1950-April 1951

When Herbert Kaiser purchased the Edgewater property in 1950, large summer estates were selling for very little. After Maybelle Swift Wichfield allowed Swiftmore to go into foreclosure in 1933, Ada Small Moore had snapped up the property for $82,000 ($1,495,000 in 2015 dollars), demolished the house and expanded her gardens. By the end of the thirties, prices had plummeted. In 1940 Eleo Sears was able to acquire Rockedge for $23,000 ($397,849 in 2015 dollars) from the Frederick Alger heirs and kept it as a summer estate. According to one story, she won the money for the house in a high-stakes game of backgammon with her pal Mike Vanderbilt.[177] A few years later Miss Sears used a straw buyer to acquire the Wood estate next door, which she quickly demolished.

During the period from 1939 to the mid-1950s, the founders of Endicott College purchased several summer estates in the West Farms district. The first purchases in 1939 were the Kendall Hall School (the former Sears place) and then the magnificent Gardner Stone mansion, followed by Alhambra in 1940. Endicott College archivist Barbara Broudo notes that the Gardners had expected to sell Alhambra, but didn't think anyone would purchase the impractically large stone castle which had stood vacant since 1930. In 1943, when Juliette Leiter's friend Anna Allen defaulted on Allenbank's mortgage, Eleanor Tupper added the estate to her newly founded Endicott College for a mere $10,000 ($137,000 in 2015 dollars)[178]. In 1944 Endicott added the Ryan estate for $15,000[179] ($202,000 in 2015). *

Finding a buyer for Edgewater House and the adjoining property had taken time. On June 9, 1950, Thomas Leiter finally sold the original Edgewater property, including the greenhouse lot, as well as his two adjoining waterfront lots to Herbert J. Kaiser, a bond salesman from Greenwich, Connecticut, for $66,000 ($651,250 in 2015 dollars). Kaiser immediately obtained a $30,000 mortgage from the Merchants National Bank of Salem.[180] His intention was to subdivide the property and reduce the size of the main house. It is unclear whether he ever had any intention of living there.

Herbert J. Kaiser was born in 1895 to John and Elizabeth Kaiser. The 1910 census listed John Kaiser as a wholesale leather merchant, living in Mt. Vernon, New York. Herbert was then 15.

Herbert Kaiser's first career was as a leather salesman, perhaps for his father's company. In 1920, the 25-year-old Herbert, along with his wife, Jane, and their infant son, Herbert Jr., were living in nearby New Rochelle. Ten years later they were still in New Rochelle with their son. The family employed a German couple as maid and chauffeur. Herbert is listed in that year's census as a sheepskin salesman.

---

* See Endicott's pamphlet, "The Historic Houses of Endicott: A Walking Tour" for the stories of these houses and more.

By 1940 Kaiser had a new career, a new wife, and a new home. The 45-year-old Herbert and his new 27-year-old wife Olga were living in Darien, Connecticut, in a house valued at $5000. Herbert was working as a bond salesman.

Although the 1940 census listed Kaiser as a bond salesman, he continued to be involved with his father's leather business, and through that connection became acquainted with the North Shore. In 1941 the John Kaiser Leather Company, which specialized in sheepskins, purchased a leather factory in Peabody. Herbert Kaiser was listed as treasurer. As a company officer, Kaiser would have made regular visits to the North Shore from Connecticut.[181]

As soon as Kaiser purchased Edgewater in 1950, he had plans drawn for the subdivision of the property into a total of six lots. The main property was divided into three lots on the locations of the house, the carriage house, and the potting shed/greenhouses, lots A, B and C on the subdivision plan. The vacant land that Tommy Leiter had purchased to the west of the house was divided into three additional lots: front lot #1 of 1.631 acres and rear lot #1 of 1.203 acres. The rear lot had frontage on the private road at 45 West Street (now Haven Way). The oceanfront lot had a 20-foot right of way to the same private road, as well as an 8-foot right of way to the Edgewater "avenue" (the driveway). The 3.059-acre oceanfront lot #2 also abutted the private road at 45 West Street (now Haven way).[182]

During the summer and fall of 1950, Kaiser demolished the greenhouses and began to dismantle the third floor of Edgewater House with the intention of removing it, as well as the second floor, to create a more salable one-story house. Fortunately, he did not complete the project. On November 28, 1950, Oliver and Ellen Ames purchased Edgewater House and adjoining front lot #1, and thereby preserved the integrity of the house. The Ameses paid $31,000 for the Edgewater house and lot and only $3500 for the adjacent oceanfront lot. Kaiser paid off his $30,000 Merchants Bank mortgage the same day.[183]

During the winter Kaiser sold off the rest of the lots. On November 27, Elizabeth Deichmann, a German biologist at Harvard University, purchased lot C, the 62,751-square-foot greenhouse lot, for $3000.[184] Miss Deichmann made her home in what had been the potting shed. (In 1952 Deichmann would subdivide the property and sell the inner lot.) On January 11, 1951, Catherine Walsh of Manchester purchased rear lot #1, a parcel of 1.203 acres and 6000 square feet, for $4500.[185] A month later Frederick J. and Rosanna T. Leviseur bought lot #2 — 3.05 acres with 230 feet of ocean frontage — for $12,000. They built a house toward the back of the lot, with frontage on the private road at 45 West Street.[186]

On April 25, 1951, Sally de C. Moffit bought lot B, made up of 1.17 landlocked acres and the Edgewater stable/garage/gardener's cottage. She paid $53,000, almost $20,000 more than the Ameses had paid just five months earlier for the mansion house and more than four acres of land that included 475 feet of ocean frontage.[187] Why Sally Moffit was willing to pay so much more than the Ameses had paid remains something of a mystery. The most probable explanation is that in the forties and fifties the large estate houses were considered impractical white elephants, suitable for institutions, but not for family homes.

The Kaisers had purchased the Edgewater properties for $66,000 in June 1950 and sold all of them for a total of $107,000 by the end of April 1951. They invested part of their profits in more real estate. In December 1951 they bought 26 acres of land in Ipswich, which they subdivided and sold over the next several years. During the same period, they also bought and sold a couple of lots on Valley Street in Beverly Farms.

The Kaisers did live in Beverly Farms for a brief time, though never at Edgewater. They first appeared in the Beverly City Directory in 1958 at 980 Hale Street. Through all of this time Herbert Kaiser was operating the leather factories in Peabody. Nearly all of the post-Edgewater real estate transactions are in Olga's name only. In 1960 the Kaisers purchased land on Hesperus Avenue in Magnolia and created their third subdivision, this one called Ocean Highlands.[188] In 1964 the Kaisers left Beverly Farms and moved to the first house in their new development. By 1975 there were 12 houses in the subdivision.[189]

Herbert Kaiser died at home in Ocean Highlands on June 21, 1972. He was 77 and died of hypertensive cardiac disease. Herbert Kaiser is buried in Harmony Grove Cemetery in Salem. At the time of his death he was listed as a leather broker with H .J. Kaiser, Inc.[190] At that time Herbert and Olga's son Christopher was living with them.. Olga and Christopher remained in the house for another year. By 1974 they had left Magnolia.

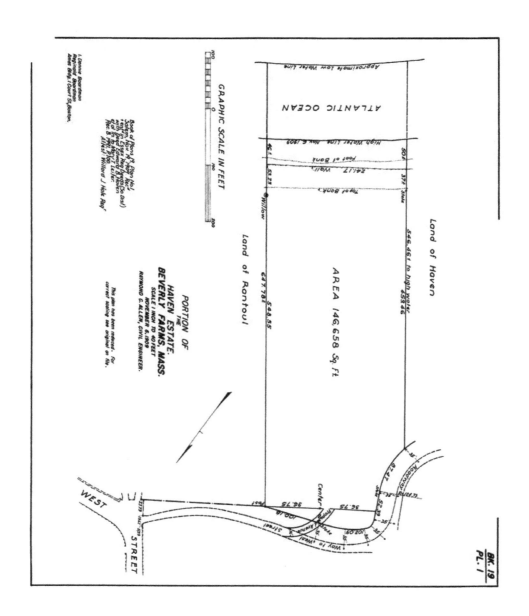

Plot plan of Mary Leiter's 1909 land purchase. Southern Essex Registry of Deeds

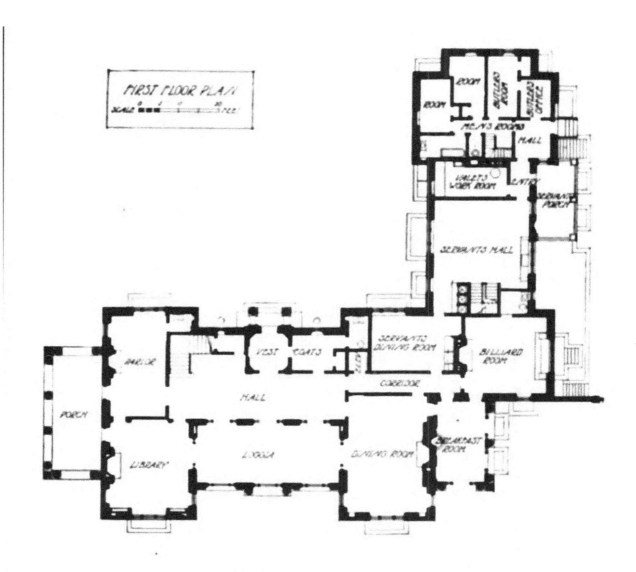

First floor plans 1910. *The Brickbuilder* Vol. XXI, #3 March 1912. Courtesy of Harvard University.

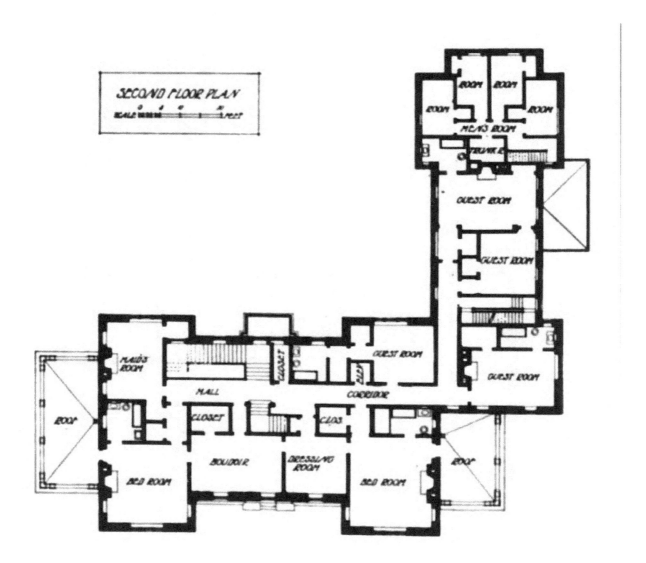

Second floor plans 1910. *The Brickbuilder* Vol. XXI, #3 March 1912. Courtesy of Harvard University

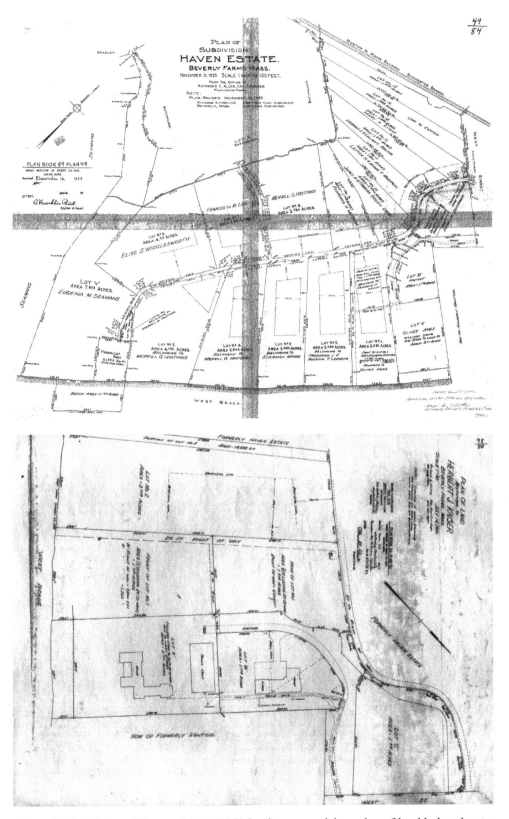

Plan of Subdivision of Haven Estate (1953 landowner revision; plan of land belonging to Herbert J. Kaiser. Southern Essex Registry of Deeds

West view of Edgewater House, 1911.
Postcard collection of Eugene Marley.

Court view of Edgewater House with
service wing on the left. *The
Brickbuilder* Vol. XXI, #3 March
1912. Courtesy of Harvard
University.

Revolving sun house, 1912. *The
Brickbuilder* Vol. XXI, #3 March
1912. Courtesy of Harvard
University

Clockwise from top left: Ocean lawn set for tea, 1912; Dining room 1912; Hall sitting area 1912; Library, 1912; the building housing the gardener's cottage, garage, and stable. All from *The Brickbuilder* Vol. XXI, #3 March 1912. Courtesy of Harvard University

INDICT LEITER HERE FOR RUM RUNNING

Chicago Millionaire and Three of His Employes at Beverly Farms Estate Named by Federal Grand Jury

Aftermath of Three Raids

Cellar Looted Twice by Hi-Jackers

Rest of Liquor Dry Agents' Prize

Charged With Smuggling and Transporting Now.

Top: Joseph and Juliette Leiter wedding, 1908; and Nancy, Joe, Jr. and Tommy Leiter, 1920; both courtesy Judy Clagett MacLennan.
Clockwise from above: *Boston Globe*, March 13, 1925; Nancy Campbell, Countess Lady Suffolk, Joseph Leiter, Image from *Chicago Daily News*. Courtesy Chicago History Museum. Glass negative DN-0080434; Mrs. Joseph Leiter's dress shop in Washington DC, 1921. Juliette in broad hat, courtesy Everett Historical.

Aerial view of total Edgewater property with greenhouses. Lawn at left is part of the Haven estate. *North Shore Breeze*, August 8, 1925. Courtesy, Phillips Library, Peabody Essex Museum

Newly built pool with the sand area. The Haven house is in the distance to the left.
Courtesy Marion Oates Leiter Charles

Joe Leiter in tank top and cap, with friends in the Edgewater pool; Joe and Juliette under the umbrella with friends; mint julep time on the West End steps; Juliette's mother, Maie Williams with friends. All c. 1928

Right: Tommy Leiter and Gertie Webb on the West End porch

All courtesy Marion Oates Leiter Charles

August 15, 1926.

Top: Nancy Leiter and Charles Thomas Clagett wedding with officiating bishop, 1941, and Joseph Leiter, both courtesy Judy Clagett MacLennan

View of Edgewater House showing the chimney that Joe Leiter added to the ocean facade in the 1920s; Tommy and Oatsie Leiter with their dog, 1947, all courtesy Marion Oates Leiter Charles

Left: "Ship" Kelley, Oatsie Leiter, Brenda Frazier Kelly, and Tommy Leiter.

Below: the last Leiter party at Edgewater House, Labor Day party, 1947.

Both courtesy Marion Oates Leiter Charles

ARCHITECTURAL MASTERPIECE ON THE OCEAN
Boston's North Shore

Built in the gilded age, this magnificent Georgian mansion is on five acres of manicured grounds with more than 500 feet of oceanfront. The 25-room residence includes elegantly detailed major rooms with high ceilings, beautiful fireplaces, parquet floor and architectural moldings. There is a four-room master suite with fireplaces, sitting room, two dressing rooms and his/her bathrooms. There are three additional master suites and room for live-in staff. The extraordinary features of this property include a 60-by-30-foot saltwater pool, off-shore boat mooring and a beautiful sandy beach. Two acres can be used as an additional building site. Plans have been approved.

This is the premier property in the Boston area and offers a life-style in the grand tradition. $6,500,000.

Indicate Inquiry Number 22-0 or Contact:

Gene R. Groves

1497 SE 17th St. Causeway
Ft. Lauderdale, Florida 33316
(305) 522-0700 or (305) 524-6397

UNIQUE HOMES   WATERFRONT LIVING   AUGUST / SEPTEMBER 87

Merrill Lynch advertisement for sale of Edgewater House; courtesy Jeffrey Horvitz

Clockwise from top left: Jeffrey and Carol Horvitz;
Caroline and Christina, 1992; Joshua's graduation from
Valley Forge Military Academy, 1999; Caroline, Carol,
Christina and Joshua, 1992; Malcolm Rogers, Jeffrey
and the French Consul Boston at Chevalier dinner 2012.
All courtesy Jeffrey and Carol Horvitz

Clockwise from top: Christina and Jeffrey, 2001; Caroline with Cheryl Lauricella and Governor Deval Patrick, 2012; Michelle and Joshua, August 20, 2011; Frago; Carol with Samuel and Oliver 2016;Christina piloting with Caroline and Cheryl Lauricella, 2014. All courtesy Jeffrey and Carol Horvitz

Chapter 7
Oliver and Ellen Ames,
Year-Round Resident Owners: 1950-1980

Unlike the Leiters and the Kaisers, Oliver Ames 2nd and Ellen Poore Moseley Ames came from the Massachusetts Brahmin establishment. Oliver Ames 2nd was a descendent of the Oliver Ames who founded the Ames Shovel Company in 1803. His grandfather, Oliver Ames III, was the Massachusetts governor who vetoed the bill that would have divided Beverly Farms off from Beverly in 1887 as a separate town. During the early part of the twentieth century an uncle or cousin, also named Oliver Ames, had owned High Wall, an impressive waterfront mansion in Prides Crossing. Ellen's paternal great-grandfathers had been among the early summer estate builders in Essex County. Between 1850 and 1890 Ben: Perley Poore [*the eccentric punctuation was his*] had built and expanded Indian Hill, one of the first great estates in Newburyport. In the 1890s, Frederick Strong Moseley built Maudslay, his 70-room country estate on the Merrimack River in Newburyport.[191]

Ellen Poore Moseley had grown up in Ipswich and Boston. Her father, Ben: Perley Poore Moseley, was a Boston banker who much preferred gardening to banking. Moseley had been a close enough friend of Joseph Leiter to have been one of the recipients of Leiter's famous cookbook.[*]

The Moseley family, which included Ellen and four younger brothers, divided their time between 327 Commonwealth Avenue in Boston and their country estate, Town Hill, on Spring Road in Ipswich. Ellen was close in age to Nancy Leiter and visited Edgewater House as a young child and as a teenager. She later told a friend that she had always coveted the house.

A photo of Ellen Poore Moseley on horseback graced the October 22, 1937, issue of *North Shore Breeze.* An article inside described her October 16 debut at the Myopia Hunt Club.

> The next night as you know was the evening of Ellen Moseley's party. The dance at Myopia was really one of the nicest of the year.... A huge tent had been built off the porch, so there was ample room for dancing inside and out. Pine trees were placed outside all around the tent, and autumn flowers were the main decorations indoors. Mrs. Thomas [*Ellen's grandmother*], Mrs. Moseley, and Ellen received against a background of beautiful flowers.

---

[*] Ben Moseley's cookbook was given to Jeffrey and Carol Horvitz by Ellen Ames's friend Jonathan Loring.

In addition to her debut at Myopia, Ellen was later presented at the annual Bachelors' Ball in Baltimore in December. During her debutante year and later, Ellen Moseley was a favorite model in local fashion shows. *North Shore Breeze* reported on all of them and frequently featured Ellen Moseley.

At a moonlight dance and fashion show at the Essex County Club ... in black taffeta is Ellen Moseley, who wears a dress with the skirt cut like a tulip and high enough to disclose her ankles. The skirt is lined with pink taffeta as is the rather low, turned over collar.[192]

At a benefit show for Boston Children's Hospital ... Ellen Mosely, who still remains the outstanding model, wore with great distinction an egg-shell crepe tea gown with much intricate and beautiful coral beading in narrow bands down the sides of the slim skirt, around the sleeves and bordering the mock bolero.....We don't mind stating that Miss Dorothy Potter and Miss Ellen Moseley make stunning models, and that only those who have tried it know how hard it is to appear naturally and yet with style.[193]

At a benefit fashion show at the Casino presented by Jonas of Magnolia and New York, Ellen Moseley and the Cochrane girls will be among the models. Nancy Leiter will pass among tables at tea distributing chances.[194]

The following November, when the Moseleys had returned to their home on Commonwealth Avenue, the *Boston Globe* reported:

Ellen Poore Moseley, one of the busier of last year's group, is hard at work at the Junior League where she is in charge of publicity for the League. Miss Moseley, daughter of Mrs. and Mrs. B. P. Moseley of Town Hill, Ipswich, and Boston, was graduated from the Beaver Country Day School and is now studying at the Child-Walker School of Design on Beacon Street.[195]

By 1941, with the United States moving toward entry into the war, social life among those in their twenties and thirties had a frantic edge. When Ellen was 21, she, along with her friends Nancy and Lucy "CZ" Cochrane and her cousin Eleanor "Sister" Frothingham, was at the center of activity. As part of the young Boston smart set, they dressed well, worked for war-related charities by day, and danced at the Ritz-Carleton by night. The *Globe*'s society pages often featured photos of Ellen modeling fashionable clothes for such charities as one providing aid for French war victims. They also described what she wore to various social events.

At the New England Premiere of Disney's *Fantasia* ... were Mrs. B. P. Moseley and her daughter, Ellen Moseley — Ellen's knee-length stole of gray kidskin something new in premier furs.[196]

During the summer, *North Shore Breeze* reported on the same people involved in similar activities on the North Shore.

Ruby Newman himself was at the Essex on Saturday night, which, although rather cold, was very pleasant. Amongst the many people there were Johnny Zinsser, Freddie and Duke Pierson, Charlie Wadsworth, Ann and Joan Friess, Dorothy Warren, Dick Fearing, Tom and Bill Moseley, Miss Lucy Pope Nichols, Ben Cole, Cizzie [*sic*] and Nancy Cochrane, Bill Walker, Budsie Cochrane and his fiancée Cynthia Dunn, Miss Ellen Moseley, Edward Moseley, and Baily Buchanan.[197]

The Boston society columns of the day were discreet regarding unmarried couples before the announcement of an engagement. Ellen Moseley and "her escort" would be noted. At some time during these years that escort must have been Oliver Ames 2nd. Once the war began, Ames, a reserve officer in the Navy, was deployed.

In June of 1943, Ellen Moseley was one of the few Boston guests at her cousin and friend Eleanor "Sister" Frothingham's small wartime wedding at the St. Regis Hotel in New York. "Sister" Frothingham had shocked the North Shore by marrying Albert Navarro, a seaman stationed at the Portsmouth Navy Yard, and former saxophone player and band leader. Woodbury Soap Company produced a full-page ad with photos of the happy couple.[198] The marriage ended within a year.

In January of 1944, Mr. and Mrs. Ben: Perley Poore Moseley announced the engagement of their daughter Ellen Poore Moseley to Lieutenant Commander Oliver Ames 2nd of North Easton.

Oliver Ames 2nd was born on May 20, 1903. His father was Oakes Ames, a well-known Harvard botanist. His mother, Blanche Ames Ames [*an Ames married an Ames*], was a respected portrait painter, women's rights and birth control advocate, writer, and inventor. Oakes, Blanche, and their four children, Amyas, Evelyn, Oliver, and Pauline, divided their time between a Boston or Cambridge apartment and Borderland, the beautiful country estate they had built in North Easton. Oliver attended the Country Day School for Boys of Boston and received his B.A. from Harvard in 1927. While at Harvard he was an avid member of the crew team.

After graduation Oliver Ames worked in a variety of business ventures, including the family-owned Ames Aircraft Corporation in East Boston. The 1940 census listed him living at the family home in North Easton and working as a family trustee. At some point he became a licensed pilot and joined the Naval Reserve. According to his son, Ollie (Oliver Ames Jr.):

> After Pearl Harbor he went active. He already knew how to fly, so I believe his first duty station was as an instructor in Florida. I don't know if that was Pensacola. He served on *USS Core* and *USS Card*, both escort carriers in the Atlantic.[199]

By 1943 Oliver Ames had risen to the rank of Lieutenant Commander and was assigned as flight officer on the newly commissioned escort carrier USS *Liscome Bay*, bound for Pearl Harbor. In his Introduction to *The Little Giants: U.S. Escort Carriers Against Japan*, William T. Y'Blood writes:

> They were called "jeeps," "baby flattops," "two-torpedo ships," "combustible, vulnerable, expendable," and other, unprintable names. They were the CVE's — the U.S. Navy's designation for aircraft carrier, escort. ...envisioned as hardly more than convoy escorts in the beginning, they evolved into remarkably versatile vessels.[200]

The USS *Liscome Bay* (CVE-56), a Casablanca-class escort carrier, was commissioned on August 7, 1943, Captain Irving D. Wiltsie in command. The ship carried 28 aircraft. In late October, after the completion of training operations, *Liscome Bay* arrived at Pearl Harbor where it joined the Northern Attack Force, under Rear Admiral Richmond K. Turner, bound for the invasion of the Gilbert Islands. As a unit of CarDiv (Carrier Division) 24, it departed Pearl Harbor on November 10 attached to TF (Task Force) 52.

> The invasion bombardment announcing the United States' first major thrust into the central Pacific began on 20 November at 05:00, and 76 hours later Tarawa Atoll and Makin A were captured.

Liscome Bay's aircraft played their part in the 2278 action sorties provided by carrier-based planes which neutralized enemy airbases, supported landings and ground operations in bombing-strafing missions, and intercepted enemy raids. With the islands secured, the U.S. forces began a retirement.

On 23 November, the group arrived off Makin. The temporary task group, built around Rear Admiral Henry M. Mullinnix's three escorts — *Liscome Bay*, *Coral Sea*, and *Corregidor* — was steaming 20 miles southwest of Butaritari Island at 15 knots. At 04:30 on 24 November, reveille was made in *Liscome Bay*. The ship went to routine general quarters at 05:05 as flight crews prepared their planes for dawn launchings.

There was no warning of a submarine in the area until about 05:10, when a lookout shouted: "Here comes a torpedo!" The torpedo struck abaft the after engine room and hit the aircraft bomb stockpile, causing a major explosion engulfing the entire vessel and sending shrapnel out 5000 yards. "It didn't look like a ship at all," wrote Lieutenant John C. W. Dix, communications officer on *Hoel*, "We thought it was an ammunition dump....She just went *whoom* — an orange ball of flame."

At 05:33, *Liscome Bay* listed to starboard and sank, carrying 53 officers and 591 enlisted men — including Captain Wiltsie — down with her. Only 272 of her crew of 916 were rescued. Lieutenant Commander Oliver Ames was the senior surviving officer (not counting Capt. John G. Crommelin, who was, as Carrier Division 24's chief of staff, technically not part of the carrier's crew). [201]

Oliver Ames was among those rescued by the *Leonard Wood*. In his *Twenty-Three Minutes to Eternity: The Final Voyage of the Escort Carrier USS Liscome Bay*, James L. Noles records the observations of Paymaster Daily.

Daily observed that his fellow survivors' reactions to the sinking seemed to fall into three distinct demographic groups. The youngest men — those under twenty — accepted their survival with a typical teenager's sense of immortality. They soon returned to their card games or jawing about girlfriends they would see again back in port. The men between twenty and thirty seemed more reflective but were also soon ready for duty. The torpedo attack and its aftermath had hit the older men the hardest. Even five days after the sinking, the older survivors were, according to Daily, still stunned by the magnitude of the disaster at sea. [202]

According to Noles, paymaster Daily spent his time reconstructing pay records for the crew so that they could be paid as soon as they reached Pearl Harbor, still several days away. In the meantime practically all the crew were without any cash, rendering them unable to buy cigarettes, candy, cards, and other items from the ship's store to pass the time during their transit back to Hawaii. Aware of the economic hardship befalling the crew, Lieutenant Commander Oliver Ames approached Daily a few days into their voyage.

"Hey Pay, are these any good?" he asked, pulling from his oily wallet every paycheck Daily had ever issued him. Ames, heir to his Massachusetts family's industrial fortune, always had plenty of money on hand. His Navy pay must have struck him as an amusing pittance in comparison, but Ames had accepted his paychecks nevertheless as a polite gesture to Daily. He had just never bothered to cash them.

"Sure, Ollie," Daily answered in amazement. "Just take them to the ship's paymaster, and he'll cash whatever you want."

Smiling, Ames tracked down the *Leonard Wood's* paymaster, cashed his checks, and distributed the proceeds to *Liscome Bay's* survivors. After that the ship's store did a brisk business for the rest of the voyage.[203]

The disaster of the *Liscome Bay* and his survival of it would stay with Oliver Ames for the remainder of his life. Its immediate effect was to convince him that he should marry Ellen Moseley as soon as possible. On January 17, 1944, the Wartime Society section of the *Boston Globe* carried a lovely cameo photo of Ellen with the announcement "Miss Ellen Moseley is the daughter of Mr. and Mrs. Ben: P. P. Moseley of Commonwealth Avenue, who have announced her engagement to Lt. Com. Oliver Ames 2nd of North Easton." Three months later the *Globe* reported on their wedding.

Ellen Moseley Wed to Lt. Commander Ames

Mr. and Mrs. Ben: Perley Poore Moseley of Boston and Ipswich announce the marriage of their daughter Ellen Poore Moseley to Lt. Com. Oliver Ames, USNR, son of Prof. and Mrs. Oakes Ames of North Easton and Ormond, Florida, on March 23 at Virginia Beach, Va. The wedding took place at 6 o'clock in the Episcopal Church at Virginia Beach.

The bride was given in marriage by her father. She wore her mother's exquisite wedding gown and an heirloom veil of Italian lace. Mrs. John P. Davis (Evelyn Ames) of New York was matron of honor for her brother's bride.

Mr. and Mrs. Moseley and Mrs. and Mrs. Ames were present at the ceremony. Com. Ames and his bride will live in Virginia Beach for the present. [204]

Oliver Ames was 40; Ellen Moseley was 24. When the war ended, the Ameses returned to Massachusetts. Their first child, Oliver Jr., (called Ollie), was born in Boston the following year. For a time Ames managed an electric company for his uncle somewhere in the Lowell area and later went on to work in finance in Boston.

In 1947 the Ameses decided to buy a house on the North Shore. It was the ideal location — an easy train ride to Boston, near Ellen's family, and best of all on the ocean, where Oliver could sail. They found the old Dexter place in Beverly Farms, a comfortable, wood-shingle house surrounded by lawn and garden with a path and view to the beach beyond a pond and marsh. At the time, oceanfront houses of modest proportions were in far greater demand than big summer estates. On June 9, 1947, they purchased the property for $59,500. The Beverly City Directory listed them as summer residents.

Three years later almost to the day, Herbert Kaiser bought the Edgewater property. News has always traveled quickly in Beverly Farms, and Ellen Ames must have soon learned that Kaiser had subdivided the property, demolished the greenhouses, and was in the beginning stages of tearing down Edgewater House's upper stories.

Somehow Ellen convinced her husband to make an offer on the house before it could be destroyed. The house they had bought three years before was simple rather than imposing, a bit primitive in some of its fixtures, and somewhat isolated. Edgewater House was majestic both in architecture and surroundings, had the added amenities of a saltwater pool and a tennis court, and was close to the center of town.

On November 28, 1950, Oliver and Ellen Ames purchased Edgewater House and the adjoining empty lot #1 for what now seems the astonishingly low price of $34,500 ($340,426 in 2015 dollars). A month later they sold the Dexter place to Robert Seamans Jr. for $77,000 ($759,792 in 2015 dollars).[205] His son, Toby Seamans, remembered that when his family moved in, it was a homey but unrenovated old house with exposed water pipes in the front hall.[206]

When the Ameses moved into Edgewater, it had been totally empty since the auction in July of 1948. Their eldest son, Oliver Jr., called Ollie, was five. Thinking back on that time, he wrote:

> I was five in 1950 but remember seeing, or perhaps at least hearing the story, that there were seven or eight bathtubs, sinks, and toilets in the front hall as a result of initial demolition starting on the third floor level to raze the structure to a one-story ranch-style house. Ugh.[207]

Ellen Ames had succeeded in rescuing the house by the sea that she had loved as a teenager. Now she had the daunting task of turning a house that had been built for summer entertaining into a year-round family home. In 1950 she was a young mother with two sons — Ollie and three-year-old Angier. A third son, Thomas, would be born in 1953.

Ollie Ames walked through the house in the late winter of 2013 and recalled the changes that his parents had made. The comfortable paneled library with its fireplace became the Ames family living room. The adjacent small parlor, which Ellen called the morning room, was used mainly for company — a room to which the women could retire while the men smoked their cigars.

The loggia was seldom used except for large parties and at Christmas. Every December a large tree from the Moseley estate in Ipswich was brought into the loggia and decorated. "We had a Christmas tree in one corner and had a fire in the fireplace. My parents also had one of those wonderful leopard-skin rugs with the head on it."

The first-floor kitchen that Joe Leiter had created was turned into an eat-in kitchen and became the center for family meals. For a very brief time when the children were young, the Ameses had a cook, but that didn't last. Ellen had always loved to cook and took every opportunity to learn more. In the spring of 1947 the *Boston Globe* had reported on her being among those taking copious notes at a lecture given by French cookbook writer and later TV personality Dione Lucas.[208]

Ellen Ames also loved plants and turned what had been the breakfast room into a greenhouse/conservatory. She was adept at forcing plants and kept the room blooming throughout the year.

The dining room was reserved for holiday meals and adult dinner parties.

> We had a big dining room table that would seat 14 or 15 people. There was a portrait of my dad in his naval uniform that his mother painted that hung over the fireplace. It was neat because he is holding a chart that shows where the ship went down in the Pacific.[209]

A couple of times a year the Ameses held large dinner parties that would be catered by Creed, the North Shore's society caterer. Cocktails were served in the loggia.

During the early 1950s television was making its way into every home, with the result that houses began to include dens or TV rooms. At Edgewater, the billiard table, long gone from the billiard room, was replaced with a television set, a couch, and comfortable chairs. The house now had the requisite den, conveniently located near the kitchen.

On his walk-through of the house, Ollie Ames looked in on the coat room and men's bathroom off the hall, remembering that in his childhood its toilet was the family dog's favorite water bowl. Farther along the hall the family piano stood next to the stairs. Mary Leiter's elevator had been inoperable and never repaired during the Ameses' time in the house.

One small change the Ameses made in the downstairs was the installation of oval brass doorknobs bearing the initials *OA* on several of the doors. The doorknobs had come from Governor Oliver Ames's house in Boston.

Ellen Ames took great pride in keeping the parquet floor in the front hall well polished. She occasionally hired Harold Jones from Manchester to help with the heavy work, including polishing the hall floor. Her son remembered that in her later years she would be down on her hands and knees polishing it herself.

The family bedrooms were on the second floor. Oliver and Ellen used the rooms on the oceanfront at the center and west end of the house. What had been Mary Leiter's lady's maid's room became the bedroom. Ellen used the southwest corner oceanfront room as her studio. Oliver kept the former dressing room as his retreat, decorating it with naval pictures. Ollie, Angier, and Thomas used the two larger bedrooms at the east end of the house and the center bedroom that faced the driveway.

The tubs in the bathrooms connected to the east corner room, and the former guest room next to it still had faucets for both freshwater and seawater, though the seawater had been disconnected. When the Ameses moved into the house all of the original bathroom plumbing was still there. The toilets had wood-covered wall tanks.

In the late 1950s, when he was in his early teens and particularly adventuresome, Ollie Ames had the front bedroom that faced the driveway.

> My bedroom had the original sink. I had one of those inch-and-a-half firecrackers and I put it in an old plastic pill bottle, got some cherry bomb fuse and married it to the firecracker, put some clay around the top and sunk it in the water and it truly was amazing! It looked like a depth charge had detonated — it lifted up and then a V-shaped piece of porcelain fell out and everything came crashing down. My mother wasn't very happy. I was about 13 or 14.

> A small room next to that bedroom "had a couple of hundred lightbulbs — it was like a sauna to help you get rid of whatever was going on the night before."[210]

Beyond the family bedrooms at the east end of the house and over the servants' wing were a guest bedroom and Ellen's sewing room. A door led to the three rooms and a bath that the family called the maids' rooms (even thought there were no maids). Aside from the very brief time in the 1950s when the Ameses had a live-in cook, any household help lived out and came in by the day.

By the time the Ameses bought Edgewater, Herbert Kaiser had stripped out all of the bathroom fixtures from the third floor. The walls and fireplaces remained in the front guest rooms, but the finished flooring was gone. In the third floor of the servants' wing only the studs remained. Sometime in the 1960s Ellen Ames decided that the third-floor rooms on the ocean side would make pleasant summer bedrooms and did some basic rebuilding.

Throughout the time the Ameses lived at Edgewater, the basement remained pretty much unchanged. Ollie Ames remembered that the section under the main part of the house was dark and a little scary. He recalled:

> One night in 1953 when my youngest brother was born, my father was down there fooling around with the wiring for one of the furnaces and a rat bit him. He went to his friend who took care of our dog, Doc Fanning the veterinarian, to give him a shot.[211]

Not far from the stairwell, Oliver Ames set up a shooting gallery with a target near the west wall. Everyone in the family learned to shoot.

> You put the target in front of a steel bullet trap. When the bullet goes in, it's deflected — the trap is angled iron so that the bullet deflects into the trap. The problem was we didn't have the right ventilations so after a half an hour or 45 minutes you could taste powder residue. We learned to shoot as kids. My father was draconian in teaching us gun safety. You always assumed the gun was loaded. I had two brothers. My mother was the only girl with 4 brothers, so she was male oriented.

> After my father died, my mother, in the evening, would come down before having a cocktail and pace off 50 feet and shoot her 22 or 38.[212]

When the Ames boys were children, there was also an American Flyer electric train set up on a large table in the main part of the basement. Beyond, on the ocean side of the room, loomed the two huge metal tanks that had been used in the Leiter days to settle seawater for the saltwater baths. Ollie remembered that in his childhood there had also been two large coal bins. At some point his father had the heating system converted to oil.

The basement under the service wing was much brighter. The old kitchen and scullery remained, unused and pretty much unchanged. Ollie recalled the dumbwaiters, the old black stove, and the toads living outside in the window wells on front side of kitchen. Oliver Ames turned the former laundry room into a workshop and tool room. The old drying room became the repository for the dozen or so large fire extinguishers on wheels — the kind seen in airports —that Ames had collected from somewhere. Other things were as they had been: the toilet at the end of the hall beyond the stove, the wine cellar, and the kitchen storerooms. The old, now unused electric board remains in the small hall near a stairway that once led up to a bulkhead leading to the back driveway. Oliver Ames did make one important addition: either following or in anticipation of Hurricane Carol in September of 1954, he installed a backup generator.

In August 1954, Oliver Ames and his neighbor Catherine Walsh negotiated a mutually beneficial land swap. It is not clear how much, if any, money changed hands. The Ameses owned front lot #1 from the Kaiser subdivision. Catherine Walsh owned rear lot #1. Walsh deeded to Ames an 8940-square-foot strip of her land abutting the Edgewater avenue (driveway). Ames in return released:

93

> ... to Catherine F. Walsh the rights to use so much of said "20 Foot Right of Way" as crosses her said remaining land and all other rights, if any, I may have in her said remaining land , and agree to remove the fence now situated on or substantially on the northwesterly boundary of the granted premises.

In addition, Ames granted Walsh the right of foot passage over the 20-foot right of way through front lot #1 as well as over the eight-foot path from that right of way to the Edgewater avenue. These rights of way were granted "only for and so long as she or any successor in title does not subdivide the remaining land."[213]

Kaiser had done nothing to the exterior of the house or to the immediate grounds. The tennis court and swimming pool were still in good order. The Leiter sand pile, once raked every morning by the gardener in preparation for sunbathing ladies, became a giant sandbox, often filled with small boys and their trucks.

The Ameses maintained and used the saltwater pool. In a note to his daughter Chilton, Ollie Ames described it:

> The pool was 60'x 30' and saltwater was pumped in from a pipe that was exposed when the tide was low. Your grandfather took the gasoline engine apart and rebuilt it, but I think your grandmother had the pump electrified after he died. The pool would be emptied and refilled a number of times during the summer, and the discharge of water onto the beach made for wonderful attempts to dam and redirect the water flow. The outflow was powerful and always won. We usually left the pool almost full during the winter, and I've memoires of cutting a hole in the ice and swimming underwater with a wetsuit and aqualung a number of times when I was older.[214]

During the summer months, Ellen Ames spent as much time as she could working outside. Her largest garden was at the head of the pool. Ellen's parents were enthusiastic horticulturalists, and she had grown up with extensive gardens. According to one story, Ben: P. P. Moseley hired so many gardeners to work on his estate that he was the largest employer in Ipswich.[215] Unlike her parents, Ellen never joined the North Shore Horticultural Society in Manchester and for many years did all of her own gardening. Only in her later years did she hire Archi Fiore of Beverly Farms as a part-time gardener. Roger LeBlanc, who worked at the estate in the 1970s, recalled that Mrs. Ames knew a tremendous amount about plants and had beautiful gardens. Roger especially remembered espaliered trees and trellised vines growing against the house. One of his tasks was carrying potted trees and plants into the house in the fall and back out in the spring.[216]

Oliver Ames was a devoted yachtsman and spent his leisure time on the ocean. For a while he owned a #9 cutter along with two friends. In 1952 or 1953 they were Class C winners of the Bermuda Cup Race. After the cutter was sold he owned a Rhodes 18. Ames kept his boat at the Manchester Yacht Club. Ollie recalled sailing with his father one day early December and nearly freezing to death.

When hurricanes struck, Oliver Ames raced to Manchester to look after his boat. Ellen remained at home, stuffing rags around leaking windows. Fortunately, Edgewater never suffered hurricane damage.

It seems Oliver Ames also had a prankish bent. His friend Burnham Porter told his nephew Alan Bigelow a story about a joke gone wrong.

> He somehow got hold of a weather balloon, filled it with hydrogen, and attached a long paper tail which he ignited. His intent was to create a great explosion over the ocean. A backdraft sent the balloon overland above the house of his friend and neighbor Sam Batchelder. The balloon exploded with a deafening boom and blew out windows from the Batchelder house. Fortunately no one was home.[217]

Apparently the friendships survived the joke.

Like most children in Beverly Farms, the Ames boys spent their summers outdoors. They rode bicycles around the vacant land on the Haven estate, swam in the pool or ocean, and puttered around in a small dinghy equipped with a 15-horsepower motor. During the school year the boys attended Shore Country Day in North Beverly.

Ellen Ames was a capable woman and a creative artist. Decoupage and cutwork were popular crafts among women in the early fifties. Ellen became highly skilled in both. The ocean-facing southwest bedroom became her studio. During the months that she could not spend in the garden, she created intricately designed shadow boxes and cutwork lampshades, many of them of city scenes. Her friend Jonathan Loring described a shade that included designs of buildings with meticulously cut-out windows that the lamplight shone through.

Ellen Ames's most ambitious artistic undertaking was the creation of four bas relief panels depicting the natural world in each of the four seasons that were then installed in the loggia.

> She drew the design on plywood and then placed nails in it for a base — then used a plaster compound called Seavagrim to build up the bas relief. When it was semi-soft, she hand carved it. She spent three to five years working on it.[218]

Throughout the time Oliver Ames lived at Edgewater he worked in Boston and served on many boards. He was president of the Ames Aircraft Corporation, and a director of the First National Bank of Easton and of the Ames Shovel and Tool Company. He was also a trustee of the North Easton Savings Bank and of the Woods Hole Oceanographic Institute. On October 8, 1971, Oliver Ames died of cancer. He was 67 years old. During his final illness he used the downstairs den as his bedroom.

In June of 1971, before Oliver died, the Ameses had hired Bill and Bob's Contracting Service to build a new seawall at an estimated cost of $18,000. They also had hired Connolly Brothers to build a wood fence at the rear of lot A along 45 West Street.[219]

In the years after her husband's death, when her sons had moved on, Ellen Ames lived alone at Edgewater. She proved herself to be a practical, self-reliant woman of great fortitude. When the oil crisis hit in the 1970s, she closed off a large part of the house, stockpiled firewood, and made do. In order to maintain the beautiful parquet floor in the front hall, she bought herself an industrial-sized floor polisher. The kitchen became her favorite place for entertaining dinner guests.

During those later years Ellen Ames hired Bill and Bob's to do necessary maintenance work. When Roger LeBlanc was a teenager, he worked at Edgewater House as an employee of Bill O'Hearn. Roger remembered Ellen Ames as a very smart and shrewd woman who demanded excellence and could be very stern. He also recalled that if she liked you, you could do no wrong. She liked and trusted Bill O'Hearn, who worked for her over many years, doing mostly outdoor work, including cleaning and maintaining the swimming pool.

Roger recalled two stories that illustrated Ellen Ames's relationship with people who worked for her. One late spring day, when Bill and Roger were working in the empty pool, a workman from the awning company was installing a shade awning for Mrs. Ames's sitting area. Bill noticed that the awning was a little out of line and told the man he'd better fix it. The workman replied that it was "close enough" and that the owner would never notice. Just then Ellen Ames came walking up from the beach, looked at the awning, and told the workman it wasn't right. He replied with, "Where isn't it right?" Mrs. Ames pointed to the problem and said, "Right there. Now pick up your tools and get off of my property." The awning company had worked for Mrs. Ames for many years. Roger had no doubt that the sloppy workman was fired as soon as his boss heard the story.

Bill and Bob's crew often referred to Ellen Ames as "Ma Ames" behind her back. One day when Roger was working near the house, she stuck her head out the window and spoke to him. Taken by surprise, Roger said something like "Oh hello, Ma Ames." As soon as the words were out of his mouth he got worried. Ellen Ames's response was unexpected. "Ma Ames — I kind of like that." During all of the time he worked for her, Roger found Ellen Ames demanding but pleasant. He remembered her as always friendly and talkative, not stuffy like some of the other people he worked for.[220]

Maria DiFazio, an Italian-born seamstress who worked for Mrs. Ames in her later years, also remembered her fondly.

> Mrs. Ames was old school — the way we were brought up in Italy, strict — you've got to show respect, use your manners on everything ... even like the way you sit down; she was perfect on everything, that woman. She was a good dresser. I usually did alterations for her. When I knew her she was very thin. She walked very straight like a model. She was very, very fussy. She respected me, and I respected her back.
>
> If I went there when she was cooking, she would still have on a suit that she wore in town with an apron in the front. She would never use a mug to drink, always a cup and saucer. She hated mugs. She liked my cooking. One day she was cooking an artichoke, so she asked me how I cook mine — so I explained, and she began to cook them my way. She was a very good cook. One day she gave me a panetonne she made in a two-pound coffee can. It was perfect, puffed up like a mushroom, just like you get in Italy. I am a good cook, but I will never ever try to make panetonne, it's too difficult. Mrs. Ames used to take me out to lunch; then I would take her out. She didn't want me to, but I didn't feel right. We told jokes and laughed. We both loved "Dallas" — she used to call me up and we'd talk about it. She was a wonderful lady.

In 1975 Ellen Ames hired J. W. Linehan Company to repair the slate roof. The estimated cost on the building permit was $2800.[221] Later in the 1970s Ellen Ames purchased more of the old Leiter property. On February 2, 1977, she bought the late Elizabeth Deichmann's converted potting shed and lot for $25,000. This was lot A of a three-lot subdivision of the property that Diechmann had created in 1956. The property is referred to in later deeds as the Shelter. In July of 1978, Mrs. Ames paid $80,000 to purchase rear lot #1, the former Catherine Walsh lot, which fronted on the private drive, 45 West Street, and was an extension of her oceanfront lot.[222]

In 1979, at age 60, Ellen Ames decided that it was time to move to smaller house. It was a good time to sell; the real estate market had risen to unheard-of heights. In December she purchased a small house on Cutler Street in Hamilton and put Edgewater on the market. On August 28, 1980, Denis and Susan Fabry purchased the Edgewater house lot, the strip the Ameses had purchased from Catherine Walsh, and front lot #1 for $400,000 ($1,154,393 in 2015 dollars). It was reportedly the highest dollar amount ever paid for a property on the North Shore.[223] During a last run-through of Edgewater at the time of the sale, Ellen Ames removed the heirloom doorknobs marked with *OA*.[224]

Ellen Ames had been ready to leave Edgewater, but not prepared to give up all of her ties to the property. She held on to the Shelter and wrote into the Edgewater deed an easement that gave her the right of passage from the Shelter, through a gate in the fence, over part of the old Walsh property and the Avenue, over the right of way to front lot #1, and down the 20-foot right of way

> ...to the beach which is part of the land, and to use said beach for sitting, swimming, sunning, picnicking, and launching small boats, and to use during the time said beach is being used, that part of the above described easement next to said beach to park a car.
>
> Excluded from the above described easements are the rights to litter, make loud noise or music, or bring animals upon the subject premises.
>
> The grant of the within described easements shall be binding on the Grantors' successors and assigns.
>
> The consideration for this conveyance is less than $100.
>
> The above described easement does not extend to guests of right.[225]

Ellen Ames enlarged her Hamilton house and transformed the interior, doing much of the decorating herself. Her friend Jonathan Loring remembers that she incorporated dried grass into the paint for the walls of her fabulous plant room. For the next 20 years, she lived in the handsome home she had created for herself. Ellen Poore Moseley Ames died on December 5, 2000, at the age of 81.

Chapter 8
Dennis and Susan Fabry: 1980-1991

Why did Dennis and Susan Fabry, who had spent most of their married life in the western United States, purchase Edgewater House and move to Beverly Farms? The decision had very little to do with a desire to own a mansion by the sea and join the Eastern establishment. The Fabrys were real estate speculators who hoped to make a killing in a rising market.

Dennis Walter Sidney Fabry was born in Plymouth, England, on January 13, 1928. He arrived in the United States on the *Ile de France* on March 10, 1950. In April he crossed the border into Canada. His border-crossing card indicated that he was a permanent United States resident alien living in Buffalo, New York. On June 27, 1955, the 27-year-old Dennis married 45-year-old Ethel E. Hunter in Inglewood, California. At the time of his naturalization on July 25, 1958, he was listed as a gardener, married to Ethel, and living at 928 Ninth Street in Santa Monica, California.

Dennis and Ethel divorced in June of 1970. On January 11, 1971, Dennis married Susan Lee Roper in a civil ceremony in Las Vegas. At the time of their marriage Dennis was 43 and Susan was 31.

During the height of the real estate boom of the early seventies, the Fabrys invested heavily in independent hotels and motels in the western United States.* By the late seventies, real estate values in the West (with the exception of California) had begun to flatten and in some cases actually fall.[226] In addition, a reduction in travel due to the oil crisis further diminished the real value of the Fabrys' motels. In the spring of 1980, legislation that Congress passed deregulating thrifts made home purchase a promising option for the investors like the Fabrys. They began looking for a region where real estate values were on the rise.

The Fabrys' search for a rising real estate market led them to Massachusetts. During the summer of 1980, they discovered the Edgewater House listing and made an offer. While the price was high for the North Shore, by national standards it was relatively inexpensive for shorefront property.

Ellen Ames and the Fabrys passed papers on the Edgewater property on August 28, 1980. The deed listed the Fabrys as residents of Tonopah, Nevada, an old mining town halfway between Reno and Las Vegas that was by then a modest tourist destination.[227] Inquiries to the Tonopah Town Hall failed to uncover any evidence or memory of the couple's having ever lived or owned property there. Their address on the deed was a post-office box. The Fabrys had likely established Nevada residency for tax purposes.

---

* Jeffrey Horvitz found information about the Fabrys' investments in file cabinets left behind at Edgewater.

The record $400,000 the Fabrys paid for the Edgewater property was financed with $110,000 cash and a $290,000 mortgage from Ellen Ames.[228] A month after they purchased the property, they obtained a $240,000 mortgage from Melrose Bank and discharged the Ames mortgage.[229]

The story of the Fabrys' eight-year tenure at Edgewater is revealed through a dizzying succession of mortgages and of deed transfers between Dennis and Susan and the various trusts they created. S&Ls were in fierce competition to grant mortgages, and the law encouraged reckless lending. The Fabrys had no difficulty obtaining mortgages on top of mortgages. Their story also included at least two futile attempts to sell at a huge profit.

The property they had purchased from Ellen Ames consisted of three separate lots: lot A, the house lot; front lot #1, on the ocean, adjacent to lot A; and the "Walsh lot," the strip of land along the driveway that Oliver Ames had acquired from Catherine Walsh in 1954. During the course of their ownership of the property, the Fabrys sometimes broke up the lots with separate ownership; and at times they mortgaged them separately, at other times as a whole, and occasionally both at the same time with different mortgage holders.

It is not clear how soon the Fabrys moved in. It was a quiet arrival. They did not appear in the Beverly list of residents until 1983. At that time Dennis was 55 and listed as retired; Susan was 43 and listed as an investor.

Few people in Beverly Farms appear to have known them. One resident remembered Dennis as a pleasant and rather dapper man. Another recalled that the Fabrys drove around in a beat-up station wagon. Paul and Jean Bonner, neighbors at 67 West Street, had only a nodding acquaintance with the couple. Jean recalled that the Fabrys had an intercom system that was on the same frequency as their baby minder and that she would occasionally hear the Fabrys' voices. She also remembered that there were always impatiens flowers in front of the house. Former West Beach resident Charlie Sherrill never saw any signs of life at Edgewater during the Fabry years and thought of it as a ghost house.[230]

Apparently on Ellen Ames's recommendation, the Fabrys hired Bill and Bob's to do maintenance work. Their employee Roger LeBlanc remembered going there early on to do some project and speaking to an older man in work clothes who was working outside in the garden. Roger told him what he had come to do, and the man said fine, go ahead. When Roger said he had better check with the owner first, the man said, "I'm Dennis Fabry. I *am* in the owner." As Roger was to later learn, Dennis may have been one of the owners, but Susan Fabry was definitely the dominant spouse. Roger came to know Dennis Fabry as a quiet man and a very hard worker who did all of the gardening and landscape maintenance by himself.[231]

The Fabrys appear to have made no improvements. The one thing they may have done was to repaint some of the walls; at the time Jeffrey Horvitz bought the house, many of the interior walls had been painted white with bargain-basement paint. At some point they also demolished the tennis court, which had been unused and allowed to deteriorate during the Ames years.

On July 27, 1981, a year after they had purchased the house, Dennis and Susan took out another loan, a $220,000 mortgage on lot A (the house lot) from the National Shoe Workers Pension Fund.[232]

On April 28, 1982, they transferred ownership of lot A to Susan. During that year the Fabrys decided to turn Edgewater House into a small, exclusive hotel, catering to western millionaires drawn to the prestigious North Shore of Massachusetts. Edgewater House already had attractive amenities: a spectacular oceanfront location in an upscale neighborhood, a sandy beach, a boat mooring, and a saltwater pool. The Fabrys hired Bill and Bob's to install a spa and build an exercise balcony in what had been the first-and-second-floor male servants' rooms at the far end of the service wing. Roger LeBlanc worked on the project. He remembered that Susan Fabry was in charge. If Dennis offered suggestions, he was instantly silenced. Roger found Susan to be an extremely arrogant woman who insisted that everything be done her way — "her way or the highway, whether it made any sense or not." From what Roger could gather, Susan Fabry was planning a "sneaky deal" to open a fancy inn without anyone knowing about it.[233] There is no record that the Fabrys ever applied for a variance to create a hotel or for a building permit to construct the spa. When they stopped paying Bill and Bob, the work ended. Perhaps the Fabrys had come to the realization that their plan wasn't going to work.

By the end of 1983, the Fabrys were apparently facing some kind of financial crisis. On January 23, 1984, the city placed a lien on the property for unpaid water and sewer fees.[234] It was probably around this time that Chapman's Greenhouse and other local vendors put the Fabrys on a cash-only basis.[235] The next five months brought a flurry of mortgage activity. On January 30 Susan Fabry obtained a mortgage on lot A, this one from Liberty Mortgage Associates of Lexington. Curiously, the dollar amount of the Liberty mortgage is x'd out on the mortgage deed.[236] The same day Susan obtained a $500,000 mortgage on lot A from the Commonwealth Federal Savings Bank with an initial rate of 13.375% and a three-year graduated payment rider.[237] A day later Susan paid off the $220,000 mortgage from National Shoe. Two weeks later the Fabrys paid off the $240,000 Melrose Bank mortgage.

The next year and half were quiet. Perhaps it was during this quietus that the Fabrys came up with their next plan for making money from Edgewater. In the spring of 1985, they were borrowing money again.

On May 5, 1985, despite the fact that lot A of the Edgewater property carried loans of about $700,000, Liberty Mortgage Associates granted Susan Fabry two additional mortgages: a $250,000 mortgage on lot A and a $100,000 mortgage on the total property.[238] On May 20, 1985, the original (1984) Liberty mortgage was discharged.[239]

On September 19, 1985, Dennis established the T.I. Realty Trust with himself as trustee, and M.I.N.E. trust, also with Dennis as trustee. Susan immediately deeded front lot 1 to T.I. trust and lot A and the Walsh lot to M.I.N.E. Trust.

On October 3, Dennis Fabry of T.I. Realty Trust took out a building permit for a new masonry dwelling to be erected on lot #1. The proposed two-story building was slated to have ten rooms and six full baths. Its dimensions were to be 69'5" x 74'4" x 34', a total area of about 10,000 square feet. (Edgewater House has an area of about 19,000 square feet). The city required Fabry to present the contractor's license to practice in Massachusetts. He listed Scotsdale Inc., Box 357, Marblehead, as the contractor. It is not recorded whether the license was ever presented, but the building permit was renewed on February 24, 1986.[240]

At the end of 1985, Susan Fabry had three active mortgages: a $500,000 mortgage from Commonwealth Federal and two from Liberty (one at $250,000 and the other at $100,000), for a total of $850,000. On February 17, 1986, Dennis Fabry of T.I. Realty Trust and Susan Fabry obtained a $465,000 mortgage on the entire property from Mortgage Company of New England. Three days later, the city of Beverly put a lien on the property for $843 in unpaid water and sewer fees. The Edgewater property was now mortgaged for a total of $1,315,000 in four separate mortgages. It is doubtful that the Fabrys were keeping up with any of their payments.

The remainder of 1986 was quiet. It is perhaps during this period that the Fabrys removed the large saltwater tanks from the basement and sold them for scrap.* Guerdon Davis, one of the firemen called around this time to Edgewater to put out a minor fire in the loggia, said the firemen were startled to discover that there was almost no furniture in the house.[241]

Sometime in the summer of 1987 the Fabrys decided it was time to test the national real estate market. They listed the entire Edgewater property with Merrill Lynch Realty. A two-page advertisement in the "Unique Homes" / "Waterfront Living" section of an August/September Merrill Lynch publication carried a large photo of Edgewater House with the caption *Architectural Masterpiece on the Ocean / Boston's North Shore*. The text of the ad is effusive.

> Built in the gilded age, this magnificent Georgian mansion is on five acres of manicured grounds with more than 500 feet of oceanfront. The 25-room residence includes elegantly detailed major rooms with high ceilings, beautiful fireplaces, parquet floor, and architectural moldings. There is a four-room master suite with fireplaces, sitting room, two dressing rooms, and his/her bathrooms. There are three additional master suites and room for live-in staff. The extraordinary features of this property include a 60x30 foot saltwater pool, off-shore boat mooring, and a beautiful sandy beach. Two acres can be used as an additional building site. Plans have been approved. This is the premier property in the Boston area and offers a lifestyle in the grand tradition.

> *Offered for sale at $6,500,000 U.S. Dollars*

An additional page went into more detail, describing the configuration of rooms and observations regarding possible uses: "…originally designed to provide an elegant lifestyle, this home is quite flexible in its accommodations. One couple can feel very comfortable here, without assistance. Then again, a business gathering, of any size, would be very easy. …Schedule any size dinner party with confidence. The 22 by 20 foot kitchen is ready with its commercial-quality appliances…." Although the Fabrys had done little or no renovation of the house, the ad referenced the ill-fated spa project in the hope it would appeal to a potential buyer. "The west wing will have a health spa, complete with 7' tub, sauna, and an exercise balcony overlooking the tub area."[242]

Apparently there were no takers. A later, undated Merrill Lynch advertisement listed the property for $4,500,000. The new agent was Katherine Pickering of the Beverly office.[243] In 1987 Edgewater house

---

*Charlie Mann, who oversaw the Horvitz renovations in 1991, believes that the tanks were probably copper.

was assessed at $1,062,350 ($2,223,160 in 2015 dollars) —a little less than the $1,315,000 it was mortgaged for. It is unclear how long the property remained on the market.

In the fall of 1987 the Fabrys were again in financial trouble. On September of 1987, the city of Beverly again placed a lien on the property for unpaid property taxes and fees.

October 7, 1987, was an extraordinarily busy day for the Fabrys. First, Dennis transferred lot #1 from T.I. Realty Trust and lot A and the Walsh lot from M.I.N.E. Trust to Dennis individually. Next, Dennis obtained a $1,000,000 mortgage on lot A and the Walsh lot from the Centrust Mortgage Corporation of Deerfield Beach, Florida.[244] That same day the Golden Gate Mortgage Company of Andover granted the Fabrys a $500,000 mortgage on all three lots.[245]By the end of the day, the Edgewater property carried a staggering $2,815,000 of mortgage debt split among six separate mortgages. The Fabrys repaid only one of them: on May 26, 1988, the $500,000 Commonwealth Federal Savings Bank loan, taken out in 1984, was discharged.[246]

On August 1, 1988, nine months after it had written the mortgage, the Centrust Mortgage Corporation * informed the Fabrys, T.I. Realty Trust, M.I.M.E. Trust, Liberty Mortgage Associates, the Mortgage Company of New England, and Golden Gate Mortgage Company of its intent to foreclose.[247] On August 29, Golden Gate announced it too would foreclose.[248]

The Fabrys continued to shuffle Edgewater among trusts. On November 11, Dennis, as trustee for M.I.N.E. Trust, transferred Edgewater to PRIMM Partnership of Marblehead. Four months later PRIMM transferred the property to Secundus Partnership at another Marblehead post office box. The fancy footwork accomplished nothing; things continued to fall apart. On November 23, a federal tax lien for $27,320 was placed on the property. It was released on the 30th. On the 29th, there was a court order for the sheriff to attach goods for payment of $3,000 to a local fence company.

The Fabrys had held out at Edgewater for as long as they could. According to local stories, during their final weeks there they were pilfering water and electricity from their neighbors.[249] Contractors who worked on the house after Jeffrey Horvitz's purchase believe the house had not been heated for a couple of years.

The end came on September 23, 1991, when the land court made a judgment for Centrust Mortgage Company to sell lot A and the Walsh lot for default.[250]The Edgewater Realty Trust, Jeffrey Horvitz, trustee, purchased the property at auction for $1,775, 000. A Bank of New England mortgage (formerly Liberty) was paid off on the same date. The Mortgage Company of New England mortgage was discharged on April 24, 1992.

----

* By this time Centrust itself was dangerously overextended. In February of 1990 the bank failed with a loss of $1.7 billion, the nation's fourth-largest financial institution to collapse. In June the bank was sold to Great Western Bank of California. In November of 1993, Centrust's former president, David Paul was convicted on 68 counts of fraud. He had spent bank money to support an extravagant lifestyle that included luxuries ranging from a $13M Rubens painting to a $9M estate with gold plated plumbing. (*NYT, Business Day, 11-15-1993*)

On June 4, 1992, the land court ruled in favor of Golden Gate Mortgage Company, giving them the right to sell the Fabry property.[251] Centrust had already sold lot A and the Walsh lot — only front lot #1 remained. The auction was held on June 27, 1992. Jeffrey Horvitz, who was away on business the day of the auction, gave his lawyer, John E. Rattigan Jr., authorization to bid up to $330,000, two and half times the amount Horvitz thought anyone would pay for an unbuildable lot.[252] He was outbid. Evan Wile purchased the lot for $335,000 ($567,816 in 2015 dollars).[253]

How Dennis and Susan Fabry used the mortgage money they had received and never repaid is open to conjecture. One real possibility is that it was used to pay debts they had accumulated in their highly leveraged purchases of hotels and motels in the seventies. They may have used some of it to start over. The Fabrys stayed in Massachusetts for a time after they lost Edgewater. Public records list them as living in Boston, at 304 Newbury Street in 1992 and at 71 Marlborough Street in 1995. Carol Horvitz knows that they returned to Edgewater at least once, because one evening when she was home alone they looked in a window and frightened her.

Eventually the Fabrys moved to Florida, where they appear to have done well financially. In April of 2003 Dennis Fabry registered Manage, LLC as a limited liability corporation in the State of Florida. The company filed its last report in 2011. Dennis was also listed as having had a previous relationship with Manage Living Trust.[254] The two businesses were listed at the same address in Naples, Florida.[255] Susan Roper Fabry died in Miami on January 23, 2011. In 2013 Dennis Fabry was listed as living on Marco Island. Attempts to reach him were unsuccessful. There was no active business listing for Dennis Fabry in 2015.

With the sale of Edgewater House, the city of Beverly renumbered the street address. The old gardener's cottage kept the old number, 47 West Street. Edgewater House itself became 65 West Street, a more logical number in relation to the houses on the street.

Chapter 9
Jeffrey and Carol Horvitz:
The Rebirth of Edgewater, 1991-Present

Jeffrey Horvitz purchased Edgewater House with full knowledge that the house required substantial work. He also recognized that the restoration and renovation would require not only further financial investment, but also careful planning and considerable time. Edgewater House had been built in six months in 1910. Jeffrey hoped to complete the work within a year.[*] He came to the task with the skills, temperament, experience, and resources required for its rebirth.

Jeffrey Horvitz grew up in Shaker Heights, Ohio, in a family of means. The story of his grandfather, Samuel Horvitz, is the stuff of an American immigrant's dream. Jeffrey's great-grandfather, Hillel Horvitz, and his wife, Jennie, were born in the old Russian Empire, in Lithuania near the Belarus border, and emigrated to the United States in the 1880s. They were part of the first big wave of Jewish immigrants who left during the pogroms that swept through Russia following the assassination of Tsar Alexander II in 1881.[256] The couple settled in Elyria, Ohio. Twins Samuel and Lilly were born in 1891, daughter Mary in 1893, and son Isadore in 1899. When his children were still young, Hillel Horvitz became blind. His son Samuel left school when he was in seventh grade and found work laying bricks for roads in Cleveland in order to support the family. Within a few years Samuel had his own subcontracting crew. In 1910 he broadened his experience by working as a bookkeeper for an express company.[257]

By the early 1920s Samuel was president and treasurer of his own business, Highway Construction Company, later called the Horvitz Company. Samuel Horvitz was a highly competent and aggressive man who saw opportunities within and beyond his own field. In the early 1920s he acquired two Ohio newspapers in the cities of Loraine and Mansfield. During the same period he expanded his contracting business to Florida at a time when that state was being developed. He bid for and won contracts for building roads and sewers from Coral Gables developer John Merritt. From there Horvitz went on to win further contracts from Californian Joseph Young, who was then developing the new community of Hollywood-by-the Sea between Miami and Fort Lauderdale. The timing was bad for Young: a devastating hurricane and the Florida slump that preceded the 1929 stock market crash led to Young's bankruptcy. In a complex and lengthy foreclosure Horvitz acquired about half of the land in Hollywood-by-the-Sea, which at that time consisted of a beach hotel and a fledgling community. Horvitz's new property included three miles of beachfront, 400 acres in Port Everglades, and much of the land west of what is now Route I-95. Horvitz allowed individuals who had purchased from Young to hold on to their homes and lots through the Depression. Not much happened in the further development of Hollywood until after World War II.

---

[*]The process took just ten months. The planning, permitting, and hiring was four months; actual construction six months.

104

The 1940 census indicates that the 50-year-old Samuel Horvitz was doing very well. He and his family lived in a $40,000 ($668,000 in 2015 dollars) house on upscale Parkland Drive in Shaker Heights. In addition to his wife and their sons, Harry 20, Leonard 17, and Bill 13, there were three live-in servants.

Samuel Horvitz died in 1956. The business interests were left in a family trust. His three sons, who had been working in the business since soon after World War II, although still young and relatively inexperienced, took over. The eldest son, Harry, took charge of the newspapers. Bill, the youngest, moved to Florida to oversee the real estate business. Jeffrey's father, Leonard, managed the original business, the Horvitz Construction Company in Cleveland. The company grew dramatically during the building of the interstate highway system in the 1960s; Horvitz Construction built the majority of the highways in northern Ohio and became both the largest and most highly respected highway contractor in the state. The media branch of the business grew to include four newspapers in Ohio (Lorain, Mansfield, Dover-New Philadelphia, and Willoughby) and one in Troy, New York. In the 1970s, when cable television was in its infancy, it acquired a cable business in Ohio and expanded it to include networks throughout Ohio and Virginia. In Florida, Bill Horvitz was building real estate developments, primarily planned residential communities in Hollywood, since there was no buyer for so much vacant land. Although the businesses were highly successful, personal relations among the three brothers were often contentious. According to Jeffrey, "The brothers didn't get along as children and didn't harmonize very well in business." A major crisis was reached in the mid-1970s resulting in a decade of on-and-off litigation.

Jeffrey Edwin Horvitz was born on February 26, 1950, the older of Leonard and Barbara Horvitz's two sons. Richard was born three years later. Jeffrey attended public high school in Shaker Heights while his brother Richard went to an all-boys private school. For decades Shaker Heights had one of the highest per capita incomes in America due to its concentration of professionals — doctors, lawyers, accountants, professors — very highly educated and affluent. As a result, the public school system was well supported and for many years was ranked as one of the top three school systems in the nation. Shaker Heights also had the distinction of being perhaps the first American city to attempt affirmative racial integration starting in the late 1950s. Jeffrey's public school experience played a large role in his development.

Leonard Horvitz, like Joseph Leiter, hoped his sons would follow him in the family business. After high school in Shaker Heights, Jeffrey enrolled in the Wharton School of Business at the University of Pennsylvania along with his first cousin Michael Horvitz. The cousins were following the same college path as the three senior Horvitz brothers. But very early on, Jeffrey realized that he was not interested in studying business and transferred to Penn's college of liberal arts, where he began to study sociology. By his junior year he was taking mostly graduate courses. He was also a varsity epee fencer until his course load made it difficult to keep up with team practice.

Jeffrey became interested in the sociology of psychiatry and did field work at the Institute of Pennsylvania Hospital in Philadelphia and at Mt. Sinai Hospital in Cleveland. Disillusioned with the unscientific Freudian practice of psychiatry that still dominated treatment into the 1970s, he changed his course and decided to leave the field to enter a Ph.D. program in social psychology. Having had taken no undergraduate psychology courses, he was rejected at most of the universities to which he applied, but finally, in 1972, he was accepted as a doctoral candidate in psychology at UCLA, where he had been recruited. The department had the country's second-largest academic computer center for social science research.

In September 1972, on his return from a five-week trip through the South Pacific and New Guinea just before relocating to Los Angeles for the start of the academic year, Jeffrey met Linda Susan Hill while looking for a rental near the UCLA campus. They were married in 1974. In the course of picking out possible wedding gifts, he became interested in twentieth-century fine arts prints from his contact with an art dealer in Cleveland.

In 1974, Jeffrey began buying and selling twentieth-century prints. What started as a sideline soon became a profession. In 1976 he abandoned his Ph.D. program at UCLA with an M.A. in social psychology to become a full-time private art dealer, specializing in twentieth-century art, working from his apartment. Later he opened his own public gallery at 806 North La Cienega Boulevard in West Hollywood.

In 1977 Jeffrey and Linda bought a house in the Hancock Park area of Los Angeles, and Jeffrey undertook his first renovation project. He recalled with some amusement that the workers on that project were all Scientologists. The renovations came in 10% over budget, but the result was a "jewel box" of a modest-sized Spanish-style house, common in the area. A few years later, after being on the market only a short while, it sold for the highest price per square foot yet achieved in Hancock Park.

It had always been assumed that the younger generation of Horvitz cousins would eventually take charge of the family business. Jeffrey's brother and all of his cousins had graduate degrees in law, business or art, and all became highly successful in their fields. But in 1980 simmering disagreements among the older generation led Jeffrey to decide it was time for him to assume a role. Rather than work directly for his father in Cleveland, he chose to move to South Florida and work in that branch of the business devoted to real estate development and building materials. Jeffrey and Linda left California on July 18, 1980. They settled in Golden Isles, a subdivision of Hallandale, Florida, where Jeffrey bought and renovated his second house.

Jeffrey settled into working for his uncle Bill Horvitz at the family real estate business, Hollywood, Inc., along with his cousin, David Horvitz, Bill's son. Although completely inexperienced with real estate development, Jeffrey learned quickly and took on substantial responsibilities.

At first Jeffrey continued to deal in art part time, but soon stopped entirely. He kept acquiring art for his own collection, but with a new focus. In 1983 he began collecting old master drawings. In a 2008 interview Jeffrey recalled, "I was a dealer in twentieth-century art in Los Angeles in the 1970s, and my experience was that almost all of the dealers of twentieth-century art that I knew had drawings in their collections. I think it has something to do with the immediacy of the objects. I always loved drawings and fell into collecting old masters, which were relatively plentiful at the time, and not very expensive."[258]

In 1984, Jeffrey's and Linda's first child, Christina, was born.

In the mid-1980s the feud among the elder Horvitz brothers started up again. In 1986 it was finally resolved with a decision to sell all of the businesses and split the proceeds evenly to the penny. No brother could buy any of the businesses. Buyers were funded by Drexel, under financier Michael Milken, so the purchases were very highly leveraged. Astutely for the Horvitz brothers, they were paid in cash; within the next few years most of the buyers went bankrupt or very nearly so.[259] In October of 1988, *Forbes* listed Harry, Leonard, and Bill Horvitz among the 400 richest American families.

In 1987 Leonard Horvitz and sons Richard and Jeffrey founded the Moreland Management Company to manage family assets, one of the earlier "family offices" in the country. Harry's and Bill's families also set up family offices to manage their investments for the newly liquid wealth. Jeffrey's brother Richard took on the primary responsibility of developing the administrative aspects of the office, while Jeffrey concentrated on investment management.

From knowing virtually nothing about investments Jeffrey set about learning as much as he could as fast as he could, but in a systematic way, starting with basic finance theory and progressing through the various asset classes. Today, he successfully oversees his family's investment portfolio (they do not manage outside money). As Jeffrey likes to quip, "This is the longest I have ever held the same job." He is also a well-respected speaker at investment conferences and has authored numerous articles in professional investment journals and for the Chartered Financial Analysts.

Jeffrey and Linda's second daughter, Caroline, was born in the spring of 1988 with severe cerebral palsy and profoundly deaf.

In October of the following year, Linda and Jeffrey separated, with plans to divorce. Linda and their daughters remained in Hallandale. Jeffrey moved to a condominium on Williams Island, south of Hollywood. By early 1991 it had become clear to Jeffrey that Florida did not have the combination of pediatric medical expertise that Caroline needed. Although he and Linda were no longer living together, they agreed that they both needed to move to a place that had some combination of first-rate pediatric medical facilities, deaf education, physical therapy, and technology. They chose the Boston area, and both made plans to relocate to North Shore where the Beverly School for the Deaf is located.

Jeffrey's first task was to purchase a house in the Prides Crossing section of Beverly for Linda and their daughters.

I had to purchase the Richard "Dick" Sears (America's first tennis champion) estate to induce Linda to move the children. I flew up and made a deal with the family members though one of them, an attorney, was on the phone in Rhode Island. They assured me we had a deal and their word was their bond as a distinguished New England family. I was barely home a day when I got word that they were reneging on the price. We eventually settled on a slightly increased price to avoid litigation. The house was called Governor's Landing, which was not its historic name but one concocted by the realtors to make it seem more attractive. The purchase of this house and Edgewater in 1991 constituted two of the largest residential sales that year in the whole Boston metro area — mostly because the local real estate market was in a depression.[260]

In 1992 Linda and Jeffrey were divorced in Florida. Upon moving to Massachusetts, Linda hired the well-connected and famously relentless divorce attorney Monroe Inker who was allowed to reopen the Florida divorce and keep the divorce case in Massachusetts alive for several years. The notorious case became front-page news for the local press and even national TV coverage due to the publicity engineered by Linda and Inker. Eventually, the case was settled in 1996. During the lengthy proceedings Jeffrey was able to obtain first shared custody of his daughters, and finally full custody.

While still living in South Florida, Jeffrey had met Carol Louise Sunday on a blind date on December 14, 1990.

Carol was born in Rochester, New York, on April 3, 1961, the third of Evelyn and Loy Jones's four children. Her father had served as a tank commander in Korea and later worked for a company that built storage tanks for chemical companies. When Carol was three the family settled in Terrace Park, Ohio, a child-friendly suburb of Cincinnati that "was a wonderful place to grow up — swim club, tennis club, great schools. We could bicycle everywhere."[261] It was here that, at age 11, Carol bought her first camera, using money she earned from a paper route and collecting bottle caps. Much later in life she took up photography seriously, and now she exhibits locally. From age 14 on, Carol became a very serious swimmer and was expecting to be on the U.S. Olympic team going to Moscow in 1980. When the Soviet Union invaded Afghanistan and the United States boycotted the Moscow Olympics, Carol was devastated. Her life abruptly changed course and she no longer swam competitively. Nonetheless, Carol's high school swimming records remained unbroken for the next quarter century.

By the time she met Jeffrey in 1990, Carol had become a successful professional woman and a single mother living in South Florida with her son, Joshua Sunday. After high school she had earned a degree in health information management from Cincinnati Technical College to better support herself and young son. In 1982 she was working with a consortium of hospitals in a three-state region (Ohio, Indiana, and Kentucky) collecting oncology data. That data would be used in conjunction with the National Cancer Data Base in Washington as part of the government-funded "War on Cancer". Carol would often travel from Cincinnati to Washington to work with the epidemiologists and computer programmers involved in this statistical research at the National Cancer Institute. In addition to working, Carol attended the University of Cincinnati at night, studying biochemistry with the intention of going to medical school.

In 1985 Carol was offered an Air Force ROTC scholarship to medical school. Sadly, she had to decline because her mother, who was her only help with Joshua, had just been diagnosed with terminal cancer. In 1986 Carol made the painful decision to leave Cincinnati for a position with a New Jersey hospital that needed help in bringing its oncology department back into compliance with national accreditation standards. Her mother's health was rapidly declining, but Carol needed a higher salary in order to care for her son.

Though the pay in New Jersey was excellent, the area where she was living proved not to be ideal for raising a young son. In 1990, after being recruited by the 1500-bed Hollywood Memorial Hospital, Carol and son Joshua moved to South Florida.

> When people ask how I met Jeffrey, I usually say through infection control. The infection control nurse in our department, who worked for me, kept telling me I had to go out, I had to go out. One night that nurse literally dragged me out, and that's how I met Jeffrey.[262]

By the summer of 1991 Jeffrey was dividing his time between South Florida, where he still had his business office, and the North Shore, where he was house hunting. By this time Carol's and Jeffrey's relationship had deepened.

***

In early fall, Jeffrey's realtor took him to see Edgewater House which was scheduled to be sold at a foreclosure auction. He liked the idea of being on the ocean and realized how little shorefront property was available. Most importantly, he would be very near his children, who had relocated with their mother to Prides Crossing.

Although Edgewater House needed substantial renovation, Jeffrey recognized that he knew how to do that work. If he later decided that he didn't want to stay at Edgewater, he could resell it. Jeffrey went to the auction on September 21, 1991, and was astonished that there were other serious bidders. At first there were four; then, after $1 million, it was down to him and one competitor. He purchased Edgewater with a final bid of $1,775,000 ($3,099,150 in 2015 dollars).

As noted in the previous chapter, the prior owners, Susan and David Fabry, had owned both Edgewater House and the adjacent vacant lot, but had mortgaged the two properties separately. When the banks finally foreclosed, Edgewater was auctioned first and the vacant lot was auctioned the following year. Jeffrey was out of town and had his attorney bid for him at a price he thought was sure to be successful for a lot that was unbuildable because it lacked frontage. However, he was outbid by a developer, Evan Wile, who got it for $335,000.[*]

* * *

Now that he owned the house, Jeffrey began to analyze it. Edgewater House was designed for entertaining and for six months he puzzled over the proportions of the first floor rooms until he understood how the house had originally functioned. The main hallway was a reception space as large as the loggia. The loggia (now used as a living room) was designed as an indoor-outdoor room facing the ocean and is long and narrow to emphasize the ocean view and Misery Island offshore. Its ends are slightly asymmetrical around two facing French doors leading on the north side into the dining room and on the south side into the library. The dining room is a large and grand space with an exquisite plaster ceiling crafted by a group of Italian artisans who did other similar work in Boston at the time. On the south side of the loggia is the library, originally done in yew wood, now painted. Adjacent to the library is the parlor with its entrance through a tall doorway at the base of the main stairs in the front hall. Originally these two

---

[*]Wile's property was landlocked and lacked access by road. His first dispute with the Horvitzes concerned an easement over the Edgewater driveway, and this set the stage for litigation still-ongoing for nearly a quarter of a century. Wile, a man used to getting what he wanted from local building departments, was able to get a building permit under mysterious circumstances in 1998, but it was soon overturned. Frustrated with the situation, Wile embarked on a "campaign of retaliation," as the Massachusetts Supreme Judicial Court found in the landmark case *Rattigan v. Wile* that details the extraordinary measures Wile undertook to force the Horvitzes to drop their opposition to his permit. Despite repeated rejections of Wile's building permit applications, the litigation still percolates in the Land Court.

rooms were connected with a small door (undoubtedly, after large dinner parties the men would retire to the library and women to the parlor to socialize). The parlor and library also exhibit strange asymmetries as to window placements.

Jeffrey hypothesizes that the time pressure to complete the original construction in six months per Mrs. Leiter's requirements gave the architects no opportunity to work out the complex interplay between the exterior proportions and the interiors. The service wing seems to be crowding the front façade, and the grand Georgian style would normally have been for a house elevated on a rise.

Edgewater House had deteriorated over the years. During her later years in the house, Ellen Ames had done no major repairs. Not only had the Fabrys made no significant renovations, they had made things worse. Jeffrey remembered his first impression:

> The master bathroom was baby-blue shag carpet, a cheap toilet, a free-standing sink, and a plywood armoire. There was junky carpet in some of the bedrooms. The paint was a low-quality matte white — kind of chalky-gray looking. There were cracks in the ceilings. All of the bathrooms were shot; no plumbing work had really been done. The service wing was substantially unfinished and they were putting in a spa. You could see the framework; there was no drywall. The area behind the kitchen had been gutted. What I saw was basically just a mess. The third-floor bedrooms looked like terrorists had been there. I guess the Fabrys ran out of time and money. There were holes punched in the walls, wallpaper dangling down. No one had attended to the mechanical systems of the house.
>
> It hadn't been totally neglected; it wasn't the worst I saw. I saw houses with people living in them that were on the market for a million dollars in 1991, and you couldn't believe what you were seeing. I have lived in five cities, and what I saw here in some of the old estate houses were conditions unlike anything I'd ever seen anywhere. Families really cash poor and house rich. No ability to maintain the houses at all.[263]

Once he had passed papers, Jeffrey rented a house from Dan Senecal in Manchester for the first year so that he could spend time with his daughters as well as be present as needed during the house renovations. Carol visited frequently during this time, but remained in Florida to complete the accreditation at Hollywood Memorial Hospital.

Jeffrey wanted to create a functional house that would serve not only his own needs but also those of his family, which now included his two daughters Caroline and Christine and Carol Sunday and her son Joshua. His first task was to figure out how he was going to get everything done. He came to the job with a depth of experience. Over the previous 20 years not only had he bought and overseen the renovation of two houses, but Hollywood, Inc. was building about 80 houses a year when he worked there. In his work in real estate development in Florida, Jeffrey had learned the pitfalls and had developed strategies for avoiding them. He entered the process of renovation knowing what he wanted and how to go about doing it.

"The basic strategic approach to the house was to gut all the bathrooms, gut the kitchen, replace all plumbing, electrical, heating, and ventilation, and add air-conditioning." The first floor would undergo two major changes: the total gutting and reconfiguration of the kitchen and the removal of the fireplace from the loggia. On the second floor there would be a complete reconfiguration of the master bedroom suite. A major consideration in planning the renovations was the commitment to making

Edgewater House fully accessible to Caroline. This included the construction of a large wheelchair-accessible elevator and bathroom at the end of the service wing. In addition to the work on the house itself, Jeffrey's overall plan included construction of a six-car garage at the end of the service wing, replacement of the saltwater pool with a heated pool, and construction of a pool house.

With his basic plan in place and still commuting back and forth from Florida, Jeffrey found the people to do the work.

I purchased the house in August 1991 and probably closed on it the next month. October and November 1991 was the search for an architect, engineers, and a general contractor. By December 1991 or January 1992, I had hired Buzz Brannen at Jung/Brannen as the architect and hired Jim Ansara's Shawmut Design & Construction as the general contractor. The planning, permitting, and collecting of bids from subcontractors went on until approximately the end of March. Charlie Mann was the project supervisor, and Chet Walsh was the job foreman.

Based on his experience and vision, Jeffrey developed a unique organizational plan.

Instead of the standard pyramid with the architect at the top, I drew two wagon wheels. The center of the first wheel had me and my representative (I was back and forth from Florida) and around them the architect, the structural and electrical engineers, and the general contractor, Shawmut. The second wheel had the general contractor at the center with all the subcontractors around it. I put control in the hands of the general contractor and said if at all possible there would be no change orders. The deal I made with Jim Ansara, the general contractor, was: "If you give me full information, I will make 80 percent of all decisions on the spot, 90 percent of all decisions in 24 hours, and 95 percent of all decisions in 48 hours." He said, "Nobody will." I said, "We'll see." At the end of the job he said, "You have exceeded expectations." I had said, "If you need a change order approved by the architect, although I don't recommend it, I will pay for it, but you are the one responsible for the job. Try to figure it out by yourself. I'm not going to change much."

Before construction began, Jeffrey laid out plans for materials purchase that would simplify and expedite the decision-making and ordering process, as well as lessen the margin of error in construction:

All tile would be from American Olean to ensure easier and faster reordering if necessary.

All marble would be in Boston and purchased in full so it couldn't be sold out from under.

All plumbing would be American Standard, Kohler, or other U.S. companies, all basic line. Horvitz would pick it. All measurements would be in inches and feet to avoid confusion.

All paint would be Benjamin Moore. High quality, medium price, readily available, big color spectrum.

All hardware would be Baldwin. Door handles would be egg shaped, since they have better torque and go with both modern and traditional furnishings.

What really matters is good design, not necessarily expensive materials. As a further efficiency measure, I assured Shawmut that I would pay for both a plumber and an electrician to be on the job every day so that decisions could be made without delay. I got part of the idea from high-school chemistry: a reaction can't go faster than the rate-determining step — the slowest step in the chain. So what I thought through was how to anticipate and eliminate the things most likely to go wrong. I got two ideal men from Shawmut. Charlie Mann, the project manager, is easygoing, gets the big picture; Chet Walsh is much more a type A personality, a micromanager who didn't let a single little detail slip. They both had a great deal of authority and there were virtually no change orders. [264]

Construction began at the beginning of April, 1992. On an average day there were 35 workers on the job. On a few occasions there were as many as 100. Charlie Mann, the project supervisor, recalled that one major problem was discovered with the original construction.

When we went in there we had to replace all of the window lintels. They were rusted and the bricks were cracking, coming apart, so they weren't very well protected or flashed. That was a lot of work. You have to shore the windows up and take everything apart, so that was one thing. Then there were persistent roof leaks, but the roof was old enough so that it may not have indicated shoddy building. [265]

Removing the loggia fireplace and chimney and replicating the original limestone façade proved to be challenging. Mann recalled:

The limestone on the front was a real challenge. Only half of the carving of the basket of fruit remained. We could only make a mold of part and then someone had to go from there and communicate to someone else what the thing should look like. There was a limestone-carving company in Indiana, where they have a lot of limestone. The mason we had gave them photographs and the mold we made, and sent the whole package out and they did it. Those tradespeople still exist out there and distribute nationwide. The fireplace never fit the house; they just slapped it in. If the owner was smart he would have saved that piece of limestone.

The bulk of the interior work was the replacement of all plumbing, electrical, and ventilation systems and the addition of air conditioning. Mann recalled that the biggest challenge was fitting everything in.

There are something like 32 or 34 air handlers and zones, and they are put into all these spaces — under the eaves, up in the attic, over closets, and in hard-to-get-at spaces. So getting all that in was a real challenge, because in all of those rooms you had to preserve things like moldings, molded plaster, crown moldings, and all those things, so you had to pick where you could put in those chases. Then in the end with things like the paint, it was just that there was so much of it and so much prep with that problem of it being unheated during the last of the Fabrys' years. [266]

During the construction process, Jeffrey was still commuting between South Florida and the North Shore. He approached his time with the contractors with the mind of a frugal efficiency expert. His description of a meeting regarding the secondary bathrooms is illustrative.

When we did the secondary baths, I told them, "I'm coming up from Florida. Get me all the American Olean samples and lay them out on the tables in the dining room and here is what we are going to do. Give me the plans for all the secondary bathrooms. The basic tile is going to be white or off-white, and I am going to make decorative choices for colored tile on the walls and on the floors. And we'll specify all of this in one morning." Between 9:00 am and 12:30 they had catalogued everything on the plans and it was all done. All bathrooms are basically the same. The only differences are in the powder room off the parlor and the lavatory off the coatroom, where I saved the old toilets because these would be the least used. [267]

Some of the original bathroom fixtures were sold to a salvage company from Montreal. In addition to pedestal sinks and toilets with wall tanks, Mann remembered the magnificent tub in Mary Leiter's suite.

The tub was very nice. It was huge. It was a job to get it out of the house because it was basically solid ceramic. Most tubs are like a vessel with legs that go down, but this tub had sides that went straight down with a tub-shaped interior, so every bit in between was solid ceramic. It was over a foot thick in places.[268]

The kitchen was completely gutted and reconfigured to meet the family's needs.

The kitchen needed a dual-purpose floor plan. I designed the seemingly strange layout with an embedded cooking triangle so that one person can cook. I like to cook, and I do most of the cooking for the family. Because I knew that Carol and I would entertain often, I also needed a kitchen in which you can have a large catering group and they don't get in each other's way. That's why you have the large rectangular and hexagonal islands. The sink-stove configuration is like a galley kitchen, and then as you move farther back it gets bigger and bigger. I think this is the caterers' favorite house. [269]

The configuration of the downstairs rooms in the main part of the house remained unchanged. The butler's pantry stayed as it was, complete with its polished-wood serving table, dish cupboards, silver safe, and plate warmer. Mary Leiter's original electric annunciator still hangs on the wall. The old billiard room, which later had been the Ameses' den, became an art storage area.

The breakfast room was decorated to become the most whimsical room in the house.

It was stark white with a little bit of trim, so I redesigned it so there would be much more trellis — only the diamond pattern around the edge was there. I wanted something that was formal enough for the house, but was sort of indoorsy-outdoorsy, and also a little cute for Caroline, because she would be eating most of her meals in there. She was about four at the time. We chose a Japanese style wallpaper with rabbits, with a soft green background. The trellis was painted to match.

Jeffrey followed an unusual method in choosing paint colors for the remaining rooms on the first floor.

The paint colors were decided deductively. Basically the ocean is black at night. So in the day you do have the ocean and the wall color doesn't need to fight with it, but at night wall color is very important. So I wanted to animate this house. I wanted each room to feel different, but not like a designer showcase where you are going from one style to another. I created a theory in my head about using generalized opposite colors in adjacent rooms. Think of starting with green and red, so the loggia and the dining room are the highest key of that. The loggia is a cream undercoat, take cherry red, dilute it by half, and then take a sea sponge to put it on to give it texture. The main dining room is also a cream linen undercoat, then Kelly green, then spray it all with black enamel. That's when the painters got Carol and said, talk to your husband. "He's crazy." And she said, "Just listen to him and do what he says. He knows what he is doing and it will be fine." They didn't realize until they finished that it worked. If they had just used green it would look garish. The tiny little dots of black enamel give it texture and at night give it a reflective quality. The library is actually a gray-green. It's a terribly complex color. I worked for days with the painter. It changes at different times of the day and goes from battleship gray to green. I kind of reverse-engineer what is in my head so I can convey it to the painter. Then the parlor was aubergine, which is also a complex color. Carol and I eventually chose a dark paper with large stars, reminiscent of a Napoleonic style.[270]

Jeffrey's choice of furniture reflects his imagination, wit, and eclectic tastes. The dining room is a telling example.

> I like watching British murder mysteries from the 1930s and the furniture was then-contemporary Art Deco. You'd see these manor homes decorated with contemporary furniture. So I thought that would be a fun idea for the dining room. I bought a couple of actual Art Deco things — the torcheres and the buffet — but the rest of the things are absolutely modern. The silver tazzas that are on each table are Ettore Sottsass, an architect from the 1980s Memphis Design in Milan. The tables were made in South Florida, and if I put them in a sunny room with palm trees they would look absolutely different. They are made of wood with a white gold finish and the chairs are made of horn and were crafted in Brazil in 1992. A large gilded Buddha from Southeast Asia completes the room.

Jeffrey worked closely with his interior designer, Dick Reese, in acquiring furniture. Together they purchased most of it from Boston design showrooms. The most difficult room to furnish was the loggia. Jeffrey described converting the long, narrow room with French doors, originally designed for indoor-outdoor entertaining into a comfortable year-round space as a nightmare.

> At first we didn't have so much furniture or so much French art, so the house started out a little bit lighter, and the look was a little more American and neutral. For the windows, I chose sheers with a horizontal pattern to maintain the view and to reiterate the horizon line and the beach line.

The second floor was redesigned to fit the needs of the family.

> We changed the orientation of the master bedroom suite from a series of parallel rooms, with access perpendicular to the ocean, to two end points: family room on one side and master bedroom on the other, and the three small rooms in the middle became a closet, a hallway, and the master bathroom. The two doorways to the hall, which you can still see upstairs, we just made into panels.

> The second floor of the service wing, formerly guest suites, became Christina's and Caroline's rooms. Special accommodations were designed to make everything accessible to Caroline. We built the ramps from the garage, motion-sensor lights in all of the vestibules, ramps in all of the door entrances, built an entire handicapped bathroom. We situated the new elevator just outside Caroline's room.

> Christina's room was at the ocean-side corner with nanny's rooms in the middle section between them one with full bath and one connected directly to Caroline's room. Caroline was a child who needed constant physical care. She now has personal-care assistants.[271]

On the inland side of the second floor's main hall, the Ames's former bedroom at the west end was transformed into a comfortable study. The bedroom and bath remained a guest suite.[*]

The third-floor bedrooms, partially gutted during the Kaisers period, were re-created as three guest rooms and Josh's room so that he could have some privacy.

---

[*]This suite is now used for Carol and Jeffrey's grandchildren when they come to Edgewater to spend time with their grandmother. Samuel Jesse Sunday was born August 29, 2014. Joshua married Michelle Magdycz on August 20, 2011, and Sam was born after they relocated to Beverly. A second son, Oliver John was born on May 4, 2016.

I had this plan of making the third-floor bedrooms into something like a B&B, each of them a different style room. The rooms are a pastiche of furniture that had been in different places at different times in my life put to completely different use. There are four bedrooms: the India Raj room, the English Lady's room, the Heart of Darkness room, and then there's the sort of American room. The American room was Josh's room and that's the Viking oak bedroom furniture that was in my room when I was a little boy. The English Lady's room furniture was from my house in Hallandale, Florida. It's eclectic.[272]

The third-floor service wing had been completely gutted during the year that Kaiser planned to remove the third story. Part of the service wing now became office space with Jeffrey's personal office in the ocean-facing room with secretarial space to the side and a small conference room behind. The only exterior structural change was the addition of more windows on the ocean side.

The basement at Edgewater House was the least changed during the renovations. The walls of the rough, unfinished part were painted white to brighten the interior. The area under the main section houses the new heating and air-conditioning units as well as storage areas. The old laundry and drying rooms were fitted out as a personal office for Carol. The area that had once been the cold room houses the base of the elevator shaft. The biggest change was the transformation of the old kitchen into a modern fitness center, a room Carol calls "the torture chamber." The wine cellar was relocated to what had been an open pantry and designed to hold up to 1500 bottles in a utilitarian locked room.

The outdoor work included some changes in landscaping, the building of a garage, the replacement of the pool, and the addition of a pool house. The addition of a six-car garage at the end of the service wing resulted in a reworking of the drive. The new drive was made of pea stone, but problems with snow removal led to the decision to replace it with asphalt, accented with granite pavers.

In order to meet the needs of his family, Jeffrey eliminated the old saltwater pool and created a new one in its shell. He created an original and efficient pool design to meet everyone's needs.

We had to go to freshwater because we wanted a heated pool. The round far end, for diving, is about nine feet deep. We needed a shallow end because the girls were little, so I made the rectangle with a handicap access ramp on one side and stairs on the other. The pools were connected with a narrow lane, because Carol is an Olympic-level swimmer — so there was something for everybody. The new design reduced the volume of water to be heated by about 70 percent.

The architect's design had called for a theatrical Neoclassical-style pool house. Jeffrey scrapped that plan and chose to build a more casual and utilitarian concrete structure that included a sauna. The exterior was then softened by the addition of trellises.

In 1992 the seawall separating the Edgewater lawn from the sand was about five feet high. Jeffrey got a permit to build a handicap-access ramp that would enable Caroline to get down to the beach. Over the years sand has accreted to above the top of the seawall.

Jeffrey later cut down all of the tall pine trees that had partially blocked the view to the ocean from the pool area. He planted one Austrian pine, which is pruned to be like a bonsai.

The firm of Morgan Wheelock worked with Jeffrey to create an overall landscape design that combines a French formality with easy-to-maintain plantings. The overgrown rhododendrons along the entry drive were removed and replaced with lawn and flowering crabapples. The original design included for the circle in front of the house suggested a fountain or some other water feature. Jeffrey chose a simpler plan, replacing the circle with a rectangular island planted with low-growing yews and ten pollarded linden trees. Similar trees line the sides of the inner driveway. The dignified effect is very much in keeping with the design of the house. The front entrance to the house is flanked with graceful serviceberry trees, hydrangeas, and ground plantings of perennials.

The lawn on the ocean side of the house, which is divided into upper and lower sections, was redesigned to include rectangular slate stones forming a cross on the upper terrace. Originally Jeffrey had installed an eight-foot-tall bronze Barbara Hepworth sculpture on the upper terrace and a smaller Tony Smith sculpture on the lower terrace, both of which were eventually donated to the Museum of Fine Arts in Boston. The Hepworth was replaced with a late-nineteenth-century monumental terra cotta urn made in Cincinnati for a former psychiatric hospital in Toledo, Ohio, and the Tony Smith was replaced with a large ceramic vessel made by Timothy Rowan. To shade the upper lawn, Jeffrey planted honey locusts — trees well suited to lawn planting, since their growth habit admits enough light for the lawn to grow well beneath them, and the leaves are small enough to be chopped up by a lawn mower. The lower level that borders the beach was left as open lawn with a small slate terrace at the center. The embankment was planted with naturalized daffodils.

In September of 1992, Jeffrey and Carol moved into the renovated house.

Construction was about 98 percent complete when we moved in. The project was about two weeks over schedule and 4.5 percent over the final construction budget — that is, the budget before actual work commenced. The total cost of the renovation was about one and half times the purchase price.

Several of the subcontractors and workers suggesting that I write a small book or article about how I organized this complex renovation so successfully, as they had never seen a project work like this before.

The two percent left to be done provided Carol with a vivid memory. "I was taking a shower in the master bathroom soon after we moved in, and a contractor walked by. There was some kind of punch list, and they were checking for about a year."

Interestingly, the timeline for the renovation process was almost identical to the timeline for building the house. Construction of Edgewater House had started in April of 1910 and been completed by September 30. Actual work on the renovation began in late March or early April of 1992 and was completed at the end of September.

* * *

For six months, Beverly Farms residents had been watching the renovation process with great interest. Beach walkers had witnessed the transformation of the oceanfront façade. They had watched as the awkward and incongruous chimney was dismantled and the beautiful central doorway, capped with a limestone fruit basket, was lovingly restored. They followed the transformation of the exterior, as brick was repointed and peeling white window frames gave way to elegant black ones. For the second time in its history, Edgewater House had been saved. It had also been returned to its former grandeur.

Carol Horvitz remembered the first weeks of living in the house. A happy memory was the warm welcome she received from neighbors Jean Bonner and Mary Lockwood. A now humorous memory concerns the Horvitzes' first night out.

> We had just started to heat the house. It was all new paint and everything was just pristine. I remember we had an adult woman babysitter come over to the house. We were all excited — we had just moved in and were going to go out for the first time. We came back after two or three hours and the babysitter was at the door, absolutely terrified, and said, "I will never come back here — this house is haunted." The wood had started to crack because we were heating the house for the first time, and it sounded like guns going off in the house. We had huge cracks in the wood.[273]

During the last years that the Fabrys had owned the house, it was sparsely heated if at all. It took nearly two years before the walls were completely dry.

In October the Horvitzes held their first big party at Edgewater House to show their gratitude to all of the Shawmut employees for the fine work they had done. Over a hundred people, workers and their families, were among the first to see the fruits of their handiwork.

Later that fall Carol wrote a note to Ellen Ames, inviting her to tea. As a modern woman from the Midwest, unfamiliar with upper-class Boston etiquette, Carol addressed the envelope to *Mrs. Ellen Ames* rather than to *Mrs. Oliver Ames 2nd*.

> Mrs. Ames called and told me how very inappropriate my envelope had been and asked if my secretary had done it. She then told me that there was no such thing as a Ms., which is what I had used for my name; that I was either a Miss or a Mrs. Needless to say, I did not invite her to tea again.[274]

In December 1992, Carol and Jeffrey held the first of the holiday parties that have become an annual Edgewater tradition. Carol had grown up in an Ohio suburb where neighborhood parties were common and was eager to open her home to her new community. Starting with the people she had already met, Carol used the Beverly List of Residents to include others. About 100 people attended that first party. The evening was an overwhelming success. The neighbors not only got to meet the Horvitzes and see the interior of the newly renovated Edgewater House, they also got to see each other.

> I overheard one neighbor say to another neighbor, "Oh my goodness, I haven't seen you in 20 years. It's so good to see you." Now people say, "I'll see you next year." People see each other here and catch up with each other. And they're next-door neighbors![275]

Now that Jeffrey and Carol were living full time in Massachusetts, Jeffrey's friend Dan Senecal suggested that they might like to join the Essex County Country Club as a way to meet local people. Jeffrey was skeptical, not being interested in tennis, golf, or the country club life, but allowed Dan to propose him for membership with the understanding that if accepted he did not actually have to join. Some months went by before Dan called with the news that the application had been rejected. Jeffrey's response was, "Well, I could understand it if they had met me, but I haven't even been there," echoing Groucho Marx's famous quip "I don't want to join any club that would have me as a member." Unbeknownst to Jeffrey, Carol was being independently solicited for membership. Carol's lineage can be traced back directly to the captain of the *Mayflower* and Commodore Perry. Apparently when the club realized that Carol was living with Jeffrey they had to inform her that she too was not the sort of person they wanted as a member. Two decades later things had changed and a social acquaintance who was a member assured Carol that now they had both a Jewish and an African-American member. But Jeffrey and Carol still don't play golf or tennis, and had no interest in joining.

During their first summer Carol discovered that she and Jeffrey had inherited a tradition attached to the Edgewater pool. "For the first couple of years during the summer, we would have teenagers and young men jumping into our pool in broad daylight." Carol and Jeffrey together explained:

CAROL: When we first moved up here Jeffrey traveled quite a bit and I would be home alone sometimes during the summer. I was amazed that three or four times during the day, in broad daylight, there would be people in my pool whom I did not know. I'd run out, and they'd run away, laughing. I know it sounds innocent enough, but it was scary. They were often drinking. I'd find beer cans floating, and there were big guys I didn't know diving from the diving board.

I remember that at a cocktail party we had soon after one of the pool invasions, I mentioned it to some of the gentlemen, and a very respectable older man wearing a bow tie said, "Oh yes, we all used to do it. It's a tradition." So I realized I had to break that tradition of young men jumping into the pool.

JEFFREY: So here's what we did. I was in Monaco when I got the call that this was happening and I was going to be back in a couple days. They'd do it with workers, construction people in the yard — it didn't seem to faze them at all. A couple of days after I got home from Monaco, Carol came up to my office and said, "They're in the pool."

I went out and they had disappeared. I asked Carol if she could recognize them. "Yes." "Where did they go?" "They went toward the West Beach Club." So we went down there. Carol spots them immediately. Now, I am five-eight and about 165 pounds. They are five guys in their twenties, the smallest of whom is substantially bigger than me, all solid muscle. I'd heard the stories, the rumors about the "drug dealer from Miami" who had purchased this house. So I went over to them and said, "I understand you guys have been jumping into my pool." And they said, "No, it wasn't us." And I said, "Well, my wife, who is here behind me, says that you were." "Oh no, we weren't doing it." So I looked straight at them and said, "Are you calling my wife a liar?" All of a sudden the tone changed. I knew what my reputation was, so I said, "You know in Miami we have a lot of home invasions, and you never know who is going to be there. It's really dangerous and they are often armed, so you have to kind of do something about it if you see people in your house, because they might be armed." So now their eyes are getting really wide. I said, "Let me explain this to you one more time. If I see you in my pool again, if you are lucky, very lucky, I'll call the police. Do you understand what I am telling you?" "Yes, sir." And that pretty much ended the problem.

* * *

In the fall of 1992 when they had moved into the house, Christina and Caroline split their time between Edgewater and their mother's house in Prides Crossing. Josh was twelve, Christina was eight, and Caroline was four. In the fall of 1992, Josh was enrolled at the Cardigan Mountain School in New Hampshire and later went on to the Valley Forge Military Academy before graduating from the University of Massachusetts, Amherst. Christina attended Shore Country Day School in Beverly, then Bishop Fenwick High School in Peabody before graduating from American University. Carol remembers that Josh and Christina, and later Caroline, enjoyed having friends come to visit, but found it awkward to explain why they lived in such a big house.

In 1995 Jeffrey hired then 19-year-old Cheryl Lauricella to help take care of Caroline, the result of which was a relationship that mirrored that of Helen Keller and Annie Sullivan. As Jeffrey said, "I have made two particularly good decisions in my life: marrying Carol and hiring Cheryl." Eventually, Caroline attended the Beverly School for the Deaf, then spent two years at Beverly High School. Cheryl then became her home-school teacher. Caroline went on to Mount Wachusett Community College, then to Mount Holyoke College, where she graduated in 2015. She is currently enrolled in a Simmons College dual masters degree program held on the Mount Holyoke campus.

Carol, who had been accustomed to working full time, decided to return to school herself. In September of 1993 she restarted her college education at Tufts University, where she earned a B.A. in history. From there she continued at Boston University, where she received a combined J.D. and M.P.H., (Master of Public Health). With everyone in school most of the time and Jeffrey working from his home office, he was the primary cook for the nightly family dinners. Carol's M.P.H. thesis is referenced in China's genetic testing laws.

For several years after receiving her J.D. from B.U., Carol had a law office in Salem and did almost exclusively pro-bono and low-income cases — mostly divorce, special needs, and battered and abused women. She later became deeply involved with the stem cell controversy in Massachusetts and helped organize the world-class stem cell researchers in the region to address policy concerns.

* * *

Second only to his love for his family was Jeffrey's passion for fine art. He had begun collecting old master drawings in 1983 and had amassed an impressive collection of Italian and French drawings by the time he moved to Edgewater House.

In 1994 Carol entered the art field when she began buying gifts for Jeffrey.

I started buying antiquities as gifts for Jeffrey. The first piece was a small ancient terra cotta piece from India. I started buying them a few times a year. We had about a dozen or so before I started noticing Chinese cinnabar lacquer, and purchased the first piece as a gift for Jeffrey. That was the beginning of our collection.

A decade later Carol began to acquire contemporary works.

119

I became interested in contemporary Japanese ceramics after seeing some in a gallery window while walking back from a conference at the UN. I started buying them and giving them to Jeffrey as gifts in 2005. Immediately after he sold his Italian drawing collection in 2008 we became serious collectors when we bought about 30 or 40. [276]

In 2008 Jeffrey made an important but difficult decision regarding his collection of drawings by Italian and French old masters. He decided to sell the Italian collection. He was quoted in *Art Daily*.

Now the French outnumber the Italian drawings by a factor of ten. Nonetheless, the Italian collection may be one of the largest remaining in private hands in North America. It has been some time since I have added an Italian drawing, not because I fell out of love with them, but because the scarcity of fine works became increasingly frustrating. Meanwhile, the French collection grew into something so large and special that it required professional management. So I have decided to turn all of my efforts and attention into continuing to build a comprehensive survey of French drawings, paintings, and sculpture. [277]

* * *

The expansion of Edgewater House had been under consideration for a few years, but in summer of 2008 Jeffrey decided he might actually move forward with the project. Carol likes to tell the tale that she pointed out to Jeffrey that he had a painting in a closet, and the next thing she knew he was setting out tiki torches on the lawn to plan out a new gallery building. According to Jeffrey, "We had enough square footage in the house but not enough contiguous space to reconfigure." Carol was anxious to move out of her basement office which looked into the old laundry drying pit.

I made some conceptual decisions first — should the art and office be in the same building or separate? I decided it was best to combine them. For cost control the basic structure needed to be pretty simple, basically a box, and I could articulate the sides so that they looked like a group of Georgian townhouses.

It also had to look smaller than it was so as not to compete with the façade of the main house. There are various visual tricks that I had to make it look smaller, like breaking up the planes in different ways and softening the color on the exterior. From the air it is actually quite a large footprint, but it looks about half the size from almost any vantage point on the ground. The vines were my idea. If you look at the driveway side, there are three different planes or rectangles on the rectangular façade, and that breaks up the space, and then the window treatment is made to break it up further. All of this is to prevent it from competing with the grand façade of the main house. I had this well worked out before I hired the architect.

I chose a green-gray stucco exterior to reduce the sense of mass for the building, so it sits quietly next to the main house. The color is closely related to the oxidized copper of the gutter and downspouts and to the greenish-gray tint of the slate on the roof. The old brick has chromium, which is a toxic chemical, so it is no longer available, and any other brick would have clashed with the old brick.

We interviewed eight Boston area architects but in the end chose John Margolis, who was local. Carol pointed out that if they were going to work with me I couldn't have an architect who had strong ego investment in it being their own design. I needed someone to follow through on what I had pretty much already worked out. John was good to work with and his office was walking distance in Beverly Farms.[278]

Margolis's final interior design was a graceful interpretation of Jeffrey's general plan. Windover was the general contractor, with Charlie Mann as the project supervisor (he had left Shawmut not long before). In recalling the project, Mann was reminded of Jeffrey's practicality. "What he said at the time was, 'What I am building now has no resale value, because no next person would really have a use for this space — even the people who buy this house are a very limited number of people — so I have to be a little careful what I put into it.' He has a really sensible side to him."[279]

Jeffrey explained:

I had drawn out general schematics for all of the rooms. I also thought ahead to the future. The upper galleries have real windows in the exterior walls under the drywall, so if I ever want to expand the office space, I can take out that drywall, put in a partition wall, frame in the two doors, and create two more offices and secretarial space at the landing with a space for a single line of lateral files. We also made sure they did not have bearing walls in the conference room interior walls, because for a future buyer if they take out the interior walls facing the corridor you basically have the space for a home theater. And the bathrooms are stacked one on top of another for efficiency, but they all have enough room to be expanded to a full bath if you wanted for an in-law suite or something like that. So basically this building can be repurposed at very low cost.

The gallery construction project included the less visible but equally important task of providing a controlled environment for the art. Heating and air-conditioning units located at the main house serve both buildings. The large air-conditioning units and a backup generator are housed in a secure area off the service wing. A tunnel for pipes and ducts connects the buildings.

Construction started May 8, 2009. It was completed in December of that year, and we were fully moved in during January 2010. The project came in a little ahead of schedule and a little under budget.[280]

The new gallery building houses Jeffrey's personal office as well as gallery space. One enters through an open reception and secretarial-office area. The two main galleries on the first floor also serve as meeting areas, one a formal conference room, the other a comfortable sitting room. The galleries are two stories high, providing ample area for drawings and paintings to be displayed in the salon style.

Jeffrey's office on the second floor has a spectacular view over the pool to the magnificent sculptured pine and the ocean beyond. In keeping with his practicality, Jeffrey purchased some of its furniture from a liquidator after Gillette closed down its corporate offices in the Prudential Center in Boston. The furniture is handsome and serviceable; the money saved was spent on handcrafted pieces in the remainder of the gallery. During the recession, when craftsmen where having a hard time selling their furniture, the Horvitzes spread the money around and purchased from a variety of makers, including master craftsman Jeff Roberts, through the League of New Hampshire Craftsmen.

The addition of the gallery building freed up space on the third floor of the house. Carol and Tomoko Nakagura, part-time curator for the contemporary Japanese ceramics collection, and Heather Johnson Reid, part-time registrar, now use a portion of Jeffrey's former third floor office as their office. The remainder of the wing's third floor has been transformed into a welcoming and intimate gallery for the contemporary Japanese ceramics collection. On the floor below, a room at the back of the wing houses an interesting ancillary collection — the boxes. Each piece arrives in an individually crafted wooden box labeled by the artist. The boxes themselves are works of art, preserved as an important part of the collection.

Edgewater House and the gallery are now home to three internationally significant art collections: French old masters, Japanese contemporary ceramics, and Chinese cinnabar lacquer. The collection of French art, which began with master drawings, now includes painting and sculpture as well. It spans 300 years from the mid-seventeenth century through the mid-nineteenth century and is one of the largest private collections of French art in the United States. The French collection is overseen by Alvin "Larry" Clark, who is also the J.E. Horvitz Consultative Curator, Department of Drawings, Division of European and American Art, Harvard Art Museums/ Fogg

The collection of contemporary Japanese ceramics that Carol began in 2005 is now the largest collection of contemporary Japanese ceramics, public or private, outside Japan. Objects from both collections are regularly loaned to museums for exhibit in the United States and abroad. Jeffrey and Carol have also created traveling exhibits of works from both collections, including "Mastery and Elegance: Two Centuries of French Drawings from the Collection of Jeffrey E. Horvitz" in 1998, "Genius and Grace: Francois Boucher and the Generation of 1700," in 2014 and a survey exhibition from the Horvitz Collection scheduled to open at the Petit Palais in Paris in spring 2017.

Carol writes of the contemporary Japanese ceramics collection:

> We have a lending program with nearly 500 pieces loaned out at 15 museums, including one loan to Musee Tomo in Tokyo, with hopes to have other international venues. Planning is now in the early stages. Museums in the United States currently exhibiting works from the collection include Portland, Oregon; Cincinnati; Minneapolis; the University of Florida's Harn Museum; Phoenix Art Museum; Peabody Essex Museum in Salem; the University of North Carolina's Ackland Museum; Mount Holyoke College; San Antonio Museum; Nelson Atkins Museum; Honolulu Art Museum; and Crocker Museum in Sacramento. In the past we have loaned works to museums in Los Angeles and San Antonio and in Boston to MassArt and the Museum of Fine Arts.
>
> My intent is to collect and share the pieces with as many museums as possible, given that this type of art was not available in the U.S. except for a very few pieces at a few museums. The public response/reception has been tremendous and it is a pleasure to collect, especially art from living artists, and almost be part of the process.[281]

Asked of a memorable event at Edgewater, Carol described a dinner party in 2012 celebrating Jeffrey's induction as a Chevalier of the Ordre des Arts et des Lettres, a French cultural order founded by Charles de Gaulle in 1957. The French Consul for Boston presented the award, for which only about 20 foreigners are included each year. At the dinner were the other Boston-area Chevaliers, Malcolm Rogers (then director of the MFA), Anne Poulet (former director of the Frick), and Sue Reed (former curator of drawings at the MFA), as well as the Horvitzes' children.

* * *

During the 1990s and early 2000s, as both their children and their art collections grew, Jeffrey and Carol became involved in local nonprofits and museums. Soon after Caroline entered the Beverly School for the Deaf, Jeffrey became a member of its Board of Directors. He has served on a number of other boards, including those of the Museum of Fine Arts in Boston, Center for Applied Special Technology, and Tufts University School of Medicine, as well as on Harvard University's Art Museums Visiting Committee. He serves as vice-president of the Beverly Farms Improvement Society. Carol has served on committees of the Museum of Fine Arts, on the Harvard Art Museums Visiting Committee, as a member of the board of the Massachusetts Eye and Ear Infirmary Associates, and as an overseer at the Joslin Diabetes Center.

Throughout their time at Edgewater, the Horvitzes have generously opened their home for numerous fundraisers to benefit organizations they have supported. And of course Edgewater has long been on the "must visit" list for art groups and scholars visiting the Boston area.

Edgewater House had been built for entertaining, and the Horvitzes have continued the tradition. The annual holiday party rivals the great parties of the Leiter era. That the biggest party of the year is now held in the winter has meant that, unlike the Leiters, the Horvitzes have had to cope with the weather; but even in blizzard conditions the party goes on and most of the guests manage to arrive.[282]

Over the years the guest list for the holiday party has grown to more than 800. Between 250 and 300 guests attend a typical party. The largest attendance was over 400. In addition to neighbors, guests now include friends from all areas of Carol's and Jeffrey's lives. For the past ten or more years the parties have had themes including Old England, nautical, Japan, Cuba, Paris, and Early America. Party themes often relate to the Horvitzes' travel. One year, when Jeffrey was taking Christina to the Antarctic, the tree was festooned with stuffed penguins, most of which were given away to children as they left the party. The 2010 event was a 100th birthday party for Edgewater House. Each year a twelve-foot-tall Christmas tree next to the stairs is decorated to fit the theme. The loggia, with furniture and sculpture stored away, is furnished with high cocktail tables. An exquisite array of food, usually related to the party theme, covers the dining room tables. Beginning with a 2012 event awarding Jeffrey the Chevalier de l'Ordre des Arts et des Lettres, Carol's little dog, Frago (the nickname of the French painter Jean-Honoré Fragonard), is always in attendance to meet and greet the guests. December 2016 will be the 25th annual holiday party with no missed years no matter what the weather.

The Edgewater party Jeffrey remembers best was the surprise 50th birthday party Carol organized for him in February 2000. Unfortunately, it coincided with one of the worst storms of that winter.

> Yes, I organized it and had a hundred people, most from out of state, several from out of the country. The day before the party there was a major snowstorm with planes diverted from Boston to God knows where....people calling from all over....I'm trying to keep the secret...telling Jeffrey that it was my sister, brother, etc., on the phone — not for him. It was very, very difficult to have a surprise party at the house compounded by the storm with people stranded in various locations. In the end almost all arrived, some with unbelievable stories. Only one couple, from California, could not make it. They were stranded in the Midwest somewhere. This was the first and last "surprise" party in the winter in Beverly Farms. For Jeffrey's 65th I had a surprise party for him in Florida — much easier.[283]

Through all of it, Carol was even able to keep it a surprise. Jeffrey recalled the 50ᵗʰ birthday party with awe and gratitude.

> I am expecting dinner at home with the kids. That day Caroline says she wants to go to the ballet. I don't think much of it because she actually liked ballet even though she is deaf. When we get home Caroline says, "Let's go in the front door," which I think is strange, but I always tried to go along with what she asked. So we try the front door and it is locked. I start to walk away. Then all of a sudden the door opens, and I have this sort of surreal experience of seeing this whole group of people from all over the United States and Europe. One of my friends from London had come in on the Concorde, was diverted to New York, got a limo to drive him up from New York, and he shows up. My best friend flew up from Florida — the plane nearly crashed at Logan, went into a spin when it hit ice on the runway. Then he had a horrific taxi drive to the hotel with a Somali taxi driver who had never driven in the snow and actually spun 180 degrees on Storrow Drive. Planes couldn't land and were being diverted all over the place. What I didn't know was that, because of the weather forecast and travel disasters Carol had been in tears on the phone all afternoon.[284]

Almost two years later, on December 14, 2001, the Horvitzes celebrated another important milestone. After nine years of living together, Carol and Jeffrey were married at Edgewater by Judge Peter DiGangi. It was a small ceremony with about 50 guests — family and friends from around the country and from Europe.

The Horvitzes continue to entertain throughout the year. As in the Leiter era, summer events are held outside, around the pool or on the terrace. Salsa parties are a family favorite. As times change, so do the needs of the guests. Carol laughed when a couple attending the 2013 holiday party asked if there was a way they could recharge their car.

* * *

In Edgewater's early years labor was cheap, and labor-saving devices were all but nonexistent. Mary Leiter's staff was reputed to be over 25 people working indoors and on the grounds. All of her indoor servants were immigrants. Jeffrey and Carol have found that a permanent staff of three are able to maintain both house and gallery. According to Jeffrey:

> We have two full-time housekeepers and one houseman. People usually stay with us through retirement. The house is sealed so there isn't a whole lot of dust. Windows aren't open much and we don't use the fireplace. The housekeepers are so efficient that they clean 25,000 square feet in less than five days. Outdoor lawn and garden work is hired out to others.

The Horvitzes' first housekeeper was recommended to Jeffrey by Daniel Senecal, whose Manchester house Jeffrey had rented while Edgewater was being renovated. Dan's Albanian housekeeper, whose husband had brought his two brothers and their wives to Manchester, recommended her sister-in-law, Myhyre (pronounced ma-HE-ra) Mustafa, who had arrived from Albania in March of 1992 and was working at several part-time jobs. When the Horvitzes decided they needed a second housekeeper, Jeffrey hired the second sister-in-law, Nurie Omari.

Myhrye credits her brother-in-law Musllim Mustafa and his wife, Shermin, as being the family's saviors. In 1949 Musllim's father and uncle had both been killed by the Communists in Albania. Their sons and their families were always somewhat at risk. In 1954 Musllim fled to the United States and became a successful restaurant owner with a house in Manchester. In 1991, when George H. W. Bush expanded immigration opportunities for people in Communist countries, Musllim persuaded his brothers to flee to Greece and then come to the United States. Myhyre and Nurie and their families walked six hours at night to cross the Greek border. Three months later they arrived in Massachusetts. "Musllim and Shermin are such good people; they made a big bridge for all of us to come to the United States."

Myhrye has worked for Jeffrey and Carol since 1992. When Nurie retired in 2003, she was replaced by Myhre's second cousin's wife, Hysaije Azizj (called Nia), who came with her family as immigrants in 1995. Myhyre says she would never work anywhere else. "They are very nice. Jeffrey and Carol are very, very nice. It's not easy to find a house that is comfortable, like my own house, it's more special for me. I don't want to change — never, never." Nia agrees.[285]

In 1997, after a few years with housemen/caretakers who didn't stay, Jeffrey hired Bob Jalbert, a retired construction supervisor who wanted a part-time job. Bob worked three days a week as caretaker and general houseman. Bob did a little bit of everything: made minor repairs, hired and oversaw outside contractors, grocery shopped, took care of the automobiles, drove the girls to school … sometimes even wrapped holiday gifts. Bob loved the variety and enjoyed working for the Horvitizes. When he retired in 2011 he hated to leave, but realized it was time.[286]

It was Carol who found current houseman Don Morse. In addition to being an extraordinarily versatile handyman, Don is an expert scuba diver who had been working in a local dive shop that Carol frequented. Carol learned that he also was employed as a part-time houseman for her neighbor Helen McCarthy. Since Bob Jalbert was nearing retirement, Jeffrey hired Don part-time to learn about the house. When Bob left, Don took over the entire job.

As Jeffrey has noted, "Overall the house is a pain. It really is. With so much linear footage and relatively sophisticated complex systems, something's always broken. Luckily, Don can do anything." *Anything* could involve maintaining the heating system, solving a plumbing problem, pruning a tree in the Bonsai style, helping to pack up fragile works of art — anything. In addition Don hires, schedules, and supervises outside contractors. The upkeep on an oceanfront house is never-ending. The salt air is hard on the paint; seagulls are a constant menace to the slate roof. Don tells a story of the time he was doing work in the front yard when a seagull dropped a wrench within a few inches of his head. Don clearly enjoys the variety and challenges of the job and takes pride in his accomplishments.

* * *

Will the Horvitzes stay at Edgewater House or move on? Carol imagines living somewhere else in her later years. Jeffrey isn't sure.

I like being here — it's a cool setting, but I have no emotional attachment to this locale, because I have lived in so many other places. I am constantly fantasizing about building a house. The problems is where to build it. I like the ocean setting, but I won't have two houses. Having more things doesn't make my life better. I spend money on art, travel, food, and beverage. More stuff isn't of more interest. But, I am still adding to the art collection. [287]

It is difficult to predict the future of Edgewater after Jeffrey and Carol are no longer there. The Horvitzes have transformed it into an estate that is both a family home and a museum. Unlike Isabella Stewart Gardner's Fenway Court and Henry Frick's mansion in Manhattan, Edgewater's location in the midst of a residential neighborhood makes it most unlikely that it too will become a museum. Both Jeffrey and Carol do hope that one day the art collections they have so lovingly assembled will be housed in public museums.

* * *

Since 1991, when Jeffrey purchased Edgewater, waterfront estates in Beverly Farms have met with differing fates.

The old Rantoul properties next to Edgewater, the Robert S. Rantoul house (1850s) where Paul Bonner lives, and the Neal Rantoul house (1904) owned by Ron and Mimi Pruett, as well as Rockedge (1910) built by Marion Sargent, once the home of Juliette and Oatsie Leiter's friend Eleo Sears and now owned by the estate of Nancy Benevento, are still beautifully maintained. The old Leiter gardener's cottage, currently owned by Walter and Brenda Lee Doyle, has been a charming single-family house since the 1950s.

Others have not fared so well. Sydney Hutchinson's Sydith (1910), once a Landmark School dormitory, is greatly changed. The original oceanfront property now contains three houses, and Sydith, the old Hutchinson house, has been on the market for over a year. Sarah Wyman Whitman's much changed Old Place (1885), once occupied by Tommy and Oatsie Leiter's friends Fred and Aggie Church, was demolished by Paul and Suzanne Wright in 2009. The Elizabeth Perkins house (1886), known today as the Lockwood house, has been on the market for over a year and sits overgrown and needing renovation after convicted felon Robert Lockwood was forced into bankruptcy.

Between 1991 and 2015 new mansions have been built on the beach. In 2005, architect John Margolis built himself a contemporary stucco house — on land between Sydith and the Lockwood house — modeled after the European neoclassical precedents he admired. The house was later sold and enlarged. In 2010 Dale and Anne Fowler bought the newly built cottage-style house designed by Siemasko and Verbridge between Sydith and the West Beach Corporation property. The John Swansburg house built in 2005 is now up for sale. In 2009 Paul and Suzanne Wright replaced the demolished Old Place with a much larger, light-filled wood-frame family home designed by the firm Olson, Lewis, Dioli, and Doktor. They have maintained the lovely landscaping and carriage house. Many of the homes on the old Haven property — 45 West Street, now Haven Way — have been expanded or replaced. The old Leiter brick potting shed is now part of a large wood-frame house with a three-story tower.

Jeffrey and Carol each have their own hopes for Edgewater's future. Jeffrey writes

I hope the future owners will maintain the house structurally, mechanically, and aesthetically; that they will not radically alter the sense of an historical décor — that is, not "modernize it"; that they will allow reasonable visitor groups interested in the historic homes of the North Shore. [288]

Carol concurs, and adds:

I would hope Edgewater lives on and is loved and taken care of by a family. It is a special and unique place with a vivid history. I believe houses like Edgewater have an importance that we in America have yet to fully appreciate.

In Great Britain they have the National Trust and have many of their historic homes documented. Some are actually owned and preserved for people to tour. Maybe we will have that too in America one day. I don't think it will happen or even that it would be appropriate for many more years; more history needs to accumulate. I hope this book will help preserve what has been at Edgewater and can be used in the future when the home is even more appreciated. [289]

Epilogue
The Leiters After Edgewater House

Oatsie and Tommy Leiter

Marion Oates Leiter Charles is the only living member of the Leiter family who summered at Edgewater House. At this writing, she is living in Newport at The Whim, the beautiful waterfront home she created from the carriage house belonging to Land's End, the house she and Tommy Leiter had bought in 1952.

After leaving Edgewater in 1948, Tommy and Oatsie spent a few summers in Maine. In June of 1950, their only child, Mary Victoria, was born in a private hospital in Manhattan. They spent the last days before the birth at the Ritz-Carlton. Mrs. Charles recalled:

> The morning Victoria was born I came down the elevator and the entire staff of the Ritz was lined up saying good bye, and telling me not to worry, that everything was going to be all right about the baby and all of that sort of stuff. An hour and forty-five minutes she was born.[290]

The couple spent their years together among the set of very wealthy young people who did as they pleased. Each season found them in a different place. They summered in Newport, part of the social whirl that still existed in the early fifties. Mrs. Charles recalled:

> Mrs. Leiter [*Tommy's mother, Juliette*] had known people in Newport. When I moved there, I was given a most charming welcome. Everyone was absolutely thrilled. It was a most attractive group of people in Newport at that time. The parties were divine — very formal and very grand.

> Beverly Farms was a living community where people lived their everyday lives. Newport was completely social. There were dinners or balls every night — and certainly lunches. We used to go to Bailey's Beach. God, the people were good looking — like Cynthia Cary, who was so marvelous, who would be going into the water in her swimming suit and carrying her parasol.[291]

In the fall the young Leiters went to Aiken, South Carolina, a community noted for its polo fields. Tommy and Oatsie bought One Acre Farm from Tommy's aunt Francise and her husband Huston Rawls. While Tommy rode and played polo, Oatsie played golf "at 2:30 every afternoon," went quail shooting, and very occasionally rode. Tommy's valet, former butler George Glanville, and his wife, Annette, went with them. Remembering those days, Mrs. Charles recalled that Glanville would hide lemon drops in his pocket for toddler Victoria, whom he named "Little Miss Pickpocket."

The Leiters returned to their Washington house at 1531 New Hampshire Avenue for the holiday season. Tommy Leiter loved to entertain. After the end of World War II, he had given the first ball Washington had seen in years. Because all the greenhouses had been shut down during the war, no flowers were available. Leiter directed the florist to decorate with bunches of grapes. Meyer Davis, Washington's noted society band leader, played. He became a close friend to the Leiters.

In the late winter the family went to Jamaica, where Tommy could sail. Mrs. Charles recalled that Tommy's cousins "Baba" Curzon Metcalfe and her husband Edward (called "Fruity") came to visit them there and they became close friends. It was also in Jamaica that Oatsie and Tommy met Ian Fleming, who would later name his character Felix Leiter, an operative for the CIA and Bond's friend, in Oatsie's honor.

> T. Leiter and I used to go to Jamaica for three months every year. And we had a great friend called Ivor Bryce, Ivor and Sheila Bryce. One night they came to dinner, and we went to a cocktail party. Ian Fleming [was there]. Millicent Rogers* was so in love with Ian Fleming, and he treated her very badly. I was furious. I seem to spend of lot of my time being furious. I was introduced to Ian Fleming and I looked at him and said, "Mr. Fleming, I regard you as a cad!" He said "Quite right, Mrs. Leiter. Shall we have a drink on it?" So we did, and we never looked back. He was a great friend.

It was Oatsie Leiter who introduced the James Bond books — and later Fleming himself — to John F. Kennedy.

Although Oatsie and Tommy Leiter's marriage ended in divorce in the mid-fifties, Mrs. Charles still remembered Tommy with great fondness.

> T. Leiter was absolutely irreverent and absolutely charming. He never went to college. He could have been brilliant at any number of things, but there was never any necessity and no one ever encouraged him to. But most of Leiter's other friends didn't work either. He was funny as he could be and wildly imaginative. He had only one bad habit, and that was drink.

After the divorce, Oatsie and Victoria spent a short time back at Belvoir in Montgomery, and then returned to Washington at the behest of Oatsie's friends. Her friend Joe Alsop convinced her to return to Washington.

> Joe Alsop, who was a columnist, came to see me in Alabama and said, "Now listen to me, Magnolia, you are not to leave Washington; you are very much a part of Washington. You must not leave it. So I would like you to live in my house for a year with my servants, and I don't care how much time you spend."† And I did and had a marvelous time. I would go up and stay every now and then for a week or two. It was a wonderful house and I had a marvelous time living in it. It was very sweet of Joe. Later I moved to 3387 O Street, which was a house that Jack and Jackie had later. And they loved it. It was a sweet little house.[292]

Although Land's End in Newport had been sold, Oatsie kept the carriage house, which she transformed into a lovely cottage she called The Whim. She and Victoria continued to spend summers in Newport. Tommy Leiter moved to Aiken, and also continued to go to Newport and stayed with his sister Nancy. He died in Aiken of a heart attack on April 26, 1958. He was 46 years old. According to his niece Judy McLennan, those who knew him remembered him fondly.

> You talk to people like Nuala Pell and others who knew him, and they remember his joie de vivre and his wonderful outlook on life. He was the ultimate party man. I think one of the nicest

---

*An American oil heiress, fashion icon, and art collector.
†Alsop was going to be away on assignment in Europe.

complements Nuala Pell has ever given me was when she said I had the flair and whimsy of Tommy Leiter but my feet were on the ground.[293]

In 1959 Oatsie purchased the former Dougal House, a lovely Second Empire style house on 8/10 of an acre of land in the Georgetown section of Washington. Her engaging charm and irreverent wit kept her at the center of Washington society. A real estate ad from August 2008, when Oatsie put the house up for sale, read in part:

R Street Home Played Host to a Who's Who in Washington Society

It's not often you find a home that played host to the likes of Ian Fleming, Noel Coward, and Senator John Kerry, but the Dougal House on R Street in Georgetown, which is currently for sale, is no ordinary house.

In 1959, the home was purchased by Marion Oates Leiter, known to many as Mrs. Robert "Oatsie" Charles, a legendary Washington socialite who divided her time between Georgetown and Newport, RI, where she currently resides....

It was Oatsie who recently told *Vanity Fair* that she and a group of friends that included Teddy Roosevelt Jr., Noel Coward, and President Kennedy stripped down to their underwear in the Oval Office and stepped on a scale to determine the winner in a weight-loss challenge brought on by the President. It was Oatsie who played host to a young John Kerry and his wife when he spoke out in Senate hearings about the Vietnam War. Mrs. Charles has been a friend to nearly every president since Kennedy. For almost 50 years, the house at 3259 R Street has played host to a who's who in Washington society.[294]

Mrs. Charles herself recalled:

I sort of moved in some political circles in Washington. I was born a Democrat, so I always have been; I've seen no reason to change. One thing I regret is that Jack Kennedy asked me to go to Alabama and raise $5000 and I was absolutely appalled. I thought $5000 was so much money at the time. I couldn't think of anyone I knew who would have given. And I have regretted it all my life. I think I might have been Madame Ambassador if I had done it — literally. I was friends with the Kennedys in Washington, and here in Newport too. Jack Kennedy used to love gossip. He used to come and sit next to me under the cabana and say "What's new?" It seems like a lot more went on then than does now, or at least what went as gossip then. Now it is just life.[295]

Throughout this period Oatsie sometimes traveled abroad, where she kept up her friendship with the Tommy's English cousins Baba and Fruity Metcalfe and Irene Curzon, Lady Ravensdale. She also always visited a London book shop:

My favorite bookshop in the world is the Hayward Hill in London; it was run by an absolutely charming man named John Silver Smith. I remember we were going to lunch once and I said I wish I could work at Hayward Hill, and he said "What? *You* at Hayward Hill??" "Why not?" He said, "You're not educated enough." In order to work at Hayward Hill you had to have practically a scholarship from Oxford in all literatures. I still get a lot of books from Hayward Hill. It used to be every time I went to London one of the first places I would stop would be Hayward Hill on Curzon Street, because you were bound to meet somebody you knew.[296]

In Newport Oatsie Leiter also became a close friend of heiress Doris Duke and worked closely with her in the Newport Restoration Foundation, a nonprofit institution founded by Duke in 1968 "with the

130

express purpose of preserving, interpreting, and maintaining landscape and objects reflecting Aquidneck Island's eighteenth- and nineteenth-century architectural culture."[297] After Duke's death in 1993, Oatsie Leiter Charles would become a trustee of her friend's will and become President of the Newport Restoration Foundation.

In 1969 Marion Oates Leiter married Robert Home Charles, who was at that time Assistant Secretary of the Air Force. The couple lived at the Georgetown house and in Newport.

Robert Charles died in 2002. In 2012 Mrs. Charles then sold the R Street house and moved to Newport. She continues to live at The Whim, surrounded by the spectacular seaside gardens she has created over the years. Her daughter, Victoria Mele, and her husband, Joe, who bought Land's End from the previous owners in 1989, live next door.

A *Women's Wear Daily* report on the 2012 Newport Coaching Ball captured the irrepressible spirit of the then 92-year-old Marion Oates Leiter Charles.

> Newport is the place to go to be naughty," says Marion "Oatsie" Charles, 92, who left Georgetown for Newport back in 2007. Charles, who has charmed everyone in Washington from the Kennedys to the Reagans, grew up in Alabama, the granddaughter of Confederate Colonel William C. Oates, who became Alabama's 29th governor. Outspoken, irascible, and deliciously funny, Charles relishes naughty friends almost more than being seriously naughty herself.
>
> Tobacco heiress and Newport legend Doris Duke named Charles as one of two trustees in her last will. Today Charles serves as trustee emeritus of the Doris Duke Charitable Foundation, which has an estimated endowment of $1.3 billion. Considering Duke's over-the-top approach to collecting art, huge houses, men, and mayhem, her jewelry, while dazzling in anyone else's vault, wasn't among her passions. "Doris never cared much about jewelry. Her jewelry only sold for $15,000,000 at Sotheby's," says Charles. "She did have a tiara, though. No one knew how to pronounce it, much less wear it."
>
> Mrs. Charles's lighthearted banter captures the tenor of Newport. Leaning over to talk with her driver as her car pulls up the long driveway to the Newport estate Marble House, built by William K. Vanderbilt in 1892, she observes, "This is a moneyed crowd." The luncheon, co-hosted by Marble House's former owners Frederick and Diana Prince, is another occasion for the Preservation Society to raise money. As guests arrive, paying visitors continue to tour the house, snapping pictures of the horses, the coaches, the whips (the term used to describe both the owners and coach drivers), and the fancy guests they invite to join them.
>
> For Charles, the pageantry of a weekend of coaching offers cause for celebration. Otherwise, her typical day is far less glam. "I sit in my kitchen watching the bird feeder and I watch the people coming up and down my road," says Charles, referring to the historic three-and-a-half-mile Cliff Walk, where each year thousands of tourists come to see the town's architectural treasure trove of grand seaside houses. "Hair not combed, wearing clothes that are not ironed. That's one reason I love this coaching weekend. For once, people in Newport dress to the nines."[298]

* * *

Thomas and Nancy Leiter Clagett

After the end of World War II, Tom Clagett, who had been stationed in Maui, had dreams of returning to Hawaii to live. Although his wife Nancy was an adventurous woman, he was unable to convince her to move. They made their home in Washington. Tom's first business venture after the war was the development of a racetrack for trotters in Maryland with his friend Dick Hutchinson.

A few years later, Tommy Leiter came to Tom and Nancy with a proposition. Tommy, who had never been interested in managing a business, had inherited the Zeigler coal mine from his father, Joe Leiter. He proposed that Tom and Nancy buy him out and take over the business. According to daughter Judy Clagett McLennan:

> Dad and Mother talked about it, and he decided that, even though he didn't know anything about coal, with his engineering degree he could certainly try to make something of the company. He was very successful at it. Dad ended up building it into one of the top ten coal companies in the Midwest from this one single mine.

> At one point there was talk that Mother should move to Chicago, but she said, "You travel Monday through Friday. On the weekends you can just as easily come to Washington as Chicago.

Tom and Nancy summered in Newport. For a short period they owned Wild Acre on Ocean Avenue. Later they purchased a little bungalow on Coggeshall Avenue near the beach, where they were living at the time of Hurricane Carol in 1954.

> I remember the story of Dad's leaving in the morning and going over to Land's End and insisting everyone evacuate the house. Tommy and Oatsie were there with a houseguest from Washington. They all came to the little bungalow and rode out the storm for four or five days. I remember someone gave my parents little coasters that said *Loaves and Fishes*, because whatever they had in the house had to be made to last. One of the Land's End chimneys fell down and came through the roof into the third floor and lodged in the bedroom where the houseguest had been staying.

Judy McLennan remembers that when she was growing up her family was always in touch with her mother Nancy's Curzon cousins in England.

> The Curzon family would visit us and we would visit them. We stayed in touch with the Mosley branch. Viv, who married Desmond F. Forbes-Adam during the war, would visit me and I would visit her and her brother Michael — we visited back and forth.

Sailing was always an important part of the Clagetts' lives. They named their first boat *The Barefoot Girl*.

> My mother apparently hated wearing shoes. I don't if it was a result of her back injury, but the first boat they had they named *The Barefoot Girl*. My mother's private signal was a yellow flag with a green ladder — because Leiter is the German word for *ladder*. When they got married my dad was a good sailor but not nearly as good as Mom, and she told him he had to come up with his own private signal. So he came up with a design of the triangle and put two white bare feet on it. [299]

Tom sailed a great deal with Nancy but would seldom crew for her in a race. "She was too tough," he would later admit. They shared 37 years of marriage, cruising the waters of the East coast from Maine to the Caribbean, on various boats of their own and also with friends. They supported many America's Cup boats starting in 1964.

Nancy Leiter Clagett died in 1977. As a memorial for his wife, Tom Clagett initiated what has become a nationally important sailing event for young women.

After Nancy died, Tom also donated six Lasers and a trophy in her memory to the Ida Lewis Yacht Club. The Leiter Trophy is now for US Sailing's Junior Women's Singlehanded Championship. Later Tom saw the need for junior women to also have a doublehanded championship, and through US Sailing he initiated the Ida Lewis Trophy, which is now for US Sailing's Junior Women's Doublehanded Championship. These two very successful US Sailing models have helped to elevate the skill level of junior women racers.[300]

Tom Clagett died in 2001. During his life he served on the boards of many corporate, civic, religious, and nonprofit organizations including the Chesapeake Bay Maritime Museum in St. Michael's, Maryland, and the Mystic Museum in Mystic, Connecticut. He was a member of six America's Cup syndicates from 1974 to 1995. Tom was one of the original members of the America's Cup Hall of Fame Selection Committee (the committee responsible for recommending the nominees for selection to the America's Cup Hall of Fame).

In August 2002, a small group of people gathered to discuss how to take sailors with disabilities to an elite level of sailing in order to increase the talent pool of U.S. sailors vying for Paralympic competition. This discussion led to the formation of the C. Thomas Clagett Jr. Memorial Regatta, first held in August 2003, with the help and support of Tom Clagett's daughter and granddaughter, Judy and Stephanie McLennan. The event is sanctioned by US Sailing, and the organizing authority is Sail Newport.

For the past 13 years Judy McLennan as Regatta President and her daughter Stephanie as Vice President, have worked tirelessly to make the Clagett Memorial Regatta not only an important racing event, but also free, world-class coaching for all participants. Clagett athletes have come from across the USA (eleven states), Canada (four provinces) Israel, China, Ireland, Norway, and Puerto Rico. The elite level of training provided for these athletes has resulted in Regatta participants earning a gold and a silver medal in 2008 Paralympics and two gold and two bronze medals, as well as Yachtswoman of the Year award in 2012. Equally important, the Clagett sailors have acknowledged how sail training, improving racing skills, and enjoying the sport of sailing has significantly enhanced their quality of life. Sailing skills also translate to life skills for sailors such as teamwork, problem solving to help achieve success in other areas of life.

As a young man Tom had been stricken with meningitis, which left him paralyzed. Fortunately, this was a temporary condition, but it left Tom with a respect for the accomplishments that people with disabilities are able to achieve as well as their daily challenges.

There are three classes of boats used in the Paralympics. The Sonar is sailed with three persons, and the 2.4mR is a singlehanded boat. The newest boat, introduced in 2006, is the SKUD18, a two-person doublehanded boat with the added requirement that one of the persons must be a woman. In 2003, this event started with five New England teams, all sailing in Sonars, competing for the C. Thomas Clagett Jr. Trophy. In 2006, the Clagett Regatta was a USDST [*US Disabled Sailing Team*] qualifier for the SKUD18 class, as approved by the Olympic Sailing Committee. It was also the first part of the 2007 USDST qualifiers for the Sonar class. [301]

It is fitting that Nancy Leiter Clagett and her husband, both of whom loved sailing, are memorialized by programs that encourage sailing for those who had been previously underserved. During her years at Edgewater Nancy had proved beyond a doubt that women could compete with the best male sailors in her class at a time when women athletes were often considered less able. The idea of people with disabilities being able to sail at all would have been unimaginable. Tom and Nancy Leiter Clagett would be pleased.

Acknowledgements and Sources

The story of Edgewater House and the people who lived there is a many-layered tale drawn from a great variety of sources. One layer can be found in public records such as deeds, plans and maps, building permits, census data, city directories, court records, and wills. Another layer is revealed through newspapers and periodicals, family papers, biographies, and other published texts. The richest layer of all is made up of the personal stories of the people who lived or worked in Edgewater House. I am deeply gratefully to all who permitted me to interview them. Without their contributions, this book would be far less interesting. The Leiter family photographs, generously provided by Marion Oates Leiter Charles and Judy Clagett McLennan, added still another layer by allowing an intimate look at the family who owned Edgewater House in its first golden age.

All sources are cited in the end notes. The bibliography lists only books. .The most important written source for the Leiter period is *North Shore Breeze,* a magazine of the summer community that was published by the Cricket Press in Manchester between 1904 and 1942. The only complete run of the magazine is held in the Phillips Library of the Peabody Essex Museum. The primary source for census data, border crossings, and marriage and death records is Ancestry.com.

I am particularly grateful to those who shared their own or their families' stories with such trust and candor. Being with them was my greatest pleasure in writing the book — Carol Horvitz, Jeffrey Horvitz, Marion Oates Leiter Charles, Judy Clagett McLennan, Oliver Ames Jr., Charlie Mann, Bob Jalbert, Don Morse, Maria DiFazio, Roger LeBlanc, Myhyre Mustafa, and Nia Azizi. I also thank all who shared stories and insights outside of formal interviews — Alan Bigelow, Jean and Paul Bonner, Nancy Brewka-Clark, Guerdon Davis, Josephine LeBlanc, Jonathan Loring, Ray Maguire, Alice Malone Charlie Sherrill, Robert Seamans,III (Toby), Richard Thorndike, and Cecily Vaughan.

The staffs of the following institutions were unfailingly patient and helpful: Beverly Historical Society, Beverly Public Library, City of Beverly Assessors, Planning, and Building Departments, Manchester Historical Society, Phillips Library of the Peabody Essex Museum, Gloucester Public Library, the Essex County Registry of Deeds in Salem (Salem Deeds), the National Archives at Boston in Waltham, and the Chicago Historical Society. Captain Christopher Negroti introduced me to the Beverly Police Department's archived log books. Maggie Lidz, estate historian at the Winterthur Museum, provided references to additional stories about Mary Teresa and Joe Leiter. Endicott College archivist Barbara Broudo provided information about estate prices in the 1940's and '50s. Michael Kilborne, head of Endicott College's oral history project, provided technical assistance. Finally thanks to independent scholar Pamela Fox and the staff of the Boston Public Library, Fine Arts Department for helping me to local early photographs and plans of Edgewater House.

I am deeply grateful to my good friend and retired book editor Mary Purcell, who made it possible for the book to finally come together. She not only edited the manuscript with great skill and precision, but also provided the support and enthusiasm I needed to see it through. What promised to be a difficult process became a delight. Mary died in August of 2016.

Heather Reid and Joan Johnson were kind and careful proofreaders. Sue Goganian, director of the Beverly Historical Society, has done the final work of shepherding the book through the publication process.

Finally, I thank my husband, Dan, and daughters, Liz and Sarah, for their encouragement and patience. Dan's unwavering flexibility and good humor kept me going.

Nancy Glidden Coffey
Beverly Farms

About the Author

Nancy Glidden Coffey is an independent scholar with a strong interest in local history. *The Story of Edgewater House* is her first book. She has a degree in history from Wellesley College and a Master of Arts in Teaching from Yale University.

During her career, Coffey taught high school history, served as a Peace Corps teacher in Uganda, and for the twenty years before her retirement taught English for non-native speakers, basic literacy and GED preparation to adults in Lynn. She once played the part of Mary Leiter's friend, First Lady, Nellie Taft in "Good Heaven's Mrs. Evans", Nancy Brewka Clark's play about President Taft's eviction from the summer White House in Beverly.

Nancy Coffey is currently working on a history of the working-class people who built the great estates and served the summer community in Beverly Farms from the mid-nineteenth to the mid-twentieth century.

About the Beverly Historical Society

The Beverly Historical Society has been preserving and caring for Beverly's past since 1891. In addition to a collection of nearly a million objects and documents related to Beverly and the North Shore of Massachusetts, the Society preserves and interprets three historic properties

Decorative objects brought back from Asia by Beverly merchants; the papers of William Bartlett, George Washington's naval agent; paintings by artists such as Gilbert Stuart, Frank Benson, Luke Prince, Frederick Coffay Yohn and more than 400,000 images related to Beverly and the region are among the treasures in the Society's collections, which are used by scholars, educators, students, genealogists and residents exploring their neighborhoods.

The Balch House, built in the late 17th century for the Balch family, who were among Beverly's first European settlers, and the 1694 Hale Farm, originally home to John Hale, first minister of Beverly and a key participant in the Salem witch hysteria, evoke New England's roots, early history and the evolution of Beverly over three centuries. The 1781 John Cabot House, an Essex National Heritage Area Visitor Center, is a museum of Beverly history. The Society is committed to telling Beverly's stories through lectures, walking tours, exhibits and publications and engages the community in a variety of programs. The Society is a 501 c3 non-profit organization funded by the generosity of members and friends.

Bibliography

de Courcy, Anne, *The Viceroy's Daughters: The Lives of the Curzon Sisters*, New York: Perenniel, 2002.

Diliberto, Gioia, *Debutante: The Story of Brenda Frazier*, New York: Alfred A. Knopf, 1987.

Dinnerstein, Leonard, and David M. Reimers, *Ethnic Americans: A History of Immigration and Assimilation,* New York: Dodd, Mead, 1973.

Fox, Pamela W., *North Shore Boston: Houses of Essex County 1865-1930*, New York: Acanthus Press, 2005.

Franck, Peggy Miller, *Prides Crossing: The Unbridled Life and Impatient Times of Eleonora Sears*, Beverly: Commonwealth Editions, 2009.

Garland, Joseph, *The North Shore: A Social History of the Summers Among the Newsworthy, Fashionable, Rich, Eccentric, and Ordinary on Boston's Gold Coast, 1832-1929.* Beverly: Commonwealth Editions, 1998.

Johnston, Patricia, *Real Fantasies: Edward Steichen's Adverstising Photography*, Berkeley: UC Berkeley, 1997.

Legendre, Gertrude, *The Time of My Life*, Charleston, SC: Wyrick & Co., 1987.

Leiter, Jospeh, *Favorite Old Recipes*, Chicago: Privately Printed, 1927.

McLean, Evalyn Walsh, and Boyden Sparkes, *Father Struck It Rich*, Boston: Little, Brown, 1936.

Matt, Susan J., *Keeping Up with the Joneses: Envy in Consumer Society,* Philadelphia: University of Pennsylvania Press, 2003.

Nicolson, Nigel, *Mary Curzon*, New York: Harper and Row, 1977.

Noles, James L., *Twenty-Three Minutes to Eternity: The Final Voyage of the Escort Carrier USS Liscome Bay*, Tuscaloosa: University of Alabama Press, 2004.

Tupper, Eleanor, *Endicott and I*, Manchester: Cricket Press, 1985.

Y'Blood, William T., *The Little Giants: U.S. Escort Carriers Against Japan*, Annapolis: Naval Institute Press, 1987.

Notes

Prologue:
Setting the Scene
1   Joseph Garland, *The North Shore: A Social History of the Summers Among the Newsworthy, Fashionable, Rich, Eccentric, and Ordinary on Boston's Gold Coast, 1832-1929* (Boston: Little, Brown, 1981), p. 38.

Chapter 1
The Rise of Mary Carver Leiter
2   Levi Z. Leiter papers and Leiter estate records, 1852-1969, Chicago History Museum.
3   Nigel Nicolson, *Mary Curzon* (New York: Harper and Row, 1977) pp. 15-17. Unless otherwise noted, information about the Leiter family, up to the marriage of Nancy and Daisy, comes from this book, which was commissioned by Mary Curzon's daughter Alexandra Metcalfe.
4   Nicholson, 9-12
5   *Kansas City Star*, 2-16-1909, p. 16.
6   Nicolson, p. 9.
7   Nicolson, p. 9.
8   Nicolson, p. 59.
9   *Vanity Fair*, 1897, "Capitoline Cat Fights and Exhausting Life of the Society Beauty: 1890's." In *Mrs. Daffodil Digresses*, a blog about costume, history, and social ephemera.
10   NYT (*New York Times*) online, 4-30-1903.
11   Evalyn McLean Walsh and Boyden Sparkes, *Father Struck It Rich* (Boston: Little, Brown, 1936), p. 137
12   NYT, 7-5-1909.
13   Salem Registry of Deeds, book 1991, pp. 100-101.

Chapter 2
The Building of Edgewater House and Mary Leiter's Years There: 1910-1912
14   NYT online 2-27-1910.
15   NSB (*North Shore Breeze*) 5-15-1910.
16   NSB 8-7-1910.
17   Fiske & Company advertisement,   Internet…
18   Fiske & Company, Inc., advertisement in *The Bricklayer*, March 1912.
19   Furnishings are surmised from the 1948 auction catalogue in the possession of Marion Oates Leiter Charles.
20   The descriptions of the layout of the house are gathered from several sources: preliminary from the Levi Z. Leiter papers and Leiter estate records, 1852-1969, Chicago History Museum; a first-floor plan from *North Shore Boston* and engineering plans in the possession of Jeffrey Horvitz.
21   *American Country Houses of Today*, 1915, p. 234.
22   NSB 8-13-1917.
23   NSB 10-21-1915.
24   U.S. census, 1920, Beverly city directories 1911-1934.
25   NSB 5-26-1911.
26   Greenhouse and landscape plans from the preliminary plans in the Levi Z. Leiter papers and Leiter estate records, 1852-1969, Chicago History Museum.
27   southeasternarchitecture.blogspot.com/2014_12_01_archive.

28   NSB 8-4-1915, 8-25-1911.
29   NSB 8-6-1911.
30   NSB 9-22-1911.
31   2015 conversation with Nancy Brewka-Clark, former docent at Beauport, home of Henry Sleeper, where Mrs. Jack also liked to stay.
32   NSB Oct 1911.
33   Salem Deeds, book 1991, page 100-101. The memorandum is dated 2-24-1913, only two weeks before Mary Leiter died.
34   NSB 6-7-1912.
35   NSB 8-16-1912.
36   Beverly city directories.
37   NSB 8-9-1912.
38   NSB 8-30-1912.
39   NYT 3-19-1913.

Chapter 3
The Joseph and Juliette Leiter Years: 1913-1932

40   James Lazar and Robert Pettit, "Joseph Leiter: His Road, His House, His History" (Historical Society of Fairfax County, Virginia, vol. 16, 1980), p. 15.
41   Nigel Nicolson, *Mary Curzon* (New York: Harper and Row, 1977), pp. 100-101.
42   *National Cyclopedia*, vol. 36, p. 213, as quoted by Lazar and Pettit.
43   Leiter family papers, "Brief Biography of Joseph Leiter 1868-1932."
44   http://en.wikipedia.org/wiki/The_Pit_%28Norris_novel%29
45   Raymond Null, "Zeigler Illinois: A Breath Away from Being the Nation's Capital." *Illinois Legends online*. From genealogytrails.com 3-1-2006.
46   NYT 6-11-1908.
47   NSB 10-20-1911.
48   Lazar and Pettit, pp. 12-13.
49   *Social Register*, Summer 1913. In this and further social registers the Leiters are listed in the Chicago registry.
50   Will of Mary Leiter, Salem Probate Court.
51   For a full description of the *Niagara IV* at the time of its launch, see Frank Leroy Blanchard, "Millionaire Howard Gould Steam Yacht Niagara Captain Shackford," 9-18-2011, at http://www.digitalhistoryproject.com/2011/09/millionaire-howard-gould-steam-yacht.html
52   U.S. census 1910, 1920; Beverly city directory 1913-1914.
53   *The Gardener's Chronicle of America*, 1911.
54   Minutes of the North Shore Horticultural Society, 1911 and 1913.
55   NSB 7-30-1915.
56   Beverly city directory 1915.
57   NSB 6-16-1915.
58   http://www.archive.org/stream/secretarysreport1891harvuoft/secretarysreport1891harv
59   NSB 8-4-1916.
60   NSB 9-13-1916.
61   NSB 9-22-1916.
62   NSB 10-20-1916.
63   NSB 10-13-1916.
64   Wikipedia, "Foshalee Plantation."
65   NSB 7-20-1917.
66   NSB 5-4-1917, 5-18-1917 and 7-5-18.

67 NSB 1917-1918.
68 NSB 8-9-1918.
69 NSB 7-4-1919.
70 NSB 7-4-1919.
71 NYT 1-11-1921.
72 Marion Oates Leiter Charles interview 11-16-2012.
73 NSB 9-9-1921.
74 NSB 6-19-1925.
75 James Lazar and Robert Pettit, "Joseph Leiter: His Road, His House, His History" (Historical Society of Fairfax County, Virginia, vol. 16, 1980), p. 17.
76 *Straits Times*, Reuter's service, November 1921; *Lewiston Daily Sun* 11 21-1921.
77 James Lazar and Robert Pettit, "Joseph Leiter: His Road, His House, His History" (Historical Society of Fairfax County, Virginia, vol. 16, 1980), p. 17.
78 *Life*, vol. 78, no. 2.
79 *Lewiston Daily Sun* 11-21-1921.
80 *Beverly Evening Times* 11-22-1924.
81 *Beverly Evening Times* 11-25-1924.
82 *Beverly Police Department, daily records for 1924.*
83 *Beverly Evening Times* 12-3-1924.
84 *Boston Globe* 12-6-1924.
85 Beverly Evening Times 3-24-1925.
86 USDC-Ma Criminal Case 6014.
87 *Boston Globe* 5-14-1925, p. 1.
88 *Boston Globe* 5-15-1925, p. 6.
89 USDC-MA Criminal Case 6014.
90 NSB 8-29-1924.
91 NSB 8-14-1925.
92 NSB 7-24-1925.
93 NSB 8-7-1925.
94 U.S. Census, 1920
95 Leiter family photos from 1927.
96 Leiter, Joseph, Old Family Recipes
97 Clipping from unnamed Boston paper in Moseley copy of Joe Leiter's cookbook. It is interesting that in spite of the fact that Joseph Leiter had been living in Washington for over ten years, he is still referred to as "Chicago and Beverly Farms multimillionaire."
98 Interviews with local resident Richard Thorndike and members of the Leiter family.
99 NSB 7-22-1927 and 10-8-1926.
100 NSB 7-26-1929.
101 NSB 8-2-1929.
102 *Beverly Times* 8-11-1929.
103 Appears in several places on the Internet.
104 Susan J. Matt., *Keeping Up with the Joneses: Envy in Consumer Society*, Philadelphia: University of Pennsylvania Press, 2003, pp. 45-48.
105 Patricia Johnston, *Real Fantasies: Edward Steichen's Advertising Photography* (Berkeley: UC Berkeley, 1997), p. 270.
106 ancestry.com, "Border crossings."
107 NSB 7-25-1930.
108 Letter on record at St. Paul's School.
109 Letter from Joseph Leiter to Edward W. Forbes, 8-26-1922, copy in possession of Jeffrey Horvitz

110 *Scranton Republican* 3-24-1931.
111 Leiter family papers, "Brief Biography of Joseph Leiter 1868-1932."
112 *Poughkeepsie Daily Eagle* 1932.
113 *New Orleans Times-Picayune* 3-24-1931.
114 NSB 9-18-1931.
115 *Reading Eagle* 7-2-1931.

Chapter 4
The Widow Juliette Leiter and Her Children: 1932-1942
116 Interview with Judy Clagett McLennan, 4-16-13.
117 *Milwaukee Sentinel* 5-21-1932.
118 Marion Oates Leiter Charles interview 11-16-2012.
119 NSB 7-29-1932.
120 NSB September 1932.
121 NSB 5-19-1933.
122 NSB December 1933.
123 Beverly City directory 1929.
124 *Time* 7-23-1934.
125 NSB 8-24-1934.
126 NSB 8-2-1935.
127 Clipping from Judy Clagett McLennan files.
128 Various NSB articles 1936.
129 NSB 8-14-1936.
130 NSB 9-11-1936.
131 NSB 8-20-1937.
132 Newspaper clipping from Judy Clagett McLennan 5-15-1938.
133 NSB 6-12-1938
134 NSB 7-29-1938 and information from Nancy's daughter, Judy Clagett McLennan, 4-16-2013.
135 NSB 8-25-1939.
136 Salem Deeds, Book 3188, pp. 231-232.
137 Salem Deeds. Book 3234, pp. 203-204.
138 Marion Oates Leiter Charles interview 11-16-2012.
139 Marion Oates Leiter Charles interview 1-17-2013.
140 Interviews with Alice Malone and Josephine Fiore LeBlanc 2012.
141 NSB 8-16-1940.
142 NSB 7-12-1940.
143 Cecily Vaughn conversation 5-28-2015.
144 NSB 6-28-1940.
145 Newspaper clipping from Judy Clagett McLennan.
146 Newspaper clipping from Judy Clagett McLennan. Igor Cassini, brother to designer Oleg, later wrote under the name Cholly Knickerbocker.
147 Judy Clagett McLennan interview 4-16-2013.
148 Newspaper clipping from an interview with Judy Clagett McLennan 4-16-2013.
149 NSB 6-12-1941.
150 Marion Oates Leiter Charles interview 4-15-2013. (Mary Victoria Leiter was Lady Curzon.)
151 Gioia Diliberto, *Debutante: The Story of Brenda Frazier* (New York: Alfred A. Knopf, 1987), p. 25.
152 Marion Oates Leiter Charles interview 11-16-2012.
153 Marion Oates Leiter Charles interview 2-18-2013.
154 Marion Oates Leiter Charles interview 11-16-2012.

155 Marion Oates Leiter Charles interview 4-15-2013.

156 Marion Oates Leiter Charles interview 11-16-2012.

157 NSB 9-25-1942.

158 Marion Oates Leiter Charles interview 11-16-2012 and 4-15-2014.

159 Judy Clagett McLennan interview 4-16-2013.

160 Marion Oates Leiter Charles interviews 11-16-2012 and 2-18-2013.

161 Will of Juliette Leiter, Salem Probate Court.

Chapter 5

Tommy and Oatsie Leiter: 1942-1950

162 Marion Oates Leiter Charles interview 11-16-2012.

163 Marion Oates Leiter Charles interview 4-15-2013.

164 Gertrude Legendre, *The Time of My Life* (Charleston, SC: Wyrick & Co., 1987).

165 Unlabeled clipping from Judy Clagett McClennon.

166 Marion Oates Leiter Charles interview 11-16-2012.

167 Marion Oates Leiter Charles interview 11-16-2012.

168 Marion Oates Leiter Charles interview 1-17-2013.

169 Marion Oates Leiter Charles interview 11-16-2012.

170 Salem Deeds, book 3428, pp. 93-94.

171 Marion Oates Leiter Charles interview 11-16-2012.

172 Marion Oates Leiter Charles interview 4-15-2013.

173 Marion Oates Leiter Charles interview 11-16-2012.

174 Marion Oates Leiter Charles interview 11-16-2012.

175 Auction catalog in possession of Marion Oates Leiter Charles.

176 Marion Oates Leiter Charles interview 11-16-2012.

Chapter 6

The Kaisers: June 1950-April 1951

177 Peggy Miller Franck, *Prides Crossing: The Unbridled Life and Impatient Times of Eleonora Sears*, (Beverly: Commonwealth Editions, 2009), p. 181, and conversation with Charlie Sherrill.

178 Salem Deeds, book 3328,p.440

179 Salem Deeds, book 3350, page 520

180 Salem Deeds, book 3746, pp. 211ff.

181 Salem Deeds, book 32512, p. 169.

182 Salem Deeds, Plan Book 80, p. 98.

183 Salem Deeds, book 3787, pp. 81ff.

184 Salem Deeds, book 3788, p. 117ff.

185 Salem Deeds, book 3796, pp.140ff.

186 Salem Deeds, book 3804, pp. 532ff.

187 Salem Deeds, book 3813, pp.438-439.

188 Salem Deeds, book 4678, p.502.

189 Beverly and Gloucester city directories.

190 Herbert Kaiser death certificate, Gloucester City Hall.

Chapter 7

Oliver and Ellen Ames: Year-Round Resident Owners, 1950-1980

191 Pamela W. Fox, *North Shore Boston: Houses of Essex County 1865-1930* (New York: Acanthus Press, 2005), pp. 26, 44-49.

192 NSB 7-23-1937 and 8-28-1937.

193 NSB 9-8-1939.

194 NSB 8-12-1938.

195 *Boston Globe* 11-6-1938.

196 *Boston Globe* 1-29-1941.

197 NSB 8-22-1941.

198 *Boston Globe* 6-19-1943.

199 Oliver Ames Jr. email 3-30-2014.

200 William T. Y'Blood, *The Little Giants: U.S. Escort Carriers in World War II* (Annapolis: Naval Institute Press, 1987), p. vii.

201 Wikipedia, "Liscome Bay."

202 Noles, *James L. Twenty-Three Minutes to Eternity: The Final Voyage of the Escort Carrier USS Liscome Bay*, p. 198.

203 Noles, pp. 198-199.

204 *Boston Globe*, 3-25-1944.

205 Salem Deeds, book 3798, p. 559.

206 Robert Seamans III (Toby) conversation 8-15-2013.

207 Oliver Ames Jr. email April 2011.

208 *Boston Globe* 3-29-1947.

209 Oliver Ames Jr. recorded walk-through 2-27-2013.

210 Oliver Ames Jr. recorded walk-through 2-27-2013.

211 Oliver Ames Jr. recorded walk-through 2-27-2013.

212 Oliver Ames Jr. recorded walk-through 2-27-2013.

213 Salem Registry of Deeds, Book 4139/363, plan 951, 1954.

214 Oliver Ames Jr. email April 2011.

215 Jonathan Loring conversation, 2012.

216 Roger LeBlanc telephone interview 4-28-2-15.

217 Alan Bigelow recorded following a lecture 4-24-2011.

218 Oliver Ames Jr. conversation 10-16-2012.

219 City of Beverly building permits 6-9-1971 and 6-16-1971.

220 Roger LeBlanc telephone interview, 4-28-2015.

221 City of Beverly building permits 7-23-1975.

222 Salem Deeds, book 6494, pp. 544-545.

223 Jonathan Loring conversation 6-28-2012.

224 Jonathan Loring conversation 6-28-2012.

225 Salem Deeds, book 6731, pp. 277-279.

Chapter 8
Dennis and Susan Fabry: 1980-1991

226 Historical Census of Housing tables.

227 Salem Deeds book 6731, p. 281.

228 Salem Deeds book 6731, p. 285ff.

229 Salem Deeds book 6873, p. 753ff.

230 Conversations with Jean Bonner, Charlie Sherrill, and others.

231 Roger LeBlanc telephone interview 4-28-2015.

232 Salem Deeds, book 6844, p. 312ff.

233 Roger LeBlanc telephone interview 4-28-2015.

234 Salem Deeds, book 7328, p. 446.

235 Conversation with Ray Maguire (former Chapman's owner) July 2013.

236 Salem Deeds, book 7329, p. 303.
237 Salem Deeds, book 7329, p. 195.
238 Salem Deeds, book 7743, pp. 261ff.
239 Salem Deeds, book 7913, p. 462.
240 City of Beverly building permit.
241 Guerdon Davis conversation 2013.
242 Merrill Lynch ad, file of Jeffrey Horvitz.
243 Merrill Lynch ad, file of Jeffrey Horvitz.
244 Salem Deeds, book 9229, pp. 335ff.
245 Salem Deeds, book 9229, pp. 343ff.
246 Salem Deeds, book 9728, p. 440.
247 Salem Deeds, book 10951, p. 291.
248 Salem Deeds, book 10951, p. 298.
249 Jeffrey Horvitz interview 7-9-2014, stories told to him by neighbors.
250 Salem Deeds, book 96369, p. 103.
251 Salem Deeds, book 11449, p. 150.
252 Jeffrey Horvitz interview 7-9-2014.
253 Salem Deeds, book 11449, p. 152.
254 http://www.bizapedia.com/people/DENNIS-FABRY.html
255 www.corporationwiki.com/Florida/Naples/

Chapter 9
Jeffrey and Carol Horvitz: The Rebirth of Edgewater, 1991-Present

256 Leonard Dinnerstein and David M. Reimers, *Ethnic Americans: A History of Immigration and Assimilation* (New York: Dodd, Mead, 1973) p. 38.
257 1910 U.S. census.
258 "Settling on Old Masters: A Collector Winnows and Sharpens," economist.com 8-30-2008; and http://artdaily.com/news/22652/Sothebys-to-Sell-the-Jeffrey-E.-Horvitz-Collection-of-Italian-Master-Drawings
259 Jeffrey Horvitz interview 10-27-2014.
260 Jeffrey Horvitz interview 7-9-2014
261 Carol Horvitz interview 7-7-2014.
262 Carol Horvitz interview 7-7-2014.
263 Carol Horvitz interview 7-7-2014.
264 Carol Horvitz interview 7-7-2014.
265 Charlie Mann interview 8-20-2014.
266 Charlie Mann interview 8-20-2014.
267 Jeffrey Horvitz interview 10-27-2014.
268 Charlie Mann interview 8-20-2014.
269 Jeffrey Horvitz interview 7-9-2014
270 Jeffrey Horvitz interview 10-27-2014.
271 Jeffrey Horvitz interview 8-11-2014.
272 Jeffrey Horvitz interview 7-9-2014.
273 Carol Horvitz comments following Edgewater lecture 4-24-2011.
274 Carol Horvitz email 5-24-2015.
275 Carol Horvitz interview 7-7-2014.
276 Carol Horvitz interview 4-29-15
277 "Settling on Old Masters: A Collector Winnows and Sharpens," economist.com 8-30-2008; and http://artdaily.com/news/22652/Sothebys-to-Sell-the-Jeffrey-E.-Horvitz-Collection-of-Italian-Master-Drawings

278 Jeffrey Horvitz interview 7-9-2014.
279 Charlie Mann interview 8-20-2014.
280 Jeffrey Horvitz interview 8-11-2014.
281 Carol Horvitz email 5-24-2015.
282 Carol Horvitz interview 4-29-2015.
283 Carol Horvitz interview 5-16-2015.
284 Jeffrey Horvitz interview 4-29-2015.
285 Myhyre Mustafa interview 5-20-2015.
286 Bob Jalbert interview 6-30-2015.
287 Jeffrey Horvitz email, 5-30-15
288 Jeffrey Horvitz, email, 5-30-15
289 Carol Horvitz, email 6-1-15

Epilogue: The Leiters After Edgewater

290 Marion Oates Leiter Charles interview 11-16-2012.
291 Marion Oates Leiter Charles interview 11-16-2012
292 Marion Oates Leiter Charles interview 2-18-13
293 Judy Clagett McLennan interview 4-16-2013.
294 Jim Lodico, "Georgetown Landmark for Sale," georgetowner.com, August 2012.
295 Marion Oates Leiter Charles interview 2-18-2013.
296 Marion Oates Leiter Charles interview 2-18-13.
297 Newport Restoration Foundation website.
298 Susan Watters, "Newport Rules: Ball at the Breakers," *Women's Wear Daily*, 8-23-2012.
299 Judy Clagett McLennan interview 4-16-2013.
300 http://www.clagettregatta.org/about Clagett Junior
301 http://www.clagettregatta.org/readmore